REMAINS

Historical and Literary

CONNECTED WITH THE PALATINE COUNTIES OF

Lancaster and Chester

VOLUME XVII—THIRD SERIES

MANCHESTER:

Printed for the Chetham Society

1969

The Last Days of the
LANCASHIRE MONASTERIES
and the
PILGRIMAGE OF GRACE

by
CHRISTOPHER HAIGH

MANCHESTER
PRINTED FOR THE CHETHAM SOCIETY
1969

© 1969 The Chetham Society

Published for the Society by
Manchester University Press
316–324 Oxford Road
Manchester 13

Printed in Great Britain by Butler & Tanner Ltd., Frome and London

CONTENTS

PREFACE

It is the fashion among historians of the Tudor period to stress the revolutionary changes which are thought to have taken place in sixteenth-century England, and though they are surely right to do so, I feel that this approach by itself leaves too much unsaid. For 'revolution' necessarily implies a system or a way of life which is attacked, and resistance to change by the 'reactionary' elements, aspects of the problem which are too little stressed. Lancashire, which in the sixteenth century was a by-word for backwardness, immorality and violence, seemed the obvious area for a study of the impact of religious change on a predominantly conservative society. For Lancashire, the usual questions asked by Reformation historians, how and why did Protestantism develop, become the equally important how and why did Protestantism not develop.

This book is a small part of the results of my work on the Reformation in Lancashire. Although the area discussed and the numbers of monks and religious houses are comparatively small, the restricted nature of the topic allowed detailed study of the kind which is impossible on a larger canvass. It is hoped that this book will show that some accepted interpretations need re-examination, and that a comprehensive national history disguises significant regional variations.

I wish to thank Professor G. R. Elton, who taught me as an undergraduate and has maintained an interest in my work since then, Professor E. G. Rupp, who supervised me as a research student, and Professor J. S. Roskell and Dr. W. H. Chaloner of the Chetham Society, who helped with the technicalities of preparing the work for publication. All three read most of the work in typescript, and made some useful suggestions. The staffs of the archives I have visited have all been most helpful, especially those at the Public Record Office, the Cheshire Record Office, and the Borthwick Institute, York. My gratitude to the Chetham Society for publishing the work, and to the staff of Manchester University Press for providing expert advice, should also be recorded. My wife assisted with the bibliography, proof-reading, and the index, and I wish to thank her for allowing Lancashire religion to occupy so much of my time.

C. H.

Department of Ecclesiastical History,
University of Manchester.

ABBREVIATIONS

A.P.C.—'Acts of the Privy Council', ed. J. R. Dasent
B.I.Y.—Borthwick Institute, York
   R/I—Archbishops' Registers
B.M.—British Museum
Burnet-Pocock—'History of the Reformation', G. Burnet, ed. N. Pocock
C.A.P.—'Collectanea Anglo-Premonstratensia', ed. F. A. Gasquet,
   Camden Society
C.C.C.—Corpus Christi College, Cambridge
Cheth. Soc.—Chetham Society
Church Goods—'Inventories of Church Goods, 1552', ed. J. E. Bailey,
   Cheth. Soc.
Clergy List—'List of the Clergy in . . . Diocese of Chester', L. & C. Record
   Soc.
Cock. Chart.—'Chartulary of Cockersand Abbey', ed. W. Farrer, Cheth.
   Soc.
C.R.O.—Cheshire Record Office
   EDA12—Proceedings of Ecclesiastical Commissioners
   EDC1—Consistory Court Books
   EDC2—Consistory Deposition Books
   EDV1—Visitation Correction Books
   EDV2—Visitation Call Books
Corresp.—'Correspondence of Edward, 3rd Earl of Derby', ed. T. N.
   Toller, Cheth. Soc.
D.K.R.—Report of the Deputy Keeper of the Public Records
Duchy Pleadings—'Pleadings & Depositions in the Duchy Court', L. & C.
   Record Soc.
E.H.R.—English Historical Review
F.O.R.—'Register of the Archbishop of Canterbury's Faculty Office'
Furness Coucher—'Coucher Book of Furness Abbey', ed. J. Brownbill,
   Cheth. Soc.
J. Eccl. Hist.—Journal of Ecclesiastical History
Knowles & Hadcock—'Medieval Religious Houses', M. D. Knowles &
   R. N. Hadcock
Lancs Chantries—'History of the Chantries', Reports, ed. Raines. Cheth.
   Soc.
L. & P.—'Letters & Papers of the Reign of Henry VIII'
Lich. R.O.—Lichfield Record Office
   B/A/I—Bishop's Registers
   B/V/I—Visitation Books

L.R.O.—Lancashire Record Office
  DDTo—Towneley Deeds
L.R.S.—Lincoln Record Society
N.S.—New Series
O.S.—Old Series
P.R.O.—Public Record Office
  DL—Duchy of Lancaster
  DL3—Depositions and Examinations
  DL5—Entry Books of Decrees and Orders
  DL12—Privy Seals and Warrants
  DL28—Various Accounts
  DL29—Ministers' Accounts
  DL41—Miscellaneous
  DL42—Miscellaneous Books
  DL43—Rentals and Surveys
  E—Exchequer
  E101—King's Remembrancer, Various Accounts
  E315—Augmentation Office, Miscellaneous Books
  E321—Augmentation Office, Proceedings
  E334—First Fruits and Tenths Office, Composition Books
  PL—Palatinate of Lancaster
  PL25—Assize Rolls
  PL26—Indictments
  SC—Special Collections
  SC6—Ministers' & Receivers' Accounts
  SC11—Rentals & Surveys, Rolls
  SC12—Rentals & Surveys, Portfolios
Reg.—Register
Stat. Realm—'Statutes of the Realm'
Trans. Hist. Soc. L. & C.—Transactions of the Historic Society of Lancs
  & Cheshire
Trans. L. & C. Antiq. Soc.—Transactions of the Lancs & Ches. Anti-
  quarian Society
Valor—'Valor Ecclesiasticus'
V.C.H.—Victoria History of the County of Lancashire
Whalley Act Book—'Act Book of the Ecclesiastical Court of Whalley',
  Cheth. Soc.
Whalley Coucher—'Coucher Book of Whalley Abbey', ed. W. Hulton,
  Cheth. Soc.
Whitaker—'History of the Parish of Whalley', T. D. Whitaker
Y.A.J.—Yorkshire Archaeological Journal

Full details of all works mentioned in the footnotes will be found in the
Bibliography.

THE CHURCH IN LANCASHIRE

THE condition of the late-medieval Church in Lancashire was not very good. The church buildings were in consistently poor repair. In 1535 it was found that the parish churches of Croston, Standish, and Wigan were in decay,[1] but twenty years later the same churches, as well as many others, were still in serious need of repair.[2] In 1554 eleven of the thirteen churches in Warrington deanery were said to be in decay.[3] In 1527 it was reported that the chapel at Rossendale 'is not sufficiently repaired, and that it rains upon the altar and other places within the same chapel',[4] and it was ordered that the people should remedy the situation. But the need for repair was mentioned again in the next three years,[5] though the matter was dropped after 1530, so presumably improvements were made. Some of the clergy were also very bad, and in the 1530's two of the supposedly celibate vicars in Manchester deanery had families.[6] The worst was Thomas Kirkby, curate of Halsall, who in 1530 was accused of flagrantly abusing his position to persuade the dying to remember him in their wills. He had been telling his parishioners that their relations were burning in purgatory, to obtain money for praying for them, as well as dealing in cattle and tithe-corn, and frequenting the ale-house.[7] But even Kirkby did not deserve the treatment he received from his parishioners, who drove him out of the parish, and then tried to burn him to death in his bedroom.[8]

Such violence against the clergy was common, and does not reflect well on the religious state of the county.[9] In 1526 the Rector of Bury was attacked in procession, and the next day in the church itself, in a dispute over the appointment of a parish clerk.[10] In 1535 the chantry-priest at Padiham was dragged from the altar,[11] and the chaplain of Parbold was forcibly expelled from his church about the same time.[12] If the people of Lancashire sometimes despised their clergy it is hardly surprising, since they were often but poorly served. Lancashire could hope to attract only the dregs of the clerical population, for, as a backward and underdeveloped county, it could provide only meagre incomes for its priests. As many as thirty-two of the fifty-seven benefices in the county were impropriated,

[1] C.R.O., EDA12/1, fos. 8v, 6v, 9.   [2] C.R.O., EDV1/1, fos. 145, 145v, 138v.
[3] ibid., fos. 137–44v.   [4] *Whalley Act Book*, 114.
[5] ibid., 117, 124, 139.
[6] V.C.H., iv, 359; Raines, *Vicars of Rochdale*, 38.
[7] *Duchy Pleadings*, i, 198–200.   [8] P.R.O., DL3/4, K. 5, N.D.
[9] It was not, however, confined to Lancashire, and certainly went on in the diocese of Lincoln—*An Episcopal Court Book for the Diocese of Lincoln, 1514–1520*, ed. M. Bowker, L.R.S., pp. xii, 32–4.   [10] *Duchy Pleadings*, i, 151–3.
[11] V.C.H., vi, 496.   [12] *Duchy Pleadings*, i, 147.

leaving a vicar receiving only part of the tithes or a small pension, and the twenty-eight vicars given in the 'Valor Ecclesiasticus' received an average income of only £12/9/3¾d. The richer benefices were frequently held by absentee pluralists, and in 1536 twenty benefices were in the hands of absentees; sixteen of the twenty richest positions were held by non-resident clergy.[1] Even some of the poorer cures were not served properly; in 1535 the people of Pendle complained that their curate, William Seller, was never there to perform his duties,[2] and in the following year he was suspended.[3]

The religious condition of Lancashire, therefore, was certainly no better than anywhere else. But this did not produce the revulsion against the old faith which appeared in the south of England, nor any readiness to accept with equanimity the religious changes of the 1530's. In 1541 John Bird, the new Bishop of Chester, of whose diocese Lancashire formed the major part, reported to the King that for lack of doctrine and preaching the people of the diocese were much behind the King's subjects in the south, popish idolatry still continued, and the clergy still allowed the ignorant people to make offerings to images.[4] The Consistory Court Books of the diocese of Chester[5] contain no heresy cases, even for the reign of Mary, and there is no real evidence of Protestantism within the county until 1554, when there were reports of a few heretics in the major towns of south Lancashire.[6] 'Lutherous', in fact, was a popular term of abuse for those with anti-clerical leanings.[7] When endowed prayers for the dead were already in disrepute elsewhere, the people of Lancashire were still founding chantries; of ninety-one chantries or stipendiary endowments known in Lancashire, forty-four were founded after 1490, and three of them were established in the 1540's.[8] Nor was conservative attachment to the old ways confined to the first half of the century; the strength of Catholic recusancy under Elizabeth is well known, if inadequately studied, and the government certainly thought that Catholicism had a stronger hold on Lancashire than on the rest of the country. The Privy Council described the county, in 1574, as 'the very sink of popery, where more unlawful acts have been committed and more unlawful persons holden secret than in any other part of the realm'.[9]

The poor condition of the Catholic Church, then, did not prevent the people remaining strongly attached to it. This was because, as Professor Jordan noted, the religious evolution of the county was about half a century behind that of the rest of England.[10] Lancashire simply was not ready

[1] Figures from V.C.H., iii–viii, and *Valor*, v, 219–32, 259–63, 267–8, 272.
[2] *Whalley Act Book*, 176.   [3] ibid., 185, 191.
[4] L. & P., xvi, 1377.   [5] C.R.O., EDC1/1–15.
[6] C.R.O., EDV1/1, fos. 126v, 128, 133, 133v, 134v, 141v.
[7] *Duchy Pleadings*, ii, 32.   [8] *Lancs Chantries*, passim, esp. Intro. xxxiii–xxxvii.
[9] A.P.C., viii, 216.
[10] Jordan, *The Social Institutions of Lancashire*, Cheth. Soc., 75–6, 77.

for the Reformation when it came, and change had to be forced upon the county, because pre-Tridentine Catholicism was still an integral part of the life and thought of the people. The same was true of the Lancashire monasteries. There were seven independent houses in the county on the eve of the suppression: two were Cistercian, Furness and Whalley; there was one Benedictine, Holland; Cockersand was the only independent Premonstratensian house; and there were three of Augustinian Canons, Burscough, Cartmel, and Conishead. In addition, there were four dependent priories: two, Lytham, a cell of Durham, and Penwortham, a cell of Evesham, were Benedictine; the Premonstratensian Hornby was a cell of Croxton; and Kersall, the only Cluniac house, was a cell of Lenton. In all, there were about 132 regulars attached to Lancashire houses in 1536–7,[1] omitting the friars. Though it cannot be pretended that they were in any better state than other monasteries in the early Tudor period, these houses, like Catholicism, still had an important place in Lancashire life. The monasteries of the county, like those in Scotland,[2] were important social institutions which fulfilled useful functions in a backward and unsophisticated society. Twelve of the fifty-seven parish churches were actually served by monks.[3] We may contrast this position in the north with that of the religious houses in Essex, which by the sixteenth century had no useful or effective role in either the religious or the social lives of their area, and had but little impact on the lives of the people of the county.[4] Their position meant that the Lancashire houses played a significant part in the history of local resistance to Tudor reform, and they exemplify both the weakness and the strength of the old religion in the sixteenth century, that is, the fact that medieval Catholicism was an essential facet of the life of a conservative community.

[1] See Appendix A.
[2] Anthony Ross in *Essays in the Scottish Reformation*, ed. D. McRoberts, 189.
[3] Huyton (*Valor*, v, 222); Ormskirk (V.C.H., iii, 244); Blackburn (*Valor*, v, 230); Whalley (ibid.); Tunstall (V.C.H., viii, 228–9); Garstang (ibid., vii, 297–8); Dalton (cf. *Valor*, v, 272 & F.O.R., 97); Urswick (V.C.H., viii, 337); Penwortham (ibid., vi, 54); Lytham (ibid., vii, 217); Cartmel (ibid., viii, 262); and Pennington (ibid., 341).
[4] J. E. Oxley, *The Reformation in Essex*, 2, 63.

CHAPTER ONE

THE LANCASHIRE MONASTERIES
BEFORE THE DISSOLUTION

ANY historical analysis is, naturally, dependent on the evidence which survives, and in any discussion the problems of the quantity and reliability of
the sources are sure to arise. These problems are particularly acute when
surveying the condition of religious houses. Many of the sources are
'casual', documents not produced by tested official processes, in which the
motive of the writer is often in doubt; where evidence on the state of a
house comes from a complaint, we can never be sure that the complainant
was presenting an accurate version of the facts. 'Casual' evidence is also
dependent on the chance survival of letters, inventories, or accounts, so
that the standard of a monastery may appear better or worse than others
merely because of the fact that documents have survived. 'Formal'
evidence, that produced in the course of actual official processes, is con-
ditioned by the administrative or legal processes which produced it; thus
the evidence of an episcopal register is coloured by the fact that only the
lapses of a house would require action, so leaving virtue unrecorded, and
often we have only the details of a complaint made to the bishop, which
may have been biased or wilfully inaccurate, with no record of the results
of any inquiry. Visitations records, like the reports of Richard Redman,
Visitor of the English Province of the Premonstratensian Order,[1] reflect
the purpose of a visitation, to seek out and remedy lapses, and so present
the faults of a house rather than its virtues. 'Formal' records, too, are subject to the chances of survival; we have visitation records for Cockersand,
Burscough and Holland only, but other houses must have been visited,
while if the Premonstratensian records had not survived, we would have
supposed Cockersand to have been in a reasonably good condition, as its
lapses are not recorded elsewhere. Other 'formal' evidence, like that of
episcopal registers, is dependent on someone noticing the lapses, and
bothering to report them.

But a judgement must be made, and it can only be made on the basis of
such evidence as is available. The ecclesiastical authorities were usually
vigilant, so that the more serious lapses were probably recorded, and, if
this does not conflict with whatever else is known, it can surely be assumed
that where the records are silent this indicates that the house was fulfilling
the functions expected of it in a reasonably observant manner. Such
negative arguments always contain an element of risk, but so many reports

---

[1] C.A.P., ii, passim; Knowles, *Religious Orders*, iii, 39–50.

of faults were made that it is reasonable to suppose that lack of complaint means lack of fault.

In the case of all the monasteries in the south of Lancashire, there is simply not enough evidence to warrant any definite conclusions. This is especially true in the case of the four dependent cells, which were too small to attract much attention. There is no evidence at all for Kersall and Penwortham, and little more for the other two. In 1484 Elias Sherwood, Prior of Hornby, was cited to appear before Bishop Redman to answer certain articles alleged against him;[1] this must refer to some misconduct, but the details are not known, and he was still prior in 1490, when he assisted in the confirmation of an election at Cockersand.[2] Lytham appears to have been very unpopular with the neighbouring gentry and commons, but this was the result of property disputes.[3] The most serious incident was in 1530, when the people of Lytham pulled down a boundary cross bearing a picture of St. Cuthbert, to whom the Priory was dedicated, and, according to the Prior, they would have destroyed the monastery had not two monks gone out to meet them carrying the consecrated host.[4] In 1534 the Priory was again involved in a dispute, this time over enclosures and the pasture rights of the people in Lytham, Poulton, Bispham, and Hawes Waste.[5] Except for mere property transactions, this is all that is known of the cells in the period just before the dissolution.

Even for the larger houses in the south of the county, our information is little better. The most interesting record we have of Burscough is, unfortunately, far too early to form a basis for any estimation of the condition of the house in the years immediately before its dissolution. In 1454 the Prior, Robert Woodward, Thomas Fairwise, a canon, and William Bolton, Vicar of Ormskirk and also a canon of the priory, were accused of divination, sacrilege, and practising black magic. An enquiry by Bishop Boulers of Lichfield revealed that a certain Robert, reputed to be a wizard, had undertaken, for £10, to find hidden treasure; after swearing secrecy over the host, the canons passed it, in the pyx, to Robert; three 'circuli trianguli' were inscribed, and each of the canons stood inside one, the vicar having the host suspended on his chest, and holding a rod in his hand. Nothing more is recorded, though the three denied any invocation of demons or sacrifice to them. The Bishop suspended all three from celebrating or receiving the sacraments for two years, Bolton was deprived of his vicarage, and the Prior was forced to resign.[6] Not long after, however, Boulers lifted their suspensions, although Bolton and Woodward were not restored to their positions, and the ex-prior was given a pension of ten marks and adequate board and lodging in the Priory.[7] In view of the later

[1] C.A.P., ii, 154.   [2] ibid., i, 110-11.   [3] V.C.H., ii, 108.
[4] Duchy Pleadings, i, 206-9.   [5] P.R.O., DL3/6, P. 3.
[6] Lich. R.O., B/A/I, Reg. Boulers, f. 55. The same sort of thing happened at Knaresborough in Yorkshire in 1509, when a canon of Drax was involved (B.I.Y., R/I/26, Reg. Bainbridge, fos. 68-72).   [7] Lich. R.O., B/A/I, Reg. Boulers, f. 70.

importance of witchcraft in Lancashire,[1] this case is obviously significant, and there may even have been a continuing tradition in the county. In 1554 William and Janet Dunerdill of Whalley were cited before the Bishop of Chester's vicar-general 'propter devinacionem'.[2] In Lancashire, as elsewhere,[3] ignorance often led to superstition and witchcraft.

The Prior of Burscough was obviously a man of some importance in the area. In 1503 he, with two local gentlemen, was commissioned to enquire into the misdemeanours of Henry Farington, the most substantial of the local gentry, and he reported his findings to the Duchy Court.[4] The same sort of thing happened in 1527, when the Prior was commissioned to investigate a dispute between the Mollineux family and the Blundells.[5] The importance of the Priory, however, bore no connection to its condition, for there must have been something seriously wrong in 1511, when the Prior, John Barton, was not even allowed to resign, as was customary, but was dismissed for some unknown offence. The whole house must have been in a poor state, since Bishop Blyth of Lichfield appointed an outsider from Kenilworth, Robert Harvey, to the vacant office.[6] Harvey, as Prior of Burscough, was summoned to the Canterbury Convocation in 1529.[7] Under the rule of the new superior, the condition of the convent improved considerably, and when the Bishop of Lichfield's vicar-general visited the Priory in 1517, 1521 and 1524, it was found on each occasion that the house was in good order.[8] No other evidence is available, though an inventory of the goods of the house shows the canons must have led a fairly comfortable life, with a more than adequate supply of silver plate, cooking utensils, and bedding which an ordinary peasant would find luxurious.[9] In the absence of any further record for the period after 1524, we must conclude that the Priory passed its final days in a healthy, if worldly, condition.

Little, too, is known of Holland, but what is known presents a rather poor picture. It was reported to Bishop Arundel of Lichfield in 1497 that the monks did not observe the rule of St. Benedict, that their church and other buildings were in poor repair, and that their possessions were dilapidated by their negligence and excesses.[10] What action the Bishop took is not recorded, but the buildings were renovated at some stage, and in 1536 were said to be in 'good repair'.[11] But in the 1530's the monks were still disregarding at least one rule, having each a separate chamber, well supplied with sheets, pillows and pillowslips, mattresses, blankets, and

---

[1] See especially *Pott's Discovery of Witches*, Cheth. Soc., passim.
[2] C.R.O., EDV1/1, f. 154.
[3] G. Williams, *The Welsh Church from Conquest to Reformation*, 331–3.
[4] *Duchy Pleadings*, i, 21.   [5] L. & P., iv(2), 3579.
[6] V.C.H., ii, 151.   [7] L. & P., iv(3), 6047.
[8] Lich. R.O., B/V/I, pp. 8, 59; Pt. II, p. 28.
[9] P.R.O., DL41/11/36.   [10] Lich. R.O., B/A/I, Reg. Arundel, f. 236v.
[11] P.R.O., DL43/5/7, f. 5.

coverlets.[1] They seem, indeed, to have been living in even greater comfort than their brethren at Burscough, with glazed windows, hangings on the walls, and even 'a desk to write on'.[2] At Holland it must have been the custom to pay more attention to comfort than to religion, for the house had but 'four old mass-books' for the services.[3] The priory's lack of serious concern for religion seems to have affected at least one of its appropriated churches, and in 1519 the court of the diocese of Lincoln cited Holland to prove its appropriation of the rectory of Whitwick in Leicestershire, and criticised the priory for not sending a representative to the visitation and allowing the rectory to fall into ruin.[4] The monks' lack of fervour cannot have been very inviting to new recruits, for the original foundation of a prior and twelve monks[5] was down to a prior and four monks in 1536.[6] The monks, however, appear to have observed their rule, at least to the satisfaction of their Visitor.[7] But, as with Burscough, the Priory continued to fulfil its normal social and ecclesiastical functions whatever its condition; in 1527 the Prior acted with his colleague as Burscough in the Blundell–Mollineux case,[8] and was summoned with him to the 1529 Convocation,[9] while the priory church appears to have been the centre for the worship of the surrounding area.[10] The only conclusion which can be drawn is that Holland was not in a very enthusiastic state, but that it nevertheless played a part in the life of the community.

The houses in the north of Lancashire, being larger and more important, are more fully documented. In 1525 Wolsey seems to have considered suppressing Conishead to help endow his new colleges, but in April the Duke of Suffolk wrote to the Cardinal asking him to spare the house, as it was 'of great succour to the King's subjects, and the Prior is of good and virtuous disposition'.[11] This was Prior Cansforth, who retired on a generous pension in 1527.[12] But his successor seems to have been a less reputable character, if the charges made against him are to be believed. Thomas Legh complained to Cromwell in 1533 that Thomas Lord, Prior of Conishead, and others, had organised the cruel murder of John Bardsey, one of Legh's relations. Legh's informant had reported the matter at the last assizes at Lancaster, but no action had been taken, as the crime was 'colourably borne by divers gentlemen'.[13] Still nothing was done, so the accusation may have been groundless, but it occurred again when one Richard Johnson petitioned Fitzwilliam, the Chancellor of the Duchy of Lancaster, to restore him to his office as guide over the Leven Sands, from which he had been dismissed by Prior Lord, for arresting Edward

[1] P.R.O., DL41/11/47. [2] ibid. [3] ibid.
[4] An Episcopal Court Book for the Diocese of Lincoln, 1514–1520, ed. M. Bowker, L.R.S., 92.
[5] Knowles and Hadcock, 79. [6] P.R.O., DL43/5/7, f. 5.
[7] Lich. R.O., B/V/I/I, pp. 5, 58; Pt. II, p. 28.
[8] L. & P., iv(2), 3579. [9] ibid., (3), 6047.
[10] P.R.O., DL41/12/11, No. 10. [11] L. & P., iv(1), 1253.
[12] P.R.O., DL43/5/11. [13] L. & P., vi, 1124.

Lancaster who, Johnson said, had murdered John Bardsey on the orders of the Prior.[1] Whatever the truth of these charges, Lord cannot have been a very attractive character, and at the suppression of his house he showed a rather excessive enthusiasm for securing as much property for himself as possible.[2] Under such a head the state of Conishead cannot have been very good, and this impression is strengthened by the events of 1536.

A little more evidence is available for Cartmel, a larger house than Conishead. In 1497 William Hale, Prior of Cartmel, was deprived of his office and the revenues of his house were sequestrated, by Christopher Urswick, Archdeacon of Richmond, for certain alleged 'excesses'; Hale appealed to Pope Alexander VI, stating that the charges were false.[3] The result of Hale's petition is not recorded, but it seems to have been upheld, as he was certainly still prior in 1501, when he complained to the Archbishop of York, Savage, that Miles Burre[4] and William Payne[5] had left the monastery without permission, and were engaging in secular activities.[6] The next prior seems to have extended the faults of the indulgence system till they verged on blackmail; he forgave Robert Briggs and his wife all their sins against God or the Priory, or any offences committed in the future, without further payment, in return for a gift of plate to the Priory.[7] James Grigg, penultimate prior, seems to have been engaged in some sort of underhand dealings, and confessed on his death-bed to having made a number of loans from the Priory's income, without the knowledge of his brethren, to local men, including William Grigg, presumably a relation of his.[8] Clearly the rule that a prior should show his accounts to the convent each year was being disregarded.

But, as has been noticed of the other houses, Cartmel still remained significant in local life, and the last prior, Richard Preston, fulfilled the usual social and legal functions of the head of a monastery, including being commissioned by the Duchy to enquire into a dispute concerning a will.[9] But, like Prior Lord of Conishead, he got involved to his discredit in a dispute over the office of guide over the Sands. Edward Barlow claimed the office and its profits, but was refused by Preston, and, feeling he would not get justice in the common law courts, since the Prior was a great man in the area and 'greatly friended and favoured there', Barlow appealed to the Duchy Court.[10] Preston was summoned to appear in the Duchy Chamber at Michaelmas 1535, but failed to do so, and the matter was finally settled against the Prior in February 1536 by local arbitrators.[11] But although these examples are an illuminating sidelight on the social position of

[1] P.R.O., DL41/158/22.   [2] P.R.O., DL41/11/59, f. 1.
[3] C.C.C., MS. 170, f. 144.
[4] Who was later Prior, P.R.O., DL/43/4/12, f. 4.
[5] Perhaps the William Pannell who was 68 in 1536, ibid., f. 1.
[6] C.C.C., MS. 170, f. 123.   [7] P.R.O., DL43/4/12, f. 4.
[8] ibid., f. 2.   [9] Duchy Pleadings, ii, 21.   [10] ibid., ii, 70.
[11] P.R.O., DL43/4/12, f. 6.

Cartmel, they tell us little of the moral and spiritual condition of the monastery, though the general impression is one of worldliness, at least on the part of the priors. We can only conclude that Cartmel was fairly well behaved, at least after the rule of Prior Hale, and this judgement is substantiated by the behaviour of the canons in 1536.

Despite its size and wealth, Whalley Abbey's last years are less well documented than one might expect, but except for a few isolated incidents the general standard appears to have been fairly good. In 1474 the Abbey presented one John Belling to the vicarage of Eccles, but on examination he was found 'unsuitable and incompetent' and Bishop Hales of Lichfield censured the Abbey and collated Thomas Wright.[1] This does not indicate much interest on the part of the Abbey in the welfare of the parishioners of its impropriated churches. This incident occurred during the abbacy of Ralph Holden, who also fell foul of the Rector of Slaidburn and his people in a violent conflict over tithes.[2] The Abbey was involved in a number of tithe disputes, which seem to have grown more frequent in the 1530's; in 1532, for example, Laurence Forest, who held the Abbey's court for its exempt jurisdictions in the royal forests, excommunicated John Swindlehurst of Burholme for persistent refusal to pay tithes,[3] and in 1533 the people of Great Marsden, Whalley, and Colne, were refusing to pay their tithes.[4] Between 1530 and 1533, the Abbot took as many as seven cases of refusal of tithes or disputed church lands, and three mortuary cases[5] to the court of the Archdeacon of Chester, as well as those he tried in his own court, so the magnificence of Whalley's last years may have been accompanied by some alienation from the local people. In the early 1530's the Abbey officials went to great trouble to secure the conviction and punishment of those who refused to pay tithes. Some time between 1529 and 1532, Ralph Lynney, the Abbey's proctor at Blackburn and a monk of the house, wrote to one of the officers of the Archdeacon's Court at Chester to inform him that Christopher Ainsworth of Blackburn who was 'cited to appear before Mr. Official on Thursday the next', had not paid 'his tenth corns by the space of two years last passed'. Lynney asked that the court should 'lay into him' if he appeared, and that a suspension should be sent immediately if he did not, for which Lynney would pay by the first week in Lent.[6]

The last Abbot of Whalley, John Paslew, was elected in 1507,[7] and under him the Abbey entered upon the greatest period, in magnificence at least, of its history. Paslew became a man of some importance, being summoned to the Convocation of Canterbury in 1529,[8] and acting as a

---

[1] Lich. R.O., B/A/I, Reg. Hales, f. 108. [2] Whitaker, i, 105.
[3] *Whalley Act Book*, 159–60. [4] *Duchy Pleadings*, ii, 32.
[5] C.R.O., EDC1/4, fos. 13v, 16v, 59. EDC1/8, fos. 12v, 20v, and 63; EDC1/5, fos. 3v, 5, 41. EDC1/8 is misdated 1536/7 in the C.R.O. Catalogue, instead of 1531/2.
[6] C.R.O., EDC2/1, f. 41/1.
[7] B.M. Cotton MS. Vesp. D., xvii, f. 16. [8] L. & P., iv(3), 6047.

collector for the subsidy in 1532.[1] His importance, or perhaps merely his own estimate of it, is reflected in his travelling. In 1478 the only long journey Abbot Holden made was to Stanlaw, a possession of the Abbey, and he made but six short local visits to Abbey lands.[2] But in 1520 Abbot Paslew travelled to Hornby and Lathom, seats of the two nobles in the county, and to Eccles, and made a great progress to London, costing £26/5/-;[3] a contrast with the cost of the three times one of his monks, Lionel Full, went to London in 1521, £4/17/8d.,[4] gives some indication of Paslew's lavishness. In 1521 Paslew travelled even more, to Brough, Bolton, Durham, Combermere, Stanlaw, and Ripon.[5] This travelling, however, was the result of an increase in the importance of the house, rather than laxity, for where the monks of 1478 made over thirty journeys,[6] those of 1520 and 1521 made only about fourteen.[7]

In 1520 the monks spent about two-thirds of their income on food and drink, and a similar proportion had been expended in 1478; clearly the monks and their guests had been living well for some time. The brethren also kept themselves well entertained; in 1478 36/8d. was paid for minstrels, and in 1520 and 1521 £2/4/- each,[8] while in 1521 10/- was spent on bears for baiting.[9] Such jollities were, however, not unusual; the accounts of the Prior of Dunmow in Essex show payments for minstrels, players, and bear-baiting,[10] while William More, Prior of Worcester, had singers, minstrels, players, acrobats, and trumpeters visiting his priory, and he even kept a jester of his own.[11] Though there is no evidence of vice at Whalley, the Abbey does seem to have been a great country household rather than a retreat for the spiritually minded, especially where food was concerned, for in 1520 the Abbey's provisions included sturgeon, salmon, figs, almonds, cakes, spices, sugar candy, liquorice, cinnamon, and dates.[12] The height of Whalley's splendour was reached about 1530, when Paslew, apparently without permission, assumed a mitre, the expense of which forced him to begin selling off Abbey plate.[13] The Abbot certainly did not stint himself, for an inventory of the Abbey's goods taken in 1537 includes two mitres, one in silver-gilt and heavily jewelled.[14] Paslew also adapted the Abbey buildings to reflect the new dignity he felt the house had achieved; he added a Lady Chapel to the church, rebuilt the infirmary block, and adapted his hall, kitchen, solar, and chamber to meet his own requirements.[15] But all did not augur well for Paslew, and it was

[1] L. & P., v, 1506.   [2] Whitaker, i, 123–4.
[3] L.R.O., DDTo/B21, printed in Trans. Hist. Soc. L. & C., Vol. 114, 54 ff.
[4] Whitaker, i, 123.   [5] ibid.
[6] ibid.   [7] L.R.O., DDTo/B21; Whitaker, loc. cit.
[8] Whitaker, i, 121; L.R.O., DDTo/B21.
[9] Whitaker, i, 119.   [10] Oxley, *Reformation in Essex*, 54.
[11] Knowles, *Religious Orders*, iii, 115–18.
[12] L.R.O., DDTo/B21.   [13] L. & P., xii(1), 621.
[14] Whitaker, i, 187.
[15] Wallis, *History of the Church in Blackburnshire*, 143.

recorded that in 1520 one of his monks, Edmund Howard, died, and then appeared to the Abbot in a dream, predicting that he would live another sixteen years and no longer.[1] For Paslew and his Abbey, pride did indeed come before the fall.

For Cockersand, a Premonstratensian house, we have the records of eight visitations made in the last quarter of the fifteenth century by Bishop Redman, Visitor of the English Province of the Order, and a number of other records of the same period. In 1477 the canons found some difficulty in agreeing on a successor to Abbot Lucas, and one of the canons was charged with inviting lay intervention.[2] In the hope of securing a result, Redman appointed a committee of nine canons to make the election.[3] One of the nine, William Bowland, was chosen, and his election was confirmed by Redman at the first visitation of which we have record, in 1478.[4] On that occasion, the Visitor found no serious defects, stipulating only that the rule of silence and the details of ceremonies should be better observed.[5] At the visitation of 1481, Redman felt able to compliment the canons, saying that in their house 'omnia ad laudem Dei et religionis honorem directa, tam in spiritualibus quam in temporalibus, summa providencia domini abbatis'.[6] But after this, Cockersand seems to have gone into a serious decline.

The next visitation took place in 1488[7] and perhaps the long interval contributed towards indiscipline, for then Redman had to excommunicate two canons for apostacy, and order that for 'majori tranquilitate et securitate', the canons were not to discuss the secret affairs of the Order with outsiders, and the canons were not to try to gain appointment to Abbey offices through the influence of laymen.[8] This fear of lay intervention in the affairs of the house was a constant theme in the history of Cockersand, and in 1530 Norroy King of Arms noted that 'for as much as the said house was many times troubled, at the time of their election of their Abbot, with the gentlemen of the county, their neighbours, they made suit to the King for his maintainance to have free election among themselves, and bound their said house for that privilege to give to the King at every election £20, to the King and to his heirs, kings'.[9]

Only eight months after this normal visitation of Cockersand, Redman was back at the monastery again in December 1488,[10] because of the reports of bad behaviour he had received.[11] William Bentham, cellarer, was accused of incontinence with a certain Marjory Gardiner, which he did not deny, and was sentenced to forty days' penance, and banished to

[1] B.M. Cotton MS. Vesp. D., xvii, f. 18.   [2] C.A.P., i, 95–6.
[3] ibid., i, 97.   [4] ibid., ii, 113.   [5] ibid., ii, 112–13.
[6] ibid., 113.
[7] Misdated by Gasquet in C.A.P., ii, 115. See Colvin, *White Canons*, 390.
[8] C.A.P., ii, 115–16.   [9] *Norroy's Visitation of the Northern Counties*, 91.
[10] Misdated by Gasquet in C.A.P., ii, 116. See Colvin, *White Canons*, 390.
[11] C.A.P., ii, 116.

Croxton for three years.[1] James Skipton, the precentor, was accused of the same crime with Elena Wilson, but although he denied the charge he was unable to clear himself by the usual process of purgation by his brethren, and so he received the heavier sentence of seven years' banishment, as well as the forty days' penance.[2] These two were not the only offenders, and the whole house was apparently very lax; the Abbot was ordered not to allow drinking after Compline, with a punishment of three days on bread and water for those who disobeyed, the canons were censured for wearing elaborate dress, and the prior and sub-prior were ordered to exclude women from the infirmary, the refectory, and the 'jordayne chamber', or scandal and damnation would result.[3]

As Dom David Knowles has noted,[4] sentences of banishment seem to have been frequently commuted or simply disobeyed, and those found guilty of serious offences often rose to positions of authority later. When Redman next visited Cockersand, in April 1491, Bentham and Skipton were still at their old home, though even Bentham's three years' banishment had not yet expired, as sub-prior and cellarer,[5] and Skipton later became Abbot.[6] This time the Visitor punished one canon for breaking the rule of silence, and it seems that the canons were still drinking after Compline.[7] Though there were no serious offences, the election of a new Abbot, John Preston, in 1490[8] had not improved the general condition. But by 1494 there had been another serious lapse, and Thomas Poulton was punished for incontinence, and was also accused of having had a child by Alice Pilkington, but at the intercession of his brethren the sentence of banishment was lifted.[9] The failures of this individual were reflected in the general failure of the house to perform its religious services properly.[10]

Three years later, Redman found that Poulton was sub-prior,[11] though the house as a whole had improved, and the Bishop had only to censure the canons for their quarrelsomeness and their habit of staying in bed instead of attending matins, and order a stricter observance of the rule of obedience.[12] Redman clearly thought there had been some improvement, complimenting the discretion and good government of the Abbot.[13] But by the last visitation of which we have record, in 1500, there had again been some decline, probably to be accounted for by the prolonged illness of the Abbot.[14] The canons had again been drinking after Compline, and failing to observe the regulations on dress and silence, while Robert Burton, the precentor, and Thomas Kellett, the succentor, were expelled from their stalls; the only reason given is their 'faults', but these must have been very serious to warrant such a punishment.[15] Soon after this Redman reinstated

[1] C.A.P., ii, 116–17.   [2] ibid., 117.   [3] ibid., 116–17.
[4] *Religious Orders*, iii, 45–6.   [5] C.A.P., ii, 120.   [6] V.C.H., ii, 157.
[7] C.A.P., ii, 118–19.   [8] ibid., i, 110–11.   [9] ibid., ii, 121.
[10] ibid., 121–2.   [11] ibid., 125, misdated by Gasquet, Colvin, op. cit., 390.
[12] C.A.P., ii, 123–5.   [13] ibid.   [14] ibid., 126.
[15] ibid., 126–7.

Burton,[1] and at some stage Kellett too returned to become cellarer, and later Vicar of Mitton,[2] one of the Abbey's impropriated churches.

The general picture created by this rather tedious recital of offences is one of consistent laxity punctuated by occasional more serious lapses, but the only other evidence available for this period gives an impression of rather more vigour than might be expected. A house which was in a perpetually poor state would not attract many new recruits, but Cockersand continued to draw novices, and even managed to increase its size, even up to the dissolution, in contrast with the trend over the whole of the country, both for monasteries in general and for the Premonstratensian Order.[3] In 1381 there were thirteen canons,[4] but in 1488 there were seventeen canons and two novices, both of whom were professed by 1491.[5] The number had risen, by 1491, to eighteen canons and two new novices, both of whom were deacons by 1494, when another deacon had been added, and all three were full canons in 1497. There were twenty canons in 1497, with two novices, both of whom were professed by 1500; one of them, Mathew Macrell, was Abbot of Alnwick from 1519 to 1522,[6] and the last Abbot of Barlings,[7] while the other, James Dugdale, was vicar of the impropriated church of Garstang in 1535,[8] and remained there until his death in 1545.[9] In 1500, in the last list we have, until the suppression years, there were twenty monks, and three new novices, one of whom, John Holm, was still there at the dissolution of the house in 1539.[10] This gradual increase in numbers appears to have continued until the fall of the Abbey.[11] When the 1536 Commissioners surveyed Cockersand, they found the Abbot and twenty-one canons,[12] to whom must be added James Dugdale and Thomas Kellett; after the exemption from suppression, two monks either transferred to the house, or joined as novices, giving a total of twenty-six canons in 1539, the twenty-three who signed the surrender,[13] and three others who served churches.[14] It is hard to believe that such increases would have taken place if the Abbey had been in a uniformly poor condition, and it is probable that the general standard of the house was not always as bad as some individual failings might suggest. In the eight visitations discussed, Redman recommended the Abbey on two occasions, and was critical of the monastery as a whole on four, while the canons may well have behaved in a more seemly manner for at least some of the time between visitations.

[1] ibid., i, 263.
[2] Duchy Pleadings, i, 107; Cock. Chart., 1185. He was vicar there until his death in 1546. (B.I.Y., R/I/29, Reg. Holgate, f. 78v).
[3] Knowles & Hadcock, 364, 361.   [4] ibid., 164.
[5] Numbers from C.A.P., ii, 114, 120, 122–3, 125–6.
[6] Colvin, White Canons, 393.   [7] ibid., 395.   [8] Valor, v, 263.
[9] V.C.H., vii, 297.   [10] D.K.R., viii, App. 2, 16.
[11] Three new canons were ordained as late as 1536 (B.I.Y., R/I/28, Reg. Lee, fos. 195, 196v.)   [12] P.R.O., DL43/5/4, f. 1.
[13] D.K.R., viii, App. 2, 16.   [14] See Appendix A.

It does seem, however, that though Cockersand may have left much to be desired in the last quarter of the fifteenth century, there had been some improvement by the suppression years, and the Abbey which was finally suppressed was not the lax and sometimes immoral house which Redman visited. For the number of canons it contained, Cockersand was comparatively poor, and the canons could never expect the comforts which a house such as Whalley might offer. It is therefore likely that the marked increase in numbers between the last years of the fifteenth century and the 1530's indicates sincere religious enthusiasm on the part of the inmates, which was attracting more and more novices. This would agree with the suggestion that there was a quickening of religious life in these years in Lancashire generally. In 1536, at least, the canons of Cockersand were unanimous in their wish to remain in religion at their old home.[1] The Abbey appears to have been what all religious houses were designed to be, a spiritual retreat cut off from the world; for this reason it rarely appears in the records. While the worldly wise and litigious Whalley, between 1509 and 1536, took eight cases to the Duchy Court,[2] and was involved in another two disputes which led to court cases,[3] besides being defendant in yet another,[4] Cockersand was involved in only one dispute, albeit a long one, with the tenants of Westhoughton, which seems to have stemmed not from malice but from confusion over the customs of the manor.[5] In an age when almost all quarrels led either to bloodshed or the courtroom, such a record gives us some idea of the character of the Abbey.

The largest, richest, and most important of the Lancashire houses, Furness, is also the most fully documented. The story begins in 1497, when Marmaduke Huby, Abbot of Fountains and Visitor of Furness, arrived to find the community split into two groups over the election of a new abbot. The two ambitious rivals, the cellarer and a scholar of the Abbey, had both been canvassing support from local notables, and, wisely, Huby refused to recognise either of them. He persuaded the brethren to elect Alexander Banke, a young man of only thirty, but, Huby thought, well qualified for the position.[6] At Citeaux in the same year, the General Chapter of the Order confirmed Banke's election, and his installation by Huby.[7] But John Dalton, ex-cellarer and a bachelor of theology,[8] one of the new Abbot's rivals, now did his best to unseat Banke, and, according to the Chapter, seditiously promoted a conspiracy against his superior, and by false evidence cited him to appear before a secular court.[9] For the moment, Dalton's efforts were unsuccessful, but his Abbot was even worse

[1] See below, Chapters Two and Four.
[2] *Ducatus Lancastriae*, i, 133, 149, 193, 219, 220; ii, 15, 31, 57.
[3] ibid., ii, 35, 51.   [4] ibid., i, 142.
[5] ibid., ii, 28, 32, 39.
[6] C. H. Talbot, ed., *Letters from the English Abbots to the Chapter at Citeaux*, 205–7.
[7] Canivez, ed., *Statuta Capitulorum Generalium Ordinis Cistersiensis*, vi, 189, No. 69.
[8] Talbot, op. cit., 248.   [9] Canivez, op. cit., vi, 237, No. 23.

than he; the same Chapter in 1500 absolved Banke from incontinence, irregularity, simony, and other proven crimes, and in view of his penitence and promises of reform, rehabilitated him as Abbot of Furness.[1] Banke, however, did not improve, and about 1505 he seized lands held in fee of the King when the previous owner died and the heir was out of the country.[2] Then, in 1514, the Abbot of Stratford Langthorne, in trying to visit the Abbey, had to call in secular forces to fight a way through 300 of Banke's armed retainers before he could even reach the house. The Abbot of Stratford declared Banke contumacious for his refusal to recognise the Visitor's authority, and made John Dalton abbot.[3] Although he did not hold his position for long, Dalton was abbot long enough to appear in the records; he was involved in a court case in August 1514,[4] and he granted the stewardship of the Abbey to the Earl of Derby.[5]

Alexander Banke complained to Pope Leo X, who ordered the Abbots of Meaux, Byland, and Fountains to investigate Banke's claim that he had been deprived by the Abbot of Stratford at the instigation of the Earl of Derby,[6] and, though Banke's deprivation may have been deserved, Dalton's grant to the Earl and his record of seeking lay support give substance to Banke's charges. It is not clear whether it was Banke or Dalton who, as 'Abbot of Furness', attended the General Chapter of the Order in 1515,[7] but it was probably Banke, who later referred to his absence from the monastery about that time.[8] Banke now appealed to the King, and had Dalton and four of the monks imprisoned in London, and to reassert his position had another four monks imprisoned in Lancaster Castle, where one of them, the sub-prior, died.[9] Dalton then appealed to the Pope, and secured a decree in February 1516 from the Auditor of the Apostolic Chamber for himself and other monks imprisoned by Banke, during a suit touching his right to the monastery.[10] The papal decision was, however, ignored; Banke was acting as Abbot in December 1516,[11] and he remained in office until his death, while Dalton, though still in prison in 1517,[12] was later released and he continued as a monk of Furness, signing an indenture in 1532.[13]

The later history of Furness, though with no repetition of such dramatic events, shows little improvement, especially under the rule of Banke. In 1516, intent on enclosing Abbey land, Banke and twenty-two of his monks and servants ejected William Carre and his wife and family from their tenement.[14] In 1517–18 Banke seems to have tried to cheat Christopher Bardsey, by suing him in the Duchy Court for a £20 debt and arrears of

[1] Canivez, op. cit., vi, 238, No. 25.
[2] L. & P., Addenda, 1023.
[3] Talbot, op. cit., 248–9.
[4] Duchy Pleadings, i, 98.
[5] L. & P., iv(2), 4522.
[6] ibid., i, 2910.
[7] Canivez, op. cit., vi, 468.
[8] Duchy Pleadings, i, 74.
[9] Talbot, op. cit., 248–9.
[10] L. & P., ii(2), App. 20.
[11] Duchy Pleadings, i, 68.
[12] Talbot, op. cit., 249.
[13] Beck, Annales, 313–14.
[14] Duchy Pleadings, i, 68–9.

rent, which Bardsey had already tried to pay,[1] and in 1521–2 Banke again sued Bardsey, this time over tithes and a tithe barn.[2] It was alleged in 1530 by one William Tunstall that since his election Banke had kept a free port at Furness, so depriving the King of customs worth £110, while he had not paid the King his 20/- rent for holding a sheriff's tourn, had taken a tax from his tenants at Colton, and had withheld £250 from the last subsidy, though Banke denied the charges.[3] Tunstall's evidence must be treated with care, since he seems to have been involved in a running battle with the Abbot, who complained in Star Chamber in 1529 that Tunstall had been harassing the Abbey servants and trying to gain possession of its fishery on the Lune.[4]

The most disreputable case in which Banke was involved was rather like that in which Prior Lord of Conishead took part in 1533.[5] John and Roland Taylor quarrelled over an office, and Banke sided with Roland, a kinsman of his; John alleged that Banke procured Roland to murder him, and three days after the accusation, Roland did in fact murder John, and managed to obtain a pardon from the King, probably with Banke's help. The case was taken up by Thomas Kendal, who said that the Abbot was never indicted because of his power and his friends, but Banke objected to the charges as vague, and argued that a pardon granted to the principal also covered the accessories.[6] In all, Banke was involved in at least twelve cases in the Duchy Court between 1509 and his death in 1531, and was the defendant in eight of them, usually in cases of attempts to acquire lands or fisheries by force or dishonesty.[7] He cannot have made Furness popular with its tenants and neighbours, and under his rule the Abbey operated as a property company rather than a religious house.

Though most of the misbehaviour we know of was the fault of Banke rather than his monks, his influence cannot have put Furness in a very good condition, and the character of the monks becomes clear in an incident which followed Banke's death. Hugh Brown, one of the monks, was entrusted with the keys of the late abbot's chamber, but he used the keys to enter the room and steal valuable property, and then, with three other monks, he persuaded the local smith to break open the Abbey chest, removed the convent seal, and used it on a number of blank parchments which the group also took. On one of the parchments a petition for licence to elect a new abbot was written, and all but one of the others were later recovered. On this last, Brown forged a lease of the manor of Winterburne, which he apparently sold to the Earl of Cumberland.[8] When

---

[1] *Duchy Pleadings*, i, 74, 95, 97.
[2] P.R.O., DL3/5, F.1.   [3] P.R.O., DL3/6, R.1.
[4] R. Stewart-Brown, ed., *Lancashire and Cheshire Cases in the Court of Star Chamber*, L. & C. Rec. Soc., Vol. 71, 98.
[5] See above.   [6] P.R.O., DL3/3, K.1, N.D.
[7] *Ducatus Lancastriae*, i, 126, 146, 188, 195, 196, 197, 204, 205, 213; ii, 22.
[8] P.R.O., DL3/34, P.1, printed in full, Beck, *Annales*, App. IX.

Layton and Legh, the King's Visitors, were at Furness in 1536, Abbot Pyle reported the matter to them, and Brown was imprisoned in the Abbey, where he remained until he was released by the rebels during the Pilgrimage.[1]

Banke must have died in 1531, since in that year Roger Pyle paid £200 for his admission and confirmation as Abbot,[2] and in 1532 Roger, Abbot of Furness, made a grant of £4 a year to Cromwell.[3] The forged lease was dated November 6th, 1531,[4] and it was presumably soon after this, before Pyle's election, that Cumberland tried to take advantage of the vacancy to force the convent to grant him Winterburne; the monks wrote back to the Earl asking for a respite until Michaelmas, 'for so much that we, that are the body of the convent, can give no direct answer to no such matter, without some good advertisement'.[5] The Earl took no further action until 1533, when he tried to force Abbot Pyle to grant him Winterburne and two other farms, and Pyle had to increase Cromwell's £4 annuity to 10 marks, and give him a £10 'douceur', to secure the King's favour in the matter.[6] Pyle seems to have been able to withstand Cumberland's demands, and probably fobbed him off with the stewardship of Winterburne, for which the Earl drew £6.[7] Until 1536 Cumberland appears to have tried to force the Abbot to give him a new lease, but when Layton and Legh were visiting Furness he pressed his forged lease for the first time, getting his chaplain, William Bury, to persuade Legh to intercede with Pyle to allow the lease.[8] But Cumberland did not gain possession of the manor, despite some support from Cromwell.[9] Early in July 1537 Robert Southwell reported to Cromwell that 'my Lord of Cumberland pretendeth now to be the farmer of a manor called Winterburne' at a rent of £32, whereas it was worth £50; Southwell sent Cromwell statements from the monks of Furness on Cumberland's 'pretended interest therein'.[10] But despite Southwell's advice, Cumberland gained confirmation of his lease from Augmentations, though he admitted that the original was 'not of effect',[11] and he remained in possession until 1542, when the original lessee sued him, and the whole matter came to light.[12]

This complicated story illustrates the difficulties which beset Furness during the rule of its last abbot, and the trouble caused by the legacy of Alexander Banke's rule. Pyle, in fact, spent his abbacy trying to put right the problems caused by Banke, not the least being the debts incurred

---

[1] ibid.
[2] L. & P., v, 657.   [3] ibid., 1285.   [4] Beck, *Annales*, 362.
[5] Dickens, ed., *Clifford Letters of Sixteenth Century*, No. 3, p. 61.
[6] L. & P., vi, 632; printed in Beck, *Annales*, 340.
[7] *Valor*, v, 270; P.R.O., SC12/9/73.
[8] P.R.O., DL3/34, P.1; Beck, op. cit., App. IX, xci–xcii.
[9] L. & P., xii(2), 234, printed Beck, op. cit., 362.
[10] L. & P., xii(2), 206, printed Beck, op. cit., 356–60.
[11] L. & P., xii(2), 234, printed Beck, op. cit., 362.
[12] P.R.O., DL3/34, P.1.

under him. In 1536 Roger Pyle reported to Cromwell that 'my predecessor left our monastery in great debts unto the executors of Sir William Compton, wherefore they have me now in suit'.[1] Pyle was also finding it difficult[2] to pay the annuities which Abbot Banke had granted, which included £10 to the Duke of Norfolk, granted in 1520,[3] ten marks to Laurence Starkey, granted in 1525,[4] and £5 to Fitzwilliam, Chancellor of the Duchy, granted in 1530.[5]

The most serious trouble of Pyle's abbacy occurred only a little over eighteen months after his election, showing the state in which Banke had left Furness. The Abbot complained to Cromwell that three of his monks, and one looking after one of the Abbey churches, 'cannot be contented to obey me', led by a monk named Richard Banke, who may thus have been a relation of the late abbot.[6] Pyle found it necessary to imprison Banke, but he and his friends threatened to appeal to the King, and if they were successful Pyle's authority would be completely undermined.[7] But the Abbot was able to solve the problem quietly and effectively, packing Banke off to the Isle of Man, where he was paid ten marks as Vicar of the Abbey's church there.[8]

The abbacy of Alexander Banke, therefore, weakened Furness morally and financially and so naturally weakened the authority and influence of the house and its head in its temporal affairs. In an attempt to maintain his position, Pyle had to continue the annuities granted by his predecessor, and make new grants to government officials, paying £10 to the Duke of Suffolk, increasing Cromwell's pension to the same sum, in return for a promise to help the Abbey in time of need,[9] and ten marks each to the Earl of Wiltshire, Anne Boleyn's father, and to Thomas Holcroft, 'per mandatum regis'.[10] The Abbey also paid forty shillings each to six local J.P.'s,[11] as well as employing powerful local men like the Vice-Chancellor of the Palatinate, the Earl of Derby, and the Earl of Cumberland.[12] But despite his efforts to extend the influence of his house in this way, Pyle was dogged by ill luck, and by his inability to assert the traditional authority of his office, while still being expected to fulfil its functions, and carry out the obligations which it entailed. As head of the largest Abbey in the archdeaconry of Richmond, he was naturally appointed collector of the 1532 subsidy for Richmond, but one Seyton, farmer of the rectory of Aldingham, refused to pay unless Pyle reduced his quota, and threatened to turn Cromwell and others against Furness, intending, as Pyle put it,

[1] L. & P., x, 51, printed Beck, *Annales*, 339–40.   [2] ibid.
[3] Beck, op. cit., 306; P.R.O., SC12/9/73.   [4] Beck, op. cit., 308–9.
[5] ibid., 311; P.R.O., SC12/9/73.
[6] L. & P., vi, 787, printed Beck, op. cit., 317.   [7] ibid.
[8] *Valor*, v, 270; P.R.O., SC12/9/73, SC11/376.
[9] L. & P., vii, 531, printed Beck, op. cit., 318–19; payments to the King's chief minister were common—Whalley gave £22 to Wolsey in 1520 (L.R.O., DDTo/B21).
[10] P.R.O., SC12/9/73.   [11] ibid.; *Valor*, v, 270.   [12] ibid.

'to put our monastery to great hindrance and expence, as he did in time of my predecessor'.[1] Seyton had been in conflict with the Abbey for at least two years; it seems that he had refused to pay rent, and when Abbot Banke distrained Seyton's cattle to enforce payment, the Abbey servants were attacked and the cattle recaptured. Banke then sued Seyton in the Duchy Court.[2] The Abbot tried to buy Seyton's friendship, granting him a pension of £6 a year, 'for the intent that he should be loving and gentle to me and our monastery',[3] but Seyton was not to be silenced, citing Pyle in the Exchequer Court for shipping wine into Furness, and persuading Cromwell to support him against the Abbot.[4]

Pyle was always eager to ingratiate himself with Cromwell, arresting a Scot for no other reason than that he knew the landing places in the area,[5] but this too could lead him into difficulties. In December 1533 the Abbot arrested Gawain Borrodale, a monk of Holme Cultram who was accused of murdering his abbot, questioned him, put him in custody,[6] and took depositions from two other monks of Holme Cultram.[7] But though this might keep Cromwell favourable towards Furness, it made Pyle unpopular with his Order, and the Abbots of Fountains and Byland pointed out that they alone were the 'reformators and visitors of our said religion'.[8] Pyle therefore had to transfer Borrodale to the custody of the Abbot of Byland, who later reported to Cromwell that Pyle had been mistaken, and that it was clear that Borrodale was innocent.[9]

But although the Abbot was frequently involved in service for the government, he could not always rely on fair treatment for his house in return. In March 1534, after someone had told the King that Furness held the advowson of Hawkshead church, Henry demanded from Pyle letters of presentation to the benefice,[10] and Pyle had to write back to the King, after a delay which must indicate considerable thought, pointing out that Hawkshead was only a chapel of ease to Dalton parish church,[11] and asking to be able to continue to receive the tithes and profits.[12] Two days later, Pyle wrote frantically to Cromwell asking for his help, or else 'I and my brethren be utterly undone, and thereby should be compelled to leave off such power and hospitality as we have heretofore kept in the said monastery', and sending him ten royals as an incentive to intercede with the King.[13]

[1] L. & P., v, 849, printed Beck, *Annales*, 317–18.
[2] P.R.O., DL3/4, F.3, N.D.
[3] L. & P., viii, 1132, printed Beck, op. cit., 322.   [4] ibid.
[5] L. & P., vi, 215, printed Beck, op. cit., 319–20.
[6] L. & P., vi, 1557, 986; Beck, op. cit., 320–1.   [7] L. & P., Add., 866.
[8] L. & P., vi, 1557, printed Beck, loc. cit.
[9] L. & P., vi, 987.
[10] L. & P., vii, 520.
[11] Hawkshead did not become a parish until 1578—V.C.H., viii, 370.
[12] L. & P., vii, 520.
[13] L. & P., vii, 531; printed in Beck, *Annales*, 318–19.

Despite the very full documentation covering the last years of Furness, no disreputable incident involving the monks is known, except for the Brown affair and the restlessness following Banke's death. Though the circumstances of the fall of the house give no good impression of the worth and enthusiasm of the monks, the absence of any record of failings on their part leads one to conclude that things may have improved once Pyle had re-established the authority of the Abbot's position. But whatever the condition of the house, and although it remained a powerful force in the life of the area, its moral authority had been severely weakened by the mercenary and dishonest involvement in land disputes of Banke's abbacy, and it was considered fair game for a grasping noble, a farmer with a grudge, and even the Crown. Furness shared the failings of the rather primitive society in which it was situated, but, like the other houses, especially in the north of the county, it was still an important and integral element of that society,[1] and, during the Pilgrimage of Grace, it was sufficiently attached to the old religion, the independence of the Church, and the continuation of the monasteries to play a significant part in the rebellion. But the events of the period discussed must have sapped the self-confidence of the monks, and left them ill-prepared to withstand the anti-clerical attack from the south of England, however secure their position may have been in the north.

[1] See below, Chapter Five.

CHAPTER TWO

THE VISITATION OF LAYTON AND LEGH

THE preparations for the great royal visitation of the monasteries began in January 1535,[1] and Richard Layton sent Cromwell a scheme of eighty-six articles of enquiry[2] for the monasteries, based on the usual questions asked at visitations, though Layton added notes that the monks were particularly to be questioned on the Boleyn marriage and the royal supremacy. In June Layton wrote to Comwell asking that he and Thomas Legh should be appointed Visitors of the northern houses, as one or other of them 'have familiar acquaintance within ten or twelve miles' of each house, 'so that no knavery can be hid from us in that country'.[3] Clearly the Visitors began with a bias against the monks. Layton and Legh did not move northwards until early in January 1536,[4] and at their approach the head of at least one Lancashire house was seized by panic. On January 7th Abbot Pyle of Furness wrote to Cromwell pleading the debts and expenses of his house, and asking that 'it may please you now to direct your high letters unto such as shall be visitors under you, commanding them to be good unto me and our monastery'.[5] Layton and Legh were at Richmond on February 10th, and at Ludlow on February 28th,[6] and in the meantime they had visited all the monasteries of Cumberland and Lancashire; clearly they cannot have paid much attention to each house.

The Visitors reported on all eleven houses in Lancashire, and they made no accusations of moral lapse against the monks of only two, Lytham and Kersall, both small cells.[7] At Cartmel, they charged two canons with incontinence, and said that one had six children.[8] They found one canon with a licence from his brethren to live outside the house, and a convent pension of £5/13/4d., which they revoked, and ordered him to remain in residence.[9] In view of the issue of the licence, it is reasonable to suppose that this monk did have a family. But when the Suppression Commissioners visited the house three months later, they reported, in the 'Brief Certificate', that all the monks were 'of good and honest conversation'.[10] In the Commissioners' 'Declaration', all the canons were given as 'of good and honest conversation', except William Pannell, the one who wished to

---

[1] Knowles, *Religious Orders*, iii, 268.
[2] L. & P., viii, 822; articles printed in Burnet-Pocock, iv, 207 ff.
[3] L. & P., viii, 822, printed in West, *Antiquities*, App. X, No. 2.
[4] Knowles, op. cit., App. VI.
[5] L. & P., x, 51, printed Beck, *Annales*, 339-40.
[6] Knowles, loc. cit.   [7] L. & P., x, 364.
[8] ibid.
[9] P.R.O., DL43/4/12, f. 1; 43/5/7, f. 2.
[10] P.R.O., DL43/4/11.

live outside.[1] The identity of the other canon charged by Layton and Legh is not known, but the Commissioners, three of them local men, who spent more time at the monastery than the Visitors could have done, clearly thought him of sufficiently good behaviour. Only Prior Preston was not commented on by the Commissioners, but he cannot have been the other culprit charged by Layton and Legh, since where the Prior was at fault the Visitors always named him,[2] and in any case it was the Commissioners' practice not to make any remarks about priors.[3] This charge may therefore be fabricated, or perhaps the offence took place so long ago that the Commissioners did not know of it or thought it irrelevant. The general condition of Cartmel was apparently good; when asked by the Suppression Commissioners, eight of the nine canons who were asked wished to continue in religion, and if necessary to transfer to another house,[4] and the other seems eventually to have agreed with the majority.[5] There was obvious enthusiasm for the religious life, and the house was still attracting new recruits in the 1530's; of the ten monks in 1536, two were in their twenties, and six were under thirty-five.[6]

Conishead, however, was less good, or rather very bad, if Layton and Legh are to be believed. They accused five canons of incontinence;[7] Prior Lord was probably not among them, since he was not named, but five out of the seven canons normally resident[8] is a very high proportion, indicating either that the condition of the Priory was appalling, or perhaps just bad enough for the Visitors to be able to make exaggerated charges. It was reported that one canon had committed his offences with six women, and another with ten,[9] which seem improbably high numbers. Two monks asked for permission to leave the house,[10] and these may be the two charged with the serious lapses; perhaps their behaviour reflects their distaste for religion, but more probably they were so eager to go that they made false confessions to secure speedy release. Alternatively, if these two are not the same, perhaps they laid exaggerated or false charges against their brethren to ingratiate themselves with the Visitors. In any case, the moral and spiritual condition of Conishead cannot have been good, and this may be reflected in the Suppression Commissioners' failure to give the 'good and honest conversation' report of any of the canons.[11] Too much should not be read into this, for it may have been due to lapse of memory on their part, since assessment of the condition of a house was only a minor part of their task, and they similarly made no comment on the monks of Burs-

[1] P.R.O., DL43/4/12, f. 1.
[2] e.g. Furness, Hornby, Penwortham, Holland, L. & P., x, 364.
[3] e.g. P.R.O., DL43/5/4, f. 1.
[4] P.R.O., DL43/5/7, f. 2.   [5] P.R.O., DL43/4/11.
[6] P.R.O., DL43/4/12, f. 1. The two young men had only recently been ordained (B.I.Y., R/I/28, Reg. Lee, fos. 190, 191v).
[7] L. & P., x, 364.   [8] P.R.O., DL43/5/7, f. 3.
[9] L. & P., x, 364.   [10] ibid.   [11] P.R.O., DL43/5/7, f. 3.

cough,[1] where the Visitors made only one accusation.[2] There is a strong likelihood, therefore, that if the Commissioners could not commend the whole house, they mentioned no-one.

But Conishead may not have been as bad as it appears, and there does seem to have been some enthusiasm for religion on the part of a few of the canons. Of the five given the choice, by the Suppression Commission, of transferring or taking a 'capacity', two asked for capacities, and three wished to be 'further advised if this house be dissolved'.[3] Clearly, when they were told that the house would be suppressed, these three opted for 'capacities'.[4] But although they did not wish to move, their statement indicates they would have prefered to remain in their own house had they been allowed to do so. Prior Lord seems to have wanted to stay,[5] Cansforth, the quondam, was quite comfortable there, and better off than he could expect to be in the world,[6] and this would give a majority of five to two, of those normally resident, in favour of staying. This explains the Priory's offer of 1,000 marks to the King for permission to remain, which was later increased to 1,100 marks.[7] This willingness to stay is also reflected in the canons' behaviour during the Pilgrimage of Grace, for they were back in their convent soon after the rebellion began, and on October 16th they wrote to one of the rebel leaders asking for help.[8] It seems likely, therefore, that all the trouble in the house was created by the two monastic 'mis-fits' who asked Layton and Legh for permission to leave, the only monks in Lancashire to do so,[9] and then applied for dispensations from the Commissioners.[10]

At Cockersand, Layton and Legh accused two of the canons of homosexuality,[11] which is not too serious out of twenty-two monks,[12] especially as the offence could have taken place between the same two canons on one occasion long before, and still earned the same condemnation. When the Suppression Commission reported on the house a few months later, of seventeen monks interviewed all were of 'honest conversation', and fourteen of them were willing to be transferred to another house if their own was dissolved, while the other three hoped to remain at Cockersand but were unwilling to go elsewhere.[13] There was clearly considerable enthusiasm for the religious life; the Abbey offered the King 1,000 marks for exemption from suppression,[14] and later this was increased to 2,000 marks.[15] Cockersand was vigorous enough to be attracting new recruits; of the twenty-two monks, three were aged twenty-four, and ten were under

---

[1] ibid., f. 4.   [2] L. & P., x, 364.
[3] P.R.O., DL43/5/7, f. 3. A 'capacity' was a licence to leave the monastic life and serve as a secular priest.   [4] F.O.R., 67.   [5] P.R.O., DL41/11/59, fos. 8, 9.
[6] ibid., f. 11.   [7] L. & P., x, 1191; P.R.O., DL41/11/59, fos. 8, 9.
[8] L. & P., Add., 1112.
[9] L. & P., x, 364.   [10] P.R.O., DL43/5/7, f. 3.
[11] L. & P., x, 364.   [12] ibid., 1191.
[13] P.R.O., DL43/5/4, f. 1; DL43/5/7, f. 1.
[14] L. & P., x, 1191.   [15] P.R.O., DL29/2313, m. 17d.

c

thirty.[1] In view of the need to accommodate the monks who wished to continue in religion,[2] and in view of the house's good condition and financial offers, the Crown granted letters-patent of exemption from the Act of Suppression.[3] This is adequate testimony to the enthusiasm of the canons of Cockersand.

In the absence of suppression reports, less detailed discussion can be given to the other two northern houses, Furness and Whalley, and we have little against which to check the allegations of Layton and Legh. The Visitors reported that, at Furness, Abbot Pyle and three others were guilty of incontinence, and another of homosexuality.[4] The recent history of the house would not lead one to expect a good condition, but five monks who had lapsed at some time during their religious careers is not too damning for a house of at least thirty-three resident monks.[5] The charge against Pyle may not be true, since there is no other sign of scandal in the career of a well-known figure, and not even his enemies accused him of immorality. He was apparently a trusted agent of Thomas Cromwell,[6] and when he knew the Visitors were approaching his house all he was worried about was that they might put Furness to further expense.[7] At Furness the Visitors uncovered the case of Hugh Brown, and put him in prison in the Abbey under Pyle's charge, but he was later released by the northern rebels.[8]

At Whalley, Layton and Legh accused Richard Wood of homosexuality,[9] which was hardly very serious in a monastery with at least twenty-four monks normally resident.[10] Whalley, though inclined towards luxury and worldliness, attracted not one hint of scandal, and its moral condition, if not its spiritual, was obviously good. Though there is no way of comparing the Visitors' charges with other evidence, Layton and Legh do not appear to have built up a substantial charge against Whalley or Furness, and their condition was certainly no worse than might be expected for such a time and place.

The state of the houses in the south of Lancashire seems to have been less good. At Burscough, Layton and Legh accused only one canon of incontinence,[11] but this was serious in a house of only five resident canons.[12] The Suppression Commission made no comment on the monks' morality,[13] though this may be due to lapse of memory,[14] or more probably the monks

---

[1] P.R.O., DL43/5/4, f. 1.   [2] See below, Chapter Four.
[3] L. & P., xi, 1417, g. 18; *Cock. Chart.*, 1087–92.   [4] L. & P., x, 364.
[5] cf. surrender list in West, *Antiquities*, App. X, no. 7, with capacity list in F.O.R., 97, and add two imprisoned, L. & P., xii(1), 840. See Appendix A.
[6] L. & P., vi, 215, 1557.   [7] L. & P., x, 51.
[8] P.R.O., DL3/34, P.1; Beck, *Annales*, xcii.   [9] L. & P., x, 364.
[10] See capacity lists, F.O.R., 91, 96, 110, and add three tried for treason. See Appendix A.
[11] L. & P., x, 364.   [12] P.R.O., DL43/5/7, f. 4.   [13] ibid.
[14] Of five houses visited, the Commissioners commented on the monks of only two, whom it said were all of 'honest conversation' (DL43/4/11; DL43/5/7, f. 1), and it is not reasonable to suppose that all the other monks were immoral.

received no commendation unless it could be given to the whole house. Burscough cannot have been too bad, since there was at least some enthusiasm for the religious life; of the four canons given the choice of capacity or transfer by the Commissioners, two wanted capacities if the house was dissolved, one wished to be 'further advised' if the house was dissolved, and one wished to continue in religion even if this involved transfer to another house.[1] Presumably the first two were quite willing to continue if the house was not suppressed, as they did not simply ask for capacities, and though only one canon showed real enthusiasm, the others at least seem to have been satisfied with the religious life. Certainly they were not eager to escape, offering 1,000 marks to continue in their own house,[2] a very large sum for a small monastery with an annual net income of only £80/7/6d.[3]

Holland was clearly in a much worse condition. The Visitors accused Prior Prescot of incontinence with seven women, John Codling of incontinence with a young girl, and one other of homosexuality.[4] The charge against Prescot was perhaps exaggerated, but as the Suppressors found that the three monks who were asked all wanted capacities if the house was dissolved,[5] and the house offered only 250 marks to continue,[6] the spiritual condition of the house must have been rather poor, and the moral state was probably as bad. The Visitors were at Hornby on February 23rd,[7] and they reported that the Prior, William Halliday, had been incontinent with three single women.[8] This accusation may have been justified, since it would reflect the obvious distaste Halliday had for the religious life; despite the fact that his house was a cell of Croxton, and he had no legal rights over it, he attempted to surrender it to Layton and Legh.[9] Though no other offences were recorded at Hornby, Robert Derby must have shared his superior's lack of enthusiasm, as he did not return to his mother house[10] and was presumably dispensed from his vows by the Visitors.

At Penwortham, Richard Hawkesbury, the Prior, was accused of incontinence with two women,[11] and as there was probably only one other monk in the cell[12] the condition of the Priory cannot have been very good. There is no other evidence on the condition of Penwortham, and, as in the case of Furness and Whalley, we are forced to accept as definite evidence what was really only a propagandist statement. For the reliability of the 'Compendium Compertorum' has long been in doubt, and the most judicious modern estimate has inclined to the view that once the visitation was under

---

[1] P.R.O., DL43/5/7, f. 4.   [2] L. & P., x, 1191.   [3] *Valor*, v, 222.
[4] L. & P., x, 364.   [5] P.R.O., DL43/5/7, f. 5.
[6] L. & P., x, 1191.   [7] D.K.R., viii, App. 2, 23.
[8] L. & P., x, 364.   [9] D.K.R., viii, App. 2, 23.
[10] He did not sign the Croxton surrender (D.K.R., viii, App. 2, 18), nor did he receive a capacity at Croxton (F.O.R., 173), or anywhere else, but he was not dead. See below, Chapter Nine.   [11] L. & P., x, 364.
[12] Knowles & Hadcock, 73.

way, its aim became 'to extract damaging confessions',[1] and find grounds for suppression. This was certainly the case by the time the Visitors reached Lancashire, and they seem to have raced through the county, only stopping long enough to elicit information on sexual lapses, 'superstitions', income, and debts.

The 'Compendium', however, is often the only view we have of the condition of a particular house, and though its faults must be borne in mind, its findings cannot simply be ignored. The picture it paints, however, is less damaging to the monks than might be thought. Layton and Legh achieved their effect by the continued repetition of real or imagined sexual lapses by the monks, which is a simple propaganda technique. One tends to forget, as contemporaries were intended to do, that when, for example, the Visitors charged five monks at Furness, there were at least another twenty-eight against whom even they could find nothing. A comparison of lapses with the number of monks available for interview at each house will illustrate this point.

TABLE I

House	Incontinent	Homosexual	Total lapses	Total resident
Burscough	1	—	1	5
Cartmel	2	—	2	10
Cockersand	—	2	2	22
Conishead	5	—	5	8
Furness	4	1	5	33
Holland	2	1	3	5
Hornby	1	—	1	3
Kersall	—	—	—	2
Lytham	—	—	—	3
Penwortham	1	—	1	3
Whalley	—	1	1	24
	16	5	21	118

The number of guilty monks, if Layton and Legh were correct, was thus twenty-one, which appears at first glance to be a complete condemnation of the Lancashire monks, but the most which can definitely be drawn from the reports is that 17·7% of the monks were guilty of misconduct on at least one occasion during their religious lives. This is not a staggeringly high figure, and indicates that the monks of Lancashire may well have been better behaved than those in other areas. It compares very well with the figure of 25·4% who lapsed in the houses for which Layton and Legh's reports are available in the province of York as a whole[2] and for which numbers of monks are available from the signatures on the surrender

---

[1] Knowles, *Religious Orders*, iii, 269–70.   [2] L. & P., x, 364.

documents.[1] The Lancashire performance was certainly much better than
that of the diocese of Norwich, for which the comparable figure is 36%,[2]
though this may well be an unrepresentative figure, as there are surrender
lists for only three of the houses mentioned in the report.

It is also clear from the Lancashire figures that, in the northern houses,
Cartmel, Cockersand, Conishead, Furness, and Whalley, only 17·5% of
the monks were charged, compared with the southern group, where 28·6%
of the monks were said to have lapsed, despite the fact that one might
expect lower standards in the more backward and violent north of the
county. This is very significant in view of what has already been said in the
differences between the houses of the north and south. In Lancashire,
retarded social development meant that the old institutions and forms of
thought retained their vigour, so that the monasteries at least, and quite
probably the old religion as a whole, were still vital units of social and
spiritual life. Lancashire is therefore in stark contrast not only with more
advanced areas of England, but with Wales, where backwardness in
society meant that the condition of the monasteries was almost uniformly
poor, the majority of the monks were lax and indolent, and many were
involved in crime and immorality.[3] The calculations which have been
made should not be pressed too far, and probably do not prove very much,
but they do at least indicate that either Lancashire was much better
than other areas, or the charges made by the Visitors are completely
untrustworthy.

That less than one-fifth of the monks lapsed is quite a creditable performance for a society such as Lancashire, where moral standards among
the laity were habitually low. Important county figures like Sir John
Byron and Sir Richard Houghton openly kept mistresses,[4] though married,
and the notorious Ralph Rishton set up house with three different women
in rapid succession.[5] The year before Layton and Legh were in Lancashire, an Ecclesiastical Commission sat at Wigan, and convicted several
gentlemen of substance of adultery and keeping concubines, Thomas
Gerard,[6] William Gerard,[7] Gilbert Foster,[8] John Winstanley and William
Bradshaw,[9] and Sir James Stanley,[10] who was steward of Burscough Priory

[1] D.K.R., viii, App. 2.
[2] cf. ibid. and L. & P., x, 364, ii. These figures do not allow for the small number of
monks who may have died or left religion between the visitation and the suppression,
but this is equally true of the Lancashire figures. There are, however, surrender lists for
only 25 of the 136 monasteries reported on in L. & P., x, 364, and these may be unrepresentative, especially as the houses which survived the suppression of 1536 and surrendered
later were usually the larger monasteries.
[3] G. Williams, *The Welsh Church from Conquest to Reformation*, 387–402.
[4] *L. & C. Wills and Inventories*, ii, 133–6; *Visitation of Lancashire, 1533*, i, 48.
[5] Stone, *Crisis of the Aristocracy*, 663.
[6] C.R.O., EDA12/1, fos. 1, 7v. He was a J.P.—Watson, 'The Lancashire Gentry and
the Public Service, 1529–58', Trans. L. & C. Antiq. Soc., Vol. 73, Appendix A.
[7] ibid., f. 3.   [8] ibid., f. 3v.
[9] ibid., f. 4.   [10] ibid., f. 5v.

and the Earl of Derby's uncle,[1] as well as many lesser figures. The earliest extant reports of a complete episcopal visitation of Lancashire, for 1554, give a comprehensive picture of widespread sexual laxity. In the parish of Whalley, where the Abbey had been situated, thirty-one cases of adultery or fornication were reported,[2] while in the more populous, yet supposedly more advanced, parish of Manchester, there were forty-three cases of sexual immorality.[3] One can only be surprised that the Lancashire monks, none of whom belonged to the stricter and more enclosed orders, managed to avoid falling into evil ways in even larger numbers.

The Injunctions the Visitors laid upon the houses[4] were, except for the articles on the royal supremacy and the prayers for Queen Anne, which raised the 'bêtes noires' of the regime, based largely on the usual form of injunctions.[5] But some of the more common articles were made so strict as to make convent life impossible, and others seem to have been designed to erode the confidence of the religious. The monks were to be taught that 'true religion is not contained in apparel, manner of going, shaven heads, or other such marks; nor in silence, fasting, up-rising in the night, singing, and other such kind of ceremonies, but in cleanness of mind, pureness of living, Christ's faith not feigned and brotherly charity, and true honouring of God in spirit of veracity', while any monk with complaints was to be provided with his expenses to travel to Westminster to report to Cromwell or the King. The Injunctions appear to have been a threat rather than a programme to be enforced, and they were soon relaxed; certainly Whalley received 'a relaxation of certain particles of the Injunctions' from Cromwell,[6] allowing some monks to leave the house on business or for their health, permitting older monks to have rooms for themselves, and reducing the divinity lectures to three times weekly, instead of every day.

The effect of the Injunctions on the houses which were not suppressed is difficult to assess; probably when it was realised that it was not expected that they should be observed in their full rigidity they were largely ignored. This was certainly the case at Furness, as it was later alleged by the Vicar of Dalton,[7] who was himself a monk of the house.[8] At Furness a friar, Robert Legate, was put into the house to read and preach to the monks,[9] but the monks apparently would not listen,[10] and objected to the reformist content of his sermons.[11] The visitation, however, had performed its task, providing evidence to substantiate the charges in the preamble to the Act dissolving the lesser houses, demonstrating the royal supremacy, and weakening the morale of the monasteries which were allowed to remain.

[1] *Valor*, v, 223; L. & P., xi, 517.
[2] C.R.O., EDV1/1, fos. 150–5v.
[3] ibid., fos. 120–4.
[4] Printed in Burnet-Pocock, iv, 217 ff.
[5] Knowles, *Religious Orders*, iii, 275.
[6] Printed in Whitaker, i, 107.
[7] L. & P., xii(1), 841, 2.
[8] cf. *Valor*, v, 272, and F.O.R., 97.
[9] L. & P., xii(1), 841, 3.
[10] ibid., 841, 2.
[11] ibid., 842.

CHAPTER THREE

THE BEGINNINGS OF THE DISSOLUTION:
THE CELLS

WHEN Layton and Legh visited Hornby, they reported that William Halliday, the Prior, had been incontinent with three unmarried women.[1] Halliday, apparently, had no great liking for the religious life, or perhaps he was intimidated by the Visitors, for despite the fact that he had no legal rights over the house, he surrendered it to them. On February 23rd, 1536, well before the Act of Suppression,[2] Halliday, and John Fletcher and Robert Derby, canons,[3] signed a form of surrender, and on the same day the document was confirmed in the chapter house by Richard Layton.[4] Legh, apparently, took advantage of the situation to acquire tenure of a close for himself.[5] What happened to the monks then is not clear; evidently the government cancelled the surrender, when it was found that the house was a cell of Croxton, and the Priory seems to have continued until 1538. Presumably the canons had not yet returned to their house, or the surrender cancelled by August 1536, when the Lancashire Commissioners surveyed Hornby.[6] The next we hear of Hornby is on September 8th, 1538, when Croxton surrendered; William Halliday signed the surrender as a canon of Croxton, and the canons of Hornby signed, John Consyll, Prior, John Fletcher, and Thomas Edynstow.[7] Clearly the Abbot of Croxton did not trust Halliday to continue as head of Hornby after his 'surrender' and kept him at Croxton; the new set of Hornby canons must have been withdrawn to the mother house for the surrender. Consyll, the new Prior, had been a monk of Croxton in 1534,[8] and Fletcher was one of the 1536 canons; presumably Edynstow had also been a Croxton canon. What happened to Robert Derby in 1536 is not known; perhaps he was dispensed from his vows by the Visitors, and

[1] L. & P., x, 364.
[2] The Act of Suppression was passed during the session February 4th–April 14th, 1536, but it had not been introduced by March 3rd (L. & P., x, 406), and it is suggested that it went before the Commons on March 11th (Knowles, *Religious Orders*, iii, 291); Somerville's suggestion (*Duchy of Lancaster*, 288), that the Act was passed in February, cannot be sustained.
[3] There seem to have been three canons as the usual complement, e.g. in 1484, C.A.P., ii, 155; Leland refers to it as such (*Collectanea*, i, 72).
[4] D.K.R., viii, App. 2, 23; Rhymer, *Foedera*, xiv, 557–8.
[5] P.R.O., SC6/1827, m. 32.
[6] P.R.O., DL43/5/12, fos. 1–17.
[7] D.K.R., viii, App. 2, 18. Sir Robert Somerville, op. cit., 290n., found it surprising that Hornby did not pass to the Duchy in 1536; it was because it was a cell of Croxton, and therefore exempt from the Act.
[8] L. & P., vii, 376.

he is later found as a chantry-priest at Tunstall.[1] Halliday, Consyll, Fletcher, and Edynstow were issued with capacities with the canons of Croxton,[2] given pensions by Augmentations,[3] and thus departed into the world.

The other cells, though exempted from the Act of Suppression by the size of their mother houses,[4] do not appear to have lasted long. An investigation revealed that the Duchy had no right to Penwortham, as a cell of Evesham,[5] but the mother house must have withdrawn the monks immediately after the Act, since in June 1536 John Fleetwood was trying to get a lease of the Priory from Evesham, supported by Rich, Audley, and Cromwell.[6] The monks had certainly left Penwortham by 1538, when in January the Abbot of Evesham leased out the tithes of Longton to two members of the local Farington family;[7] previous leases had always been from the Prior of Penwortham with the consent of the Abbot. In February 1539, Fleetwood finally got his lease, though Evesham reserved the advowson of Leyland to itself;[8] those with tithe leases were to continue with them, though Evesham agreed to compensate Fleetwood for the tithes paid to Richard Hawkesbury, 'late farmer, custos, or [prior?] at Penwortham'.[9] Hawkesbury had been prior when Layton and Legh visited the house,[10] but he returned to Evesham when Penwortham was dissolved, and when the mother house was suppressed he was assigned a pension of £10 as kitchener of Evesham and late prior of Penwortham.[11] There were probably two monks at this time,[12] but the identity of the other cannot be found.

Much the same story is true of Lytham, a cell of Durham. There seem to have been three monks there in 1530,[13] and the last prior was Richard Blackstone.[14] Layton and Legh visited the house in February 1536, but had no complaint to make.[15] For some reason the Duchy planned to survey the house in 1536,[16] and though the survey did not, in fact, take place, this may indicate that the monks had already been withdrawn. Durham certainly withdrew its monks at some stage, and leased the property to Thomas Dannet for eighty years,[17] and he appears to have retained the farm when it passed to the Crown.[18]

The Cluniac cell of Kersall belonged to Lenton Priory. Layton and Legh were there in February 1536,[19] but the mother house must have withdrawn the monks, since later that year the Prior of Lenton reported to Cromwell

[1] *Lancs Chantries*, ii, 232–3.   [2] F.O.R., 173.
[3] L. & P., xiv(1), 1355 (p. 598).   [4] 27 Henry VIII, c. 28, sect. xv.
[5] P.R.O., DL5/6, f. 220; Somerville, op. cit., 290n.
[6] L. & P., xi, 25.   [7] *Priory of Penwortham*, 78–79.
[8] ibid., 79–83.   [9] ibid.
[10] L. & P., x, 364.   [11] L. & P., xv, 118.
[12] Knowles & Hadcock, 73.   [13] *Duchy Pleadings*, i, 209.
[14] Dugdale, *Monasticon*, iv, 283.   [15] L. & P., x, 364.
[16] P.R.O., DL43/5/14.   [17] P.R.O., SC6/708, m. 7.
[18] Dugdale, *Monasticon*, iv, 283.   [19] L. & P., x, 364.

that 'I have accomplished your pleasure touching the cell of Kersall in Lancashire',[1] and nothing more is known of monks at Kersall. The Prior of Lenton was indicted for treason in March 1538,[2] and in April Thurstan Tildesley wrote to Cromwell that he had heard Lenton was now in the King's hands, and asked for the farm of Kersall.[3] In that year the Kersall lands were assessed with those of Lenton,[4] presumably on the basis of the survey of Kersall carried out by John Assheton,[5] auditor of attainted lands under the General Surveyors.[6]

[1] ibid., 1234.
[2] Knowles, *Religious Orders*, iii, 373.
[3] L. & P., xiii(1), 789.
[4] Dugdale, *Monasticon*, v, 117.
[5] P.R.O., SC12/13/74.
[6] Richardson, *History of the Court of Augmentations*, 54.

CHAPTER FOUR

THE SUPPRESSION OF THE
LESSER HOUSES

SECTION 24 of the Act establishing the Court of Augmentations[1] provided that the monasteries in Lancashire and their possessions outside the county, and those outside the county palatine which had been founded by dukes of Lancaster, should, at the King's pleasure, be placed under the Duchy of Lancaster.[2] After the passage of the Act, a warrant was issued to Sir William Fitzwilliam, Chancellor of the Duchy, ordering him to take charge of the houses covered by the Act.[3] Professor Elton points out[4] that though the draft was written by a Duchy clerk, it was corrected by Sir Richard Rich, Chancellor of Augmentations, indicating that even at this early stage the Duchy was relying on the expertise of the newly established Court of Augmentations.

The dissolution commission for Lancashire was issued on April 24th, 1536,[5] to Sir Thomas Halsall, Sir William Leyland, Sir Henry Farington, Thomas Burgoyne,[6] and Thomas Dawtrey.[7] On the same day government instructions for the suppression were issued,[8] giving the detailed procedure for the suppression of religious houses, which the Lancashire Commissioners certainly followed, but ordering that each commission should have an auditor, a particular receiver, the clerk of the register from the last survey, and three other 'discreet persons'.[9] Under this instruction, a list of Commissioners was drawn up by the Duchy for Lancashire:[10] Sir William Leyland, Sir Richard Assheton, Sir Thomas Halsall, Thomas Burgoyne, auditor, and Thomas Armerer, receiver, for Holland and Burscough; Sir Thomas Langton, Sir Henry Farington, Sir Thomas Southworth, Burgoyne and Armerer, for Lytham and Cockersand; Sir Marmaduke Tunstall, Sir James Layburne, Thomas Sherburne, and the two officials, for Conishead and Cartmel. It is not clear why this list was drawn up, for there is no evidence that the commission named on it ever did any work.[11] Lytham ought not to have been included, being a cell of

---

[1] 27 Henry VIII, c. 27. Augmentations was a specialised department set up to administer the lands of the suppressed monasteries.
[2] *Stat. Realm*, iii, 574.
[3] P.R.O., DL41/12/10.   [4] *Tudor Revolution*, 208–9.
[5] The commission does not survive; the date is from the 'Brief Certificates', e.g. P.R.O., DL43/5/7, f. 1, though the 'Declaration' for Cartmel gives April 23rd (P.R.O., DL43/4/12, f. 1).
[6] Duchy Auditor for the North, Somerville, *Duchy of Lancaster*, 436.
[7] Later Duchy Receiver for the Lancashire monasteries, Somerville, op. cit., 496.
[8] L. & P., x, 721.   [9] ibid.
[10] P.R.O., DL43/5/14.   [11] Somerville, op. cit., 291.

Durham and therefore outside the jurisdiction of the Duchy under 27 Henry VIII, c. 27. It must have been decided to drop the second commission, and continue with the original group named on the Duchy's own initiative.

It was some time before the commission reached Lancashire. The Duchy messenger had to take the commission to Dover for sealing by the Duchy Chancellor,[1] and he was not back in London till May 6th, when he set out for Lancashire.[2] The journey north took three or four days,[3] and the commission must have reached Lancashire about May 10th. It would then take the Commissioners time to assemble and make their plans, and they began their work at Holland on May 15th.[4]

The Commissioners were certainly at Holland between the 15th and the 17th of May, when they took an inventory of the goods, which was witnessed by the Prior, Peter Prescot, and three of his monks. The inventory reveals that the Priory had had some difficulty in making ends meet in recent years. Two silver-gilt cups had been laid to pledge for loans, and in February 1536 a chalice had been pledged to Sir Edward Fitton for £10 by the Prior to raise money for the payment of the monastery's taxes. In 1535 a silver-gilt salt-cellar had been entrusted to one William Topping while the Prior was in London, but the cellar could not be found and the Commissioners had Topping committed to Lancaster Castle.[5] They must also have made a 'Declaration of the New Survey', though this does not survive, from which they abstracted the 'Brief Certificate',[6] the summary which was sent up to London. There were five monks, including the Prior, all of whom were priests; three wanted capacities if the house was dissolved, one was 'aged and impotent, desiring some living of the King's alms', if Holland was suppressed, and the Prior, who was given no choice over his future.[7] Heads of houses were not given the usual choice of 'capacity' or transfer to another house, as it was not realistic to expect them to serve as monks under another abbot or prior.[8] The income of the house was reassessed and found to be £78/12/9d., as against the £53/3/4d. of the 1535 survey.[9] The servants were enumerated, and the land and wood valued,[10] a 'commandment' was issued to the Prior,[11] and the first stage of the suppression was over.

[1] Sir William Fitzwilliam was also Lord Admiral, and so would be at Dover.

[2] P.R.O., DL28/7/5.

[3] The Earl of Derby received the King's letter of 20/10/36 on 23rd (L. & P., xi, 806 and Corresp., 28–31; L. & P., xi, 856 and Corresp., 32–3). The Earl of Sussex replied to the King's letter of 17/3/37 (L. & P., xii(1), 668) on 21st (L. & P., xii(1), 695).

[4] P.R.O., DL41/11/47.   [5] ibid.

[6] P.R.O., DL43/5/7, f. 5.   [7] ibid.

[8] G. W. O. Woodward, 'The Exemption from Suppression of Certain Yorks. Priories', E.H.R., lxxvi, 1961, 395.

[9] P.R.O., DL43/5/7, f. 5; Valor, v, 221.

[10] P.R.O., DL43/5/7, f. 5.

[11] cf. Cartmel and Conishead.

No dates can be found for the Commissioners' visit to Burscough, but it was the next house northwards after Holland, and the Commission was not at Cockersand until May 27th, so clearly Burscough was dealt with next. The Commissioners followed the same procedure as at Holland culminating in the 'Brief Certificate',[1] which gives a prior and four canons. Two wanted capacities if the house were dissolved, one wished to be 'further advised' in that event, and one wished to 'continue in religion', if necessary by transferring to another house.[2] The monks appear to have been well served, with twenty-two 'waiting servants and officers of household', as against the eighteen men employed to work the monastic demesnes.[3] This adds to the impression that some of the Lancashire monasteries were rather like comfortable country houses. The new valuation was £122/5/7d., compared with the 1535 total of £80/7/6d.[4] The Commission then moved on to Cockersand, for which our information is more complete.

The Suppressors were at Cockersand at least between the 27th and the 29th of May.[5] As specified in the instructions,[6] the Abbot, Robert Poulton, and the officers of the house, Richard Aldcliffe, prior, Edward Bethom, cellarer, and Leonard Bentham, sub-cellarer,[7] were put on oath to give a true declaration. The twenty-two canons were then listed, in order of seniority. The Abbot was not asked, and four canons were away serving cures, leaving seventeen to be asked their preferences; of these, three wished to continue in religion only if they could do so at Cockersand, and the other fourteen all wished to continue, either at Cockersand or, if that house were suppressed, at some other house of the Premonstratensian Order.[8] The servants, corrodians, and almspeople were then listed, a list of leases was drawn up, the demesnes were surveyed, and the condition of the buildings assessed; they were all in 'good reparation at this time' except for 'one little old house called St. John's Hall, the thatch at one end of the same fallen down'.[9] An inventory of the Abbey's goods was drawn up,[10] and the conclusions of the survey were abstracted from the 'Declaration of Survey'[11] on to the 'Brief Certificate'.[12] The Abbey's common seal, plate, jewels, and 'other evidences' were locked away in the convent chest with three locks, one key kept by the Abbot and the other two by the Commissioners. The canons were left with six chalices, a cross, a silver censer, and twelve silver spoons, for their services and daily use, but all the things mentioned in the inventory were to be kept 'without waste, consumption, or embezzlement of the same'.[13] Cockersand was visited by the Suppressors because its income in the survey of 1535 was said to be

[1] P.R.O., DL43/5/7, f. 4.   [2] ibid.   [3] ibid.
[4] ibid.; *Valor*, v, 222–3.   [5] P.R.O., DL43/5/4, f. 1.
[6] L. & P., x, 721, 2.   [7] P.R.O., DL43/5/4, f. 1.
[8] ibid.   [9] P.R.O., DL43/5/4, f. 2.
[10] P.R.O., DL43/5/5.   [11] P.R.O., DL43/5/4.
[12] P.R.O., DL43/5/7, f. 1.   [13] ibid., f. 3.

£157/14/0½d.,[1] which put it within the terms of the Act of Suppression, but the Commission now calculated the income at £282/7/0½d.,[2] which put it outside the Act. But it is not clear whether the £200 annual income given in the Act as the upper limit of houses to be dissolved was to refer to the assessment of 1535, or to the new survey.

The Commissioners presumably took a holiday over Whitsun, and then moved on to Cartmel, which, across the Kent Sands, was the next house northwards. Their 'commandment' to the Prior, the only Cartmel document dated, and probably issued just before they left, was given on June 7th.[3] Here, they administered the oath to Richard Preston, the prior, Brian Willan, the cellarer, James Eskrigge, sub-prior, and William Pannell, at 68 the oldest canon.[4] Except for the Prior, they all wished to continue in religion, either at Cartmel or another house, apart from Pannell, who reported that he had a licence to live outside the house from his brethren, and a pension of £5/13/4d., but both licence and pension had been revoked by Layton and Legh.[5] He wished to live in the world if possible, but otherwise he was willing to remain in the monastery.[6] The Commissioners made two different 'Brief Certificates', which may have been the result of Pannell's later decision that he wished to stay. The 'Declaration'[7] must have been drawn up first, and on this Pannell preferred to leave; so the 'Brief Certificate' in which eight monks wished to continue and the other claimed his convent pension[8] was probably made next. Perhaps Pannell changed his mind, or was persuaded to do so by the others, for on the other 'Brief Certificate',[9] which is identical with the first except for this, all the canons are said to wish to continue. The usual surveying and listing was done, and the details summarised on the 'Declaration' and then transferred to the 'Brief Certificate'; the income, valued in 1535 at £91/6/3d.,[10] was now said to be £212/12/10½d.[11] The income of the house was now above the £200 limit of the Act, though its ten canons still remained below the twelve monks mentioned in the preamble as dividing the 'little and small abbeys' of 'manifest sin, vicious and carnal living', from the 'great solemn monasteries of this realm'.[12]

The Priory seal and thirty boxes of 'evidences' were locked in a chest with two locks, one key held by the Prior, and the other by the Commissioners.[13] The Suppressors noted that as far as they could tell from their survey, and the sworn statement of the Prior, there had been no gifts or leases since February 4th, 1536.[14] Before leaving, the Commissioners issued

---

[1] *Valor*, v, 261.   [2] P.R.O., DL43/5/7, f. 1.   [3] P.R.O., DL41/11/50.
[4] P.R.O., DL43/4/12, f. 1.   [5] ibid.
[6] ibid.   [7] ibid.   [8] P.R.O., DL43/5/7, f. 2.
[9] P.R.O., DL43/4/11.   [10] *Valor*, v, 272.
[11] P.R.O., DL43/4/11.
[12] *Stat. Realm*, iii, 575; Elton, *Tudor Constitution*, 374–5.
[13] P.R.O., DL43/4/12, f. 2.
[14] P.R.O., ibid., f. 2v. February 4th was the date of the beginning of the Parliamentary session in which the Act of Suppression was passed.

to the Prior a 'commandment' on behalf of the King;[1] he was to keep for the King all the valuables of the house named in the inventory, of which he had one copy and the Commissioners another, neither of which survive, and he was to answer for shortages 'at his extreme peril'; any goods which were not mentioned in the inventory were also to be kept; all produce was to be retained, 'except only it be for the necessary expenses of the said house'; and the Prior and canons were forbidden to receive any rents, except for necessary payments. The Commissioners must then have moved on across the Leven Sands to the last house they were to visit, Conishead.

The 'commandment' to the Prior of Conishead was issued on June 13th,[2] presumably just before the Suppressors left. At Conishead the Commission found a prior, Thomas Lord, a quondam, George Cansforth, a canon 'keeping cure' at one of the monastery churches,[3] and five other canons, two of whom wanted capacities and three who wished to be 'further advised if this house be dissolved'.[4] The usual surveying and valuing was done, and the Commission found that the income assessed at £97/0/2d. at the last survey[5] was now £161/5/9d.[6] Burgoyne and Dawtrey, the two Duchy officials, were very careful and businesslike in their work; at Conishead they found two pictures of the founder, Lord Harrington, and his wife, and an alabaster tomb, but noted on their inventory that 'the said tomb and pictures not valued, because it is thought that no man will give no money for them'.[7] It is clear from the precise manner in which they conducted their survey that the Duchy officials were as efficient as Professor Elton and Professor Richardson found those of Augmentations to have been.[8]

Conishead seems to have taken advantage of advance warning to capitalise on its assets before it was visited by the Commissioners. The Suppressors made a note on their survey, 'Item, to examine Miles Robinson what plate he hath carried at divers times to Robert Garnett of Kendal to sell or lay in pledge. The said Miles carried a silver basin and ewer and a bowl of silver and gilt to one Robert Garnett of Kendal, about Candlemas was a twelvenight[9] by the Prior's commandment, as he saith, but received no money for it.'[10] About the time the Commissioners were assembling to begin their work,[11] when the monks must have known the end was very near, seventy sheep were transferred to William Rawlinson of Furness

---

[1] P.R.O., DL41/11/50.   [2] P.R.O., DL41/11/59, f. 1.
[3] This was probably Orton, of which the Prior was Vicar (*Valor*, v, 295) and which had been united with the priorship in February 1536 (F.O.R., 45). Probably Lord foresaw the fall of his house, and wanted to secure additional employment.
[4] P.R.O., DL43/5/7, f. 3.   [5] *Valor*, v, 271.   [6] P.R.O., DL43/5/7, f. 3.
[7] P.R.O., DL29/158/27; quoted by R. J. Mason, *The Income, Administration, and Disposal of Monastic Lands in Lancashire from the Dissolution to 1558*, unpublished London M.A. thesis, 1962, p. 10.
[8] Elton, *Tudor Revolution*, 205–7; Richardson, *Court of Augmentations*, 277 ff.
[9] About February 14th.
[10] P.R.O., DL29/158/27; quoted Mason, op. cit., 11.   [11] May 10th, 1536.

Fells.[1] The monks of Holland Priory, too, had been able to raise money before they lost control of their assets; the accounts show leases to the Earl of Derby and Sir William Norris, 'before the day of the dissolution of the houses'.[2] But despite the government's fears, expressed in the Act, there seems to have been no wholesale disposal of goods by the Lancashire houses. Four days' ride away from London, and always behind with news,[3] they appear to have largely been taken by surprise. The first stage of the suppression, the 'supervision',[4] was now over, and the Commissioners had to make their report.

This essay is not concerned primarily with economic questions, but a word must be said on the glaring discrepancies between the 1535 Commissioners' income assessments and those of the Suppression Commissioners. Savine found that the 1535 survey consistently undervalued monastic incomes[5] for the Northern Province. He attributed this to the difficulties of a small commission working hastily over a large and wild area, and to the sympathy of the 1535 Commissioners for the monks.[6] Savine also noted[7] that the discrepancies for Lancashire were particularly serious. Part of the difference would be due to different aims; the 1535 Commission was assessing the income of the monasteries for taxation purposes, while that of 1536 was interested in the income the Crown might be able to extract from its new possessions,[8] though this would be true for the whole country, and would not therefore explain the greater differences for Lancashire. The argument from sympathy by the 1535 local Commissioners, rather than the cold calculation of the 1536 Suppressors, does not really stand. It is true that the Commission of 1535[9] was composed predominantly of important local gentlemen, but three of the five 1536 Commissioners were also local gentry, who had been members of the earlier Commission, and their attitudes would not have changed significantly in a year. Further, all the twenty-four local 1535 Commissioners, who were supposed to be sympathetic to the monks, except Sir John Towneley, James Scaresbreck, Henry Byron, Roger Asshaw, and John Lambert, who was in any case Vice-Chancellor of the Palatinate[10] and presumably busy at Lancaster, rallied to the Earl of Derby with their forces when the Lancashire rebels rose in support of the monasteries.[11] It is clear

---

[1] P.R.O., DL29/158/27.   [2] P.R.O., DL29/2303, m. 6-7.
[3] Edward VI died on July 6th, 1553, and the Duke of Northumberland tried to suppress the news for a few days, but as late as July 12th the quarter sessions at Manchester were still dated 7 Edward VI.—J. B. Watson, 'The Lancashire Gentry and the Public Service, 1529-1558', Trans. L. & C. Antiq. Soc., Vol. 73, p. 31.
[4] Woodward, 'The Exemption from Suppression of Certain Yorks Priories', 389.
[5] Savine, English Monasteries on the Eve of Dissolution, 46-49.
[6] ibid.; in this he was followed by Dom David Knowles, Religious Orders, iii, 245.
[7] Savine, op. cit., 46.   [8] Knowles, op. cit., 311-12.
[9] L. & P., viii, 149, g. 63.
[10] Somerville, Duchy of Lancaster, 462-3, 480.
[11] cf. L. & P., viii, 149, g. 63, with L. & P., xi, 1251, ii.

from the 1536 Commission's returns[1] and from Savine's table[2] that the discrepancies from the three northern houses, Cartmel, Cockersand, and Conishead, are far more serious than those of the southern, Burscough and Holland, and this indicates the true explanation. In 1535 the work was divided by dioceses, and the twenty-four gentlemen and two auditors had to cover only Lancashire south of the Ribble, which lay in the diocese of Lichfield, and which included the monasteries of Burscough and Holland. They would have little trouble in covering the benefices of south Lancashire, and producing an accurate survey for the two monasteries; the difference between their figures and those of 1536 can be explained adequately by the difference in aim. But the three northern houses came within the diocese of York, and were covered by William Knight, the Archdeacon of Richmond, John Dakyn, his vicar-general,[3] with three laymen and three auditors.[4] Clearly this smaller group had a more difficult task, as their area also included Richmondshire and large parts of Cumberland and Westmorland, and they appear to have worked alone.[5] Their task was made more difficult when the three auditors also had to cover Durham, Yorkshire, Northumberland, and Westmorland, on other Commissions.[6] Clearly they could not hope to do the job accurately, and in May 1535 the Council in the North had to ask Cromwell for more time for the survey, as there were only three auditors north of the Trent, one of whom was very old.[7] The haste in which the small Richmond Commission of 1535 had to work explains the very serious undervaluation of Cartmel, Cockersand, and Conishead.[8]

After completing their survey of Conishead in mid-June the Commissioners had to send their report up to London. They seem to have sent in the 'Brief Certificates' of each house[9] and the 'Breviate of the Brief Certificate'.[10] Two copies of the 'Breviate' survive, each with a mistake. One,[11] a seventeenth-century copy, gives £87/0/6d. as the 1535 Commissioners' return for Burscough, instead of the correct £80/7/6d,[12] while the other[13] gives £152/13/0½d. as the first value for Cockersand, rather than the correct £157/14/0½d.[14]

When the Commissioners sent their report to London, they appear to have raised a number of problems concerning the next stage of their work, the actual suppression. Their activities indicate that they had been following the general instructions issued for suppression commissioners,[15] which

---

[1] L. & P., xi, 1191; L. & P., xii(1), 1.   [2] Savine, op. cit., 46.
[3] See L. & P., xii(1), 878.   [4] L. & P., viii, 149, g. 68.
[5] *Valor*, v, 235.   [6] L. & P., viii, 149, g. 65, 72, 73, 82.   [7] L. & P., viii, 696.
[8] Only on this last point do I agree with R. J. Mason, op. cit., 43.
[9] P.R.O., DL43/4/11; DL43/5/7, fos. 1–5.
[10] L. & P., x, 1191; L. & P., xii(1), 1.
[11] L. & P., x, 1191; B.M. Cotton MS., Cleo. E. iv, 288.
[12] P.R.O., DL43/5/7, f. 4; *Valor*, v, 223.
[13] L. & P., xii(1), 1; B.M. Harl. MS. 604, f. 102.
[14] P.R.O., DL43/5/7, f. 1; *Valor*, v, 261.   [15] L. & P., x, 721.

had been chiefly concerned with the process of 'supervision', and ensuring that the monks did not cheat the King of any of his newly acquired wealth. The instructions were, however, very vague on the actual suppression of the houses (only three articles, 19–21, covered this), and the Lancashire men must have asked for further instructions. The Duchy officials, therefore, drew up a list of twenty-two problems, under the heading 'Articles, matters, and causes, concerning the dissolution of the religious houses within the county palatine of Lancaster, assigned by the King's Highness to be dissolved, and the same to be ordered by the Chancellor of the Duchy of Lancaster and the Council of the same.'[1] The questions were all concerned with the procedure to be adopted in displacing the personnel, clerical and lay, and taking over the lands and buildings, of the Lancashire houses. The Duchy Council, however, did not feel itself able to answer these problems, and submitted them to the Court of Augmentations, thus indicating again the Duchy's dependence on Augmentations in the matter of dissolution.[2] The experts replied with 'The answers and advice of John Onley, Esquire, the King's attorney of his Court of Augmentations, to certain articles and doubts concerning the order of matters and causes for the dissolution of certain religious houses within the county palatine of Lancaster.'[3] Onley answered ten of the twenty-two questions, leaving out the purely local questions, which only the Duchy could determine, with the comment that such matters should be left to the local Commissioners, to do what 'to them, upon the execution thereof shall seem most convenient for the avoiding of clamour of the people'.[4] He did not, however, answer the question of monastic debts, and perhaps Augmentations had not yet decided its policy on this point. The questions he answered were the procedural queries, such as how the Commissioners were to obtain letters to send the monks to larger houses,[5] and the problems on which it was desirable to have uniformity of action between Duchy and Augmentations, such as the treatment of almsmen and women,[6] the treatment of decrepit ex-monks,[7] and the pensions to be given to ex-heads of houses. This last he dealt with in some detail, suggesting 10% of the clear annual income of the house, plus £10/4/4d. or £5/4/–, depending on the eminence of the person.[8] It is clear from his answers, drawn from Augmentations practice, that he was anxious to ensure that the two departments treated the major problems common to all houses in the same way.

The officials of the Duchy were clearly satisfied with the answers Onley gave, since his reply was endorsed that 'Mr. Chancellor and Master Attorney of the Duchy of Lancaster' were now 'contented that the

---

[1] P.R.O., DL41/12/11; Elton, *Tudor Revolution*, 210.
[2] Elton, *Tudor Revolution*, 210; Richardson, *Court of Augmentations*, 273.
[3] P.R.O., DL41/12/12; Elton, loc. cit.   [4] P.R.O., DL41/12/12, f. 3.
[5] ibid., No. 2.   [6] ibid., No. 17.   [7] ibid., No. 18.   [8] ibid., No. 15.

D

Commissioners shall follow the same order'.[1] The local questions were then answered by Fitzwilliam himself, as Chancellor; the endorsements on the original questions[2] show that he ordered that the parish of Cartmel should have the 'suit of copes' claimed;[3] Cartmel Church, used by both priory and parish, was 'ordered by Master Chancellor of the Duchy to stand',[4] and on Holland Church, which was 'much easy and commodious to the inhabitants', the Commissioners were 'to suffer it to stand still, for a time'.[5] These exchanges show, as others have argued, the professionalism of Augmentations, but they also show the care the Duchy bestowed on the small number of houses within its jurisdiction, and the anxiety of the Duchy officials to avoid upsetting local people.

Perhaps it was felt necessary to give this settlement some official status, for when it became apparent that the division of labour between Duchy and Augmentations envisaged in the Act establishing the Court[6] was causing difficulties,[7] the more important of the problems Onley had discussed were embodied in an agreement made between the two departments. A meeting was held on July 5th, 1536, in the White Hall at Westminster, and a definitive settlement was reached.[8] The meeting was attended by the Chancellors of the Duchy and Augmentations, and their respective officials, and it was decided that the Duchy would dissolve the monasteries in Lancashire, and Augmentations would look after all houses outside the county palatine, whether of Duchy foundation or not. A number of clauses show that Rich, Chancellor of Augmentations, was anxious to ensure uniformity, especially in the matter of leases, and the rest of the document gives official sanction to Onley's advice on pensions and gifts to the dispossessed monks, and makes a decision on monastic debts, ordering that the Commissioners should 'pay all true debts of every house, being under the value of £20'. Finally, the meeting ordered that the lessees of Conishead, Cartmel, and Cockersand should provide a bell and guides for travellers over the sands.[9] Six days

[1] P.R.O., DL41/12/12, f. 3.   [2] P.R.O., DL41/12/11.   [3] ibid., No. 12.
[4] ibid., No. 11.   [5] ibid., No. 10.   [6] 27 Henry VIII, c. 27.
[7] Elton, *Tudor Revolution*, 209; Richardson, *Court of Augmentations*, 272–3.
[8] P.R.O., DL5/6, fos. 204v–5, printed in Elton, *Tudor Constitution*, 378–80; Elton, *Tudor Revolution*, 209; Richardson, op. cit., 274.
[9] It will be seen that the account given here differs from that of Elton, op. cit., 209–10; Professor Elton has the exchange between the Duchy and Onley taking place after the White Hall meeting of July 5th, and there are certainly strong arguments in favour of this view—the Duchy questions to Onley were confined to Lancashire, though until the meeting the Duchy was also concerned with houses outside the county of Duchy foundation, and it is sensible to suppose that the Duchy Council may have raised later questions which were not covered by the meeting; but, on the first point, there is no evidence that the Duchy had done anything about the extra-palatinate houses, so problems would not have arisen, and so would not need to be answered, for any houses except those in Lancashire; on the second it would have been more reasonable for the Duchy to raise these problems—which it must have been aware of, since the Lancashire returns were already in—at the White Hall meeting. In the opinion of the present writer, there are strong grounds for dating the Duchy–Onley documents before

later, the settlement was enforced by a warrant to the Chancellor of the Duchy.[1]

The problems raised by the Lancashire Commissioners were now solved, and the officials were able to proceed with the actual suppression. They appear to have followed the decisions of Onley, the Chancellor, and the White Hall settlement, except on the guides for the Sands. The original intention had been for the lessees of Cartmel and Cockersand to provide these guides.[2] However, Cockersand was not dissolved, and in 1537 the Duchy itself agreed to pay 53/4d. per annum to the guide over the Sands, but he was reluctant to take the office at that rate, and he was given a patent under the Duchy seal with a fee of £5.[3] The only problem now left was the decision on which of the houses ought to be suppressed. Judging by the incomes as given by the 1535 Commissioners, all five houses visited came within the Act of Suppression. For some reason, the Lancashire Commissioners, unlike those for other counties, asked the monks how much they would be willing to pay the King for permission to continue in their old house, and the answers were given in the 'Breviate of the Brief Certificate'.[4] Initially four of the Lancashire houses offered a thousand marks, and Holland, the poorest, offered 250 marks. Only

---

July 5th. The problems sent in by the Lancashire Commissioners in mid-June would have been submitted to Augmentations as soon as possible, and not kept for at least a fortnight until after July 5th. If the meeting took place first, some procedural questions of the kind raised in the document would surely have been asked, and answered either informally or in the White Hall settlement, and the Fitzwilliam–Onley questions would then not have been necessary. The Duchy's questions are clearly based on the inadequacy of the original instructions (L. & P., x, 721) rather than the inadequacy of the July settlement. The Duchy would not raise again those questions, such as pensions to heads, the personal effects of the monks, and bells for the Sands (which occur in both) in the Onley document, if these had already been answered in the White Hall settlement —but Onley's original answer might have been incorporated in an official settlement. Why did Onley fail to answer the question on the payment of monastic debts? It was a very important point, on which policy ought to have been co-ordinated, and to which Fitzwilliam, in his endorsements, did not give an answer either—it is probable that official policy on debts had not yet been decided, and that the issue was only clarified on July 5th. The Duchy would not ask purely local questions, as it did in the questions to Onley, if it had already been told at the meeting that it had discretion over them— Onley left them unanswered, and then the 'discretion' was formally acknowledged in the final settlement. Important questions such as annuities and corrodies, the wages of servants, heads of houses serving impropriated churches, and almsmen, on which it was as necessary to have uniformity as it was on repairing clauses in leases or pensions for heads, were not raised at the meeting, and this can only be because they had already been answered.

Richardson, op. cit., 273 & n., in using the Duchy–Onley documents, like Professor Elton, to prove the superiority of Augmentations in dissolution questions, suggests that they ought to be dated 'during the first half of 1537'. This is clearly impossible for the reasons given above, and because the Lancashire Commissioners, for whose benefit the questions were asked, had completed their work and dispatched the monks by the middle of September 1536.

[1] P.R.O., DL12/7, No. 39; Elton, *Tudor Revolution*, 209 & n.
[2] P.R.O., DL5/6, f. 205; Elton, *Tudor Constitution*, 380.
[3] P.R.O., DL29/2317, m. 4; Somerville, op. cit., 295.
[4] L. & P., x, 1191; L. & P., xii(1), 1.

Conishead's offer is extant;[1] it is undated, but in it Prior Lord states that he is 'contented to pay to the King's Grace one thousand marks, so that he may have his priory' with 100 marks down, and the balance over nine years. The document is endorsed 'Conishead, first offer for the redemption of that house', and the government was clearly tempted to allow the monastery to continue, as Lord appears to have been invited to make a second offer. But the house was not very rich and, as the Prior pointed out, it was 'charged with a quondam and his pension', and had to provide a guide over the Sands, and the second offer, 'so that the said prior may have the said priory to stand under and by his Grace's pardon', was only for 1,100 marks.[2] 100 marks was to be paid 'now at this time, or afore the feast of St. Bartholomew',[3] and the rest over ten years. This was not acceptable either, and Conishead was dissolved along with the others.

Cockersand, too, must have been invited to make a second offer, though the documents have not survived. It was the richest of the smaller houses, and felt able to make a second offer of 2,000 marks, so it was decided to exempt it from suppression; only £400 of this was actually paid to the Duchy,[4] but the rest of the sum was guaranteed by the local gentry.[5] But Dr. Woodward has suggested[6] that in Yorkshire, where only one of the fifteen Yorkshire houses exempted paid for this privilege,[7] the government's real motive in allowing houses to stand was not profit, but the need to accommodate those religious who wished to retain their habit. The same is certainly true in Lancashire; the decisions of the monks of other houses will be discussed later, but at Cockersand, fourteen of the seventeen monks interviewed by the Commissioners wished to remain in religion, even if this involved transfer, and the other three wished to remain at Cockersand.[8] But the only other Premonstratensian house in Lancashire was Hornby, a cell of Croxton, with only three canons:[9] in which there would be room for only a small number of additional canons, if any. But if the Crown's offer of alternative accommodation was to be more than a gesture, and if the argument that the lesser houses were to be suppressed for reform and the inmates transferred to the better and larger houses[10] was not to collapse, something would have to be done for the Cockersand canons. The Commissioners and the Duchy officials were obviously worried, since they asked Onley of Augmentations what was to be done with the monks if there were no great houses of the Order left in Lancashire.[11] Onley replied that they would have to be sent to houses in other counties.[12]

[1] P.R.O., DL41/11/59, f. 8.   [2] ibid., f. 9.
[3] August 24th.   [4] P.R.O., DL29/2313.
[5] P.R.O., DL41/11/49.
[6] Woodward, 'The Exemption from Suppression of Certain Yorks Priories', 385–401, esp. 398–400.
[7] Woodward, art. cit., 392.
[8] P.R.O., DL43/5/4, f. 1.; DL43/5/7, f. 1.
[9] D.K.R., viii, App. 2, 18.
[10] 27 Henry VIII, c. 28, sect. 1.
[11] P.R.O., DL41/12/11, No. 3.
[12] P.R.O., DL41/12/12, No. 4.

But, as was pointed out, this would not answer the problem of Cockersand, for, it was said, only six or seven of the thirty Premonstratensian houses in England were outside the terms of the Act, and they would not be able to accommodate all the canons.[1] Onley was unable to answer this question.[2] There was, therefore, no alternative but to exempt the house from suppression, and the Duchy decided to make a virtue of necessity and take the 2,000 marks offered.[3]

Cockersand was the only Lancashire house exempted from the Act; in Yorkshire, however, of twenty-nine houses eligible for suppression, fifteen were spared.[4] Dr. Woodward does not suggest this, but it is clear that the large number of exemptions for Yorkshire was due to the high proportion of nunneries in the county,[5] for nuns were very reluctant to go out into the world.[6] In Lancashire, however, only one house needed to be exempted, as there were no nunneries in the county. Few Lancashire monks seem to have transferred[7] when their own monasteries were suppressed. Capacities were issued to all the monks of the four houses suppressed in 1536, and none appears again in a monastery, either in Lancashire or outside.[8] A comparison of the list in the 'Declaration of Survey' for Cockersand[9] with the surrender[10] and the pension list[11] shows that two monks arrived at the house after 1536. The two, William Lancaster and Robert Chapman, may have been new recruits, especially as they bear local names, but it is unlikely that many houses received recruits after 1536 when their position was so precarious. The two new Cockersand canons, therefore, were probably transfers, from Premonstratensian houses outside Lancashire. It is not clear if Whalley received any transfers, as there are no earlier lists for comparison with lists of monks available at its suppression, but four monks from Sawley in Yorkshire seem to have gone to Furness.[12] When Whalley was suppressed, John Estgate wanted to go to Neath,[13] but if he ever went there, no capacity was ever issued for him at that house,[14] and Christopher Cromboke, though he received a capacity at Whalley,[15]

[1] P.R.O., DL41/12/11, No. 4. In fact, there were thirty-one Premonstratensian houses, only eight of which were not liable to suppression (P. Hughes, *The Reformation in England*, i, 295).
[2] P.R.O., DL41/12/12, No. 4.
[3] Premonstratension houses in other areas also had to be exempted; six of the twenty-three houses which came within the Act were allowed to continue (Hughes, loc. cit.).
[4] Woodward, art. cit., 387.
[5] Thirteen of the fifteen houses exempted were nunneries.
[6] Knowles, *Religious Orders*, iii, 311. Thus, twenty-eight of the 100 English nunneries within the Act were exempted, but only 19 of the 191 male houses (Hughes, loc. cit.).
[7] See below.
[8] None of them received a capacity at another house in F.O.R., and none signed a surrender in D.K.R., viii, App. 2.
[9] P.R.O., DL43/5/4, f. 1.
[10] D.K.R., viii, App. 2, 16; *Cock. Chart.*, 1153-4.
[11] L. & P., xiv(1), 1355.
[12] L. & P., xii(1), 841, 3.
[13] L. & P., xii(1), 706.
[14] F.O.R., 170.
[15] F.O.R., 97.

appears to have gone to Byland, a Yorkshire Cistercian house, where someone of his name signed the surrender[1] and received a capacity.[2] At Furness, Thomas Hornby and Michael Hammerton signed the surrender,[3] but were not issued with capacities;[4] they have not been traced to another house, but presumably they transferred.[5] Cockersand, therefore, was the only house at which the problem of accommodation arose. The Duchy appears not to have given up hope of transferring the monks elsewhere, or persuading them to leave, for some time, for the monastery's patent of exemption was not issued until December 1536.[6]

The decision to reprieve Cockersand was probably taken between July 5th and July 15th. Its dissolution was still envisaged at the White Hall meeting,[7] but the process of issuing capacities for the Lancashire monks, in which Cockersand was not included, began on July 15th.[8] When the Commissioners had questioned the Lancashire monks in May–June, they asked thirty-eight monks in five houses, including Cockersand, whether they wished to remain in religion or take capacities. There were five monks at Burscough, but the Prior was not asked;[9] there were ten at Cartmel, but Prior Preston had no choice;[10] there were eight at Conishead, but the Prior and the quondam were not asked, and one was away serving a cure;[11] at Holland, Prior Prescot had no choice, and one monk, who was 'aged and impotent', was not asked;[12] and at Cockersand, of twenty-two monks, Abbot Poulton had no choice, and four did not appear as they were working outside the houses.[13] A table best illustrates their decisions.

TABLE II

House	Number questioned	Wished to leave	Prepared to continue	Wished to continue in own house only	Continue or transfer
Burscough	4	—	2	1	1
Holland	3	—	3	—	—
Cartmel	9	1?	—?	—	8
Conishead	5	2	—	3	—
Cockersand	17	—	—	3	14
	38	3?	5?	7	23

[1] D.K.R., viii, App. 2, 14.   [2] F.O.R., 181.
[3] D.K.R., viii, App. 2, 21; West, *Antiquities*, App. X, No. 7.   [4] F.O.R., 97.
[5] Not all transfers are traceable, for some houses fell by attainder, so leaving no surrender list, and not all houses, e.g. Cockersand, have capacities recorded for them.
[6] L. & P., xi, 1417, g. 18.
[7] The decisions of the meeting included that the lessee of the demesnes at Cockersand should provide a guide for the Sands, P.R.O., DL5/6, f. 205.
[8] F.O.R., 65.   [9] P.R.O., DL43/5/7, f. 4.
[10] P.R.O., DL43/4/11; DL43/4/12.   [11] P.R.O., DL43/5/7, f. 3.
[12] P.R.O., DL43/5/7, f. 5.   [13] P.R.O., DL43/5/7, f. 1; DL43/5/4, f. 1.

This indicates that the monks were not as anxious to leave their houses as has sometimes been supposed.[1] Of the monks questioned, 60·5% wished to continue in religion even if this involved transfer to another house, which was a very real sacrifice.[2] A better figure for assessing the proportion satisfied with the religious life is that of those who sincerely wanted to continue, preferably in their own house.[3] This is the very high proportion of 78·9%, indicating that four-fifths of the monks of Lancashire had some sense of vocation and an enthusiasm for the religious life. The figure for those who wished to leave in any event is correspondingly small, only three out of thirty-eight, and this may have been only two, as the real intentions of William Pannell of Cartmel are not clear.[4] It would be unwise to assume that a reluctance to leave a comfortable monastery necessarily meant a sincere commitment to the religious life, but that such a high proportion of monks wished to remain indicates at least the social importance and institutional stability of the houses, while those who were prepared to move to other houses were quite probably eager to continue in religion.

The figures available, though they do not cover large enough numbers for any firm conclusions, illustrate one of the points this essay seeks to make—that the monasteries in the south of Lancashire, like those in southern England generally, were becoming increasingly irrelevant in a changing society, while those in the north were still integrated into the life of the county and performed important functions. A comparison of the southern houses, Burscough and Holland, with those in the north, Cartmel, Cockersand, and Conishead, shows that in the south only one monk out of seven was prepared to transfer, and only another one wished to continue in his own house, while in the north, twenty-two out of thirty-one were prepared to move to another house, and another six would have liked to remain in religion if they could have stayed in their own houses. The distinction remains true even if the unusually enthusiastic Cockersand is discounted.

Clearly, then, the majority of the monks, when given a choice by the Commissioners, elected to remain in religion. It was this which led to the exemption of Cockersand, but even then many wished to stay; of the twenty-one monks in the four houses to be dissolved, only three definitely wanted to leave, and five would prefer to leave, but nine wished to continue even if they had to transfer, and another four wished to stay in their own houses. Of the twenty-one monks, thirteen wished to remain in religion; thus, when the Commissioners sent in their figures to the Duchy,

---

[1] Baskerville, *English Monks and the Suppression*, 150–1, 153, argues that 'probably more than half' of the monks chose to take capacities and leave religion, indicating lack of concern for the religious life, but this point is only valid if there was a free choice in the matter of dispensations.

[2] Baskerville, op. cit., 149; Knowles, *Religious Orders*, iii, 310.

[3] The last two columns of the table added together.

[4] cf. P.R.O., DL43/4/11; 43/4/12; and 43/5/7, f. 2.

even if all the houses were to be dissolved, thus displacing the four who wished to stay in their own houses, arrangements ought to have been made for the transference of the other nine, and capacities ought to have been issued for the twelve who wished to leave, with the addition of the priors, the quondam at Conishead, and the old monk at Holland. Perhaps places could not be found outside Lancashire for the nine who wished to continue, and perhaps the Duchy was reluctant to exempt another house from its meagre haul,[1] but in any event capacities were issued for all the monks of the four houses, whether they had asked for them or not, and those who wished to remain were not allowed to do so. Batches of capacities for the Lancashire monks seem to have been ordered in one block by the Duchy,[2] and they were all issued within a few days of each other.[3]

The Act of Suppression gave the monks a free choice over their future, but it seems that almost half the Lancashire monks in the houses to be dissolved were forced to leave religion against their will—capacities were issued for all twenty-eight of the monks normally resident in the four houses.[4] There is no evidence that the monks ever voluntarily changed their minds, and the return during the Pilgrimage of the monks of Cartmel and Conishead[5] indicates that they were angry at their ejection. The injustice is particularly clear in the case of Cartmel—eight monks expressed a wish to go to other houses,[6] but they were all issued with capacities[7] and it is hardly surprising that they were all later indicted for helping the rebels.[8] The suggestion that all the monks were given a free choice[9] is therefore not valid for Lancashire. Mr. Hodgett has argued that the monks who left in 1536, when they had the 'choice' of continuing, were those 'with the least sense of vocation for the cloistered life',[10] but this is not necessarily true of Lancashire either.

The capacities would take some time to be cleared by Chancery,[11] but as the last were enrolled in the Faculty Office on July 24th,[12] they were presumably ready to be sent up to Lancashire, with the Duchy's instructions for the Commissioners, in mid-August 1536. The Commissioners were now to move on to the actual suppression, the sale of moveables, the sending of valuables to London, and the expulsion of the monks.[13] This

---

[1] The Duchy soon became very worried about the decline in its revenues—see 32 Henry VIII, c. 57. It would therefore want as much land as possible from the Dissolution.

[2] As often happened for other areas—Chambers, intro. to F.O.R., lii.

[3] Holland, July 15th—F.O.R., 65; Cartmel, July 22nd—F.O.R., 65; Burscough, July 22nd—F.O.R., 65–6; Conishead, July 24th—F.O.R., 67.

[4] F.O.R., 65–67; P.R.O., DL43/5/7, fos. 2–5.

[5] See below, Chapter Six.   [6] P.R.O., DL43/4/12, f. 1.

[7] F.O.R., 65.   [8] P.R.O., PL26/13/6.

[9] Baskerville, *English Monks*, 150–1; even implicitly Knowles, *Religious Orders*, iii, 309–310.

[10] Hodgett, 'The Unpensioned Ex-Religious', J. Eccl. Hist., xiii, 1962, 202.

[11] Chambers, intro. to F.O.R., xxiii–xxix.   [12] F.O.R., 67.

[13] L. & P., x, 721; Woodward, art. cit., 389.

time, the Commissioners changed their itinerary slightly, visiting Burscough, which is just north of Holland, first.[1] They were at Burscough between August 16th and 20th, at Holland August 23rd to 25th, at Cartmel September 3rd to 9th, and at Conishead September 9th to 13th, and apparently also on the 21st.[2] For some reason, they also surveyed the lands of Hornby, which was outside their jurisdiction, and was not dissolved, sometime in August.[3] They had assembled and were ready to begin their work by August 13th, when Thomas Sherburne wrote to Burgoyne asking that the proctor of Garstang should be restored to his place now that Cockersand was not to be dissolved.[4] The Commissioners also visited Cockersand to give the canons the news of their exemption, and to collect what they could of the 2,000 marks.[5]

Much of the Commissioners' work was purely routine, and was duplicated at each of the houses, except that at Cartmel the Commissioners made some arrangement for the woods, which someone thought, in an unsigned and undated letter, would only cause trouble.[6] While the Suppressors were at Holland on August 25th, Sir Antony Fitzherbert wrote to Burgoyne asking that some of the 'household stuff in the abbeys suppressed' should be sent to Lancaster Castle, for the use of the King's justices and auditors there.[7] Burgoyne later sent some on from Cartmel and Conishead, the only two houses left to suppress.[8]

The suppression of Conishead is particularly well documented. A fortnight before the Commissioners even reached his house, Prior Lord wrote to Burgoyne asking him to be as good to him as 'you are unto the Prior of Burscough and others', and asking to be allowed to buy the tithe-corn of Ulverston and the corn on the Priory demesne.[9] He sent Burgoyne two gold angels 'for a remembrance of the same', and pointed out, perhaps threateningly, that 'You know my lord Admiral[10] is good lord to me.' On September 8th, the day before the Commission arrived at Conishead, Thomas Wharton of Muncaster wrote to the members asking to buy the Priory's sheep in Muncaster and Orton.[11] The wolves were obviously gathering, and it must have been about this time that Sir James Layburne approached the Chancellor for a lease of one of the benefices of Cartmel or Conishead, since he was reminding Cromwell of the matter a month later.[12] On September 11th, William Gerard(?) wrote to the Suppressors

---

[1] Burscough is near Lathom, so perhaps they had visited the Earl of Derby before starting.
[2] P.R.O., DL29/158/26; Mason, op. cit., 17.
[3] P.R.O., DL43/5/12, fos. 1–17.
[4] P.R.O., DL41/11/59. f. 2. This was Brian Furness, monk of Cockersand (DL43/5/4, f. 1).
[5] P.R.O., DL29/2313, m. 17d.; DL29/2317.
[6] P.R.O., DL43/5/12, f. 18.
[7] P.R.O., DL41/11/59, f. 3.
[8] P.R.O., DL29/2313, m. 14–15.
[9] P.R.O., DL41/11/59, f. 4.
[10] Fitzwilliam, Chancellor of the Duchy.
[11] P.R.O., DL41/11/59, f. 5.
[12] L. & P., xi, 608.

asking for the four gold angels he had lent the Prior of Conishead.[1]
While the Commission was at Cartmel, Sir William Harrington and
Richard Duckett entered into a bond before them for the lease and division
of the parsonage of Orton,[2] which was appropriated to Conishead.[3]

While they were at Conishead, George Cansforth the quondam, petitioned the Commission to be allowed to continue with his pension of £10
cash plus 'one honest chamber and garden' and food at the Prior's table
for himself, and two servants, and two horses, which he had been paid by
the Priory[4]—he was allowed the £10 cash.[5] On being issued with their
capacities, the canons were given a half-year's stipend of 17/8d., and a
'reward' of 26/8d. with an extra mark for the sub-prior.[6] Thomas Lord,
the ex-prior, was much better off than his brethren, and was able to raise
£50 as a fine for the lease of the parsonage of Ulverston.[7] All four priors, in
fact, were able to purchase corn, and were granted tithe leases,[8] while
their monks, as a rule, got 30/- or three or four marks.[9] In accordance
with Onley's suggestion, the monks were given their bedding and personal effects, 'somewhat liberally by the discretion of the Commissioners',[10]
as well as their wages. The value of the goods allowed to each monk
averaged £3/11/7d. at Holland, £9/0/1½d. at Burscough, £1/5/1d. at
Conishead, and £3/19/4½d. at Cartmel.[11] It is, perhaps, hardly surprising
that the canons of Conishead were soon to ask the northern rebels for
assistance in retaining their priory.

Onley, the Augmentations attorney, had suggested[12] that monastic
servants should be given 'their full wages and some honest reward
beside', and at Conishead the servants each submitted slips giving their
name, occupation, and wages owing, which were endorsed by the Prior.[13]
But they were given no reward, and most were paid less than a mark,[14]
while at Waltham in Essex the Augmentations Suppressors gave all the
sixty-eight servants their wages and a reward, in sums ranging from 10/-
up to 26/8d.[15] For almsmen, too, the Commissioners did not follow the more
generous policy of Augmentations,[16] and the seven men at Conishead were
given only 16/8d. between them.[17] The goods of the house were sold off to
important local men; William Collins, the bailiff of Kendal, bought up
some wool,[18] and Lord Mounteagle was given the farm of the site and
demesnes and sold the bulk of the goods.[19]

At other houses, too, the lessees bought up the moveables; Thomas

[1] P.R.O., DL41/11/59, f. 6.
[2] ibid., fos. 7, 12.
[3] Valor, v, 295.
[4] P.R.O., DL41/11/59, f. 11.
[5] P.R.O., DL29/2313, m. 8.
[6] ibid.
[7] P.R.O., DL29/158/6.
[8] P.R.O., DL29/2313, m. 12.
[9] ibid., m. 6-11.
[10] P.R.O., DL41/12/12, No. 5.
[11] Figures from P.R.O., DL29/2313.
[12] P.R.O., DL41/12/12, No. 19.
[13] P.R.O., DL29/158/27 & 28.
[14] P.R.O., DL29/2313, m. 6-11.
[15] J. E. Oxley, The Reformation in Essex, 132.
[16] P.R.O., DL41/12/12, No. 17.
[17] P.R.O., DL29/2313, m. 6-11.
[18] P.R.O., DL29/158/26.
[19] P.R.O., DL29/2273; DL29/158/26.

Holcroft was made farmer of Cartmel, where he bought the goods of the house,[1] and Sir Thomas Butler, lessee of Holland, did the same there.[2] The Commissioners themselves, though there is no evidence of profiteering at the expense of the Duchy, also made purchases, usually of tithes, Sir Thomas Halsall and Sir William Leyland from Burscough,[3] and Sir Henry Farington from Cartmel.[4] It seems to have been the usual practice for suppression officials to take advantage of their position in this way; the Essex Commissioners certainly did so.[5] Though all five Commissioners seem to have worked hard at each house during the 'supervision' process,[6] most of the work of the actual suppression appears to have been done by Leyland, Burgoyne, and Dawtrey, for these are the officers usually named on the suppression documents.[7] Burgoyne, as auditor, must have had the hardest job of all, and he clearly thought he deserved some reward. He asked the King for Conishead, half of it at twenty years' purchase, the usual price, and the rest as a gift from the King, 'in consideration of my service . . . in the surveying and dissolving of certain religious houses in Lancashire'.[8] His plea, however, went unheard.

[1] P.R.O., DL29/2228; DL29/2313.
[2] ibid.; DL29/2303.
[3] P.R.O., DL29/2198, m. 6-7.
[4] P.R.O., DL29/2228, m. 6.
[5] Oxley, *The Reformation in Essex*, 109-10, 123.
[6] P.R.O., DL43/5/7, fos. 1-5.
[7] e.g. P.R.O., DL41/11/59, fos. 6 & 11.
[8] P.R.O., DL43/5/9.

CHAPTER FIVE

THE ORIGINS OF THE PILGRIMAGE:
THE POSITION OF THE HOUSES IN
LANCASHIRE SOCIETY

THE suppression of the smaller houses sparked off the rebellion;[1] only four weeks after the canons of Conishead had been ejected, they were back in their house,[2] and the commons of Lancashire had been buying up arms a fortnight before that.[3] Lancashire had been restive for some time; there were unlawful assemblies in June 1535;[4] Sir Marmaduke Tunstall had raised 500 men in July 1535 against a much smaller group of Lord Mounteagle's retainers at Melling;[5] and Adam Hulton had raised forces to prevent Mounteagle holding a court at Westhoughton.[6] Agricultural discontent in the north-west was also serious. In June 1535 there was a riot involving 300 or 400 people in Craven, who pulled down dykes and hedges in the Giggleswick area.[7] Eighty-two men were indicted, for three different riots, and eighteen were imprisoned, but the others involved were mainly women and children, intent on pulling down recent enclosures of moors and waste.[8] There were also enclosure riots near Fressington in Cumberland in July 1535.[9] There were no agrarian riots in Lancashire, although there is evidence of some discontent; in the early 1530's there were disputes over common rights at Nuthurst, Chadderton, Oldham, Morton, Ashton, Hindley, Warton, Poulton, Bispham, Lytham, and Hawes Waste.[10] Certainly the King's instructions to the Earls of Sussex and Derby, after the rebellion, imply that agrarian grievances were thought to be one of the causes of the rising; 'if any commons have been enclosed, or any gentlemen take excessive fines that their tenants cannot live, the Earls shall labour to bring such enclosers and extreme takers of fines to such moderation that they and the poor men may live in harmony'.[11] Similarly, when Cromwell appointed deputies at Furness and in Lonsdale, they were instructed to guard against excessive fees and entry fines.[12]

But it was obviously in the government's interest to suggest that it was the greed of the gentry rather than its own ecclesiastical policy which had caused the revolt, and there is no real evidence of serious agricultural un-

[1] Knowles, *Religious Orders*, iii, 320–2.
[2] P.R.O., DL29/158/26; L. & P., Add., 1112.
[3] L. & P., xi, 563.   [4] L. & P., viii, 984.   [5] ibid., 1108.
[6] ibid.   [7] ibid., 863.   [8] ibid., 970, 992.
[9] ibid., 1133.   [10] *Ducatus Lancastriae*, i, 142, 145, 146.
[11] L. & P., xii(1), 302.   [12] L. & P., xii(2), 1216; (1), 881.

rest in the county. The common field system operated mainly in the south-western portion of Lancashire,[1] where only the smaller monasteries were situated, and where, in any case, there was little active support for the rebels. Enclosure of common land was usually achieved by negotiation in Lancashire, and with little social dislocation, because both the fields and the numbers of occupiers were relatively small.[2] The rest of the county, where the more important monasteries were situated, was conservative and unchanging in agriculture as in much else; in 1662 the copyhold rents in Pendle were the same as they had been in 1507.[3]

But in an economic climate which was never very bright, the suppression of the monasteries must have added an element of uncertainty which would be very worrying, and change was always frightening to a conservative society. Sir James Layburne was reported to have said that 'If we may enjoy our old ancient customs, we have no cause to rise,'[4] but many seem to have felt that the old customs were threatened. Robert Southwell, who suppressed Furness, realised that immediate security would save the commons from fear of the unknown future. He thought that if the surveyors had had 'some small part of the demesnes, upon their suit to the Council, distributed to the poor', the rebellion might not have taken place.[5] Southwell himself learned the lesson of the earlier dissolutions, and when he sold off the animals of Furness he allowed the local people first choice, he suggested that plots on the demesne should be leased to the unemployed ex-servants of the house, and, on Beaumont Grange, he pleaded 'that the poor men be not expelled for no gentleman's pleasure'.[6] The policies of Southwell, an Augmentations man, were much more generous than those of the Duchy officials, and if the treatment of Conishead's servants is typical of Duchy procedure, it is hardly surprising that servants were angry.

In Lancashire, at least, the course of the rebellion, and especially the close liaison between the monks and the commons, indicate that the rebels were more concerned with religious than economic issues. The county's discontent with the Crown's religious policy had been growing for some time; in 1533 at least one Lancashire clergyman was speaking out against the King's second marriage, calling Katherine the lawful queen and Anne Boleyn a whore, and predicting that there would be a rebellion against Henry's attack on the Church.[7] Though not a reliable witness, Chapuys, the Imperial ambassador, reported in December 1534 that the people of Lancashire were, like the Welsh, disaffected 'at the

[1] G. Youd, 'The Common Fields of Lancashire', Trans. Hist. Soc. L. & C., Vol. 113, 3.
[2] ibid., 34-5.
[3] M. Brigg, 'The Forest of Pendle in 17th Century', Trans. Hist. Soc. L. & C., Vol. 113, 68.
[4] L. & P., xii(1), 914.
[5] L. & P., xii(2), 205; printed in full, Beck, Annales, 356-60.   'ibid.
[7] L. & P., vi, 964; printed in full, Corresp., 7-12.

ill-treatment of the Queen and Princess, and also at that which is done against the faith'.[1] If the opinions of the monks of Furness were representative of the attitudes of the clergy of Lancashire,[2] there was considerable anger over Henry's claim to supremacy over the Church, while Cromwell's note in 1534 that a number of Lancashire priests were refusing to pay the subsidy[3] may indicate further discontent.

The Furness area, in particular, was a hotbed of religious reaction; according to Latimer, there 'pardoning doth prate in the borders of the realm', and unless reformist clergy were sent by Cromwell the people 'shall perish in their ignorance'.[4] It was reported, probably late in 1536, when the Pilgrimage of Grace was at its height, that a certain commissary and William Ashburner, one of the clergy at Dalton, had been persuading the people to pay Peter's Pence to the papacy, in defiance of the Act forbidding this. A local priest who complained at such flouting of the law, William Rede, was dismissed from keeping the school at Dalton, and ill-treated by the commissary for preaching against the authority of the Pope and teaching from Erasmus' 'Paraphrases'; as the friar who reported all this to the King put it, 'Your Grace will perceive how hopeless it is for men to be true in this country unless other manner of men be put in spiritual rooms, which your Grace may do now better than at any former time.'[5] Though Ashburner and the commissary were clearly breaking the supremacy laws and encouraging the people to disobey the King, it is hardly surprising that they attacked Rede, who seems to have held distinctly reformist views and may even have been a heretic. In 1533 he was said by Dr. Dakyn, the Vicar-General of Richmond, to have had a copy of a book called *Unio Dissidentium*,[6] a collection of texts from patristic authors which supported Protestant teachings. This book, which may have been the work of Martin Bucer, was used by a number of heretical authors, including Robert Barnes,[7] and in 1529 a London curate had been in trouble with his bishop for possessing the book, 'containing the Lutheran heresy'.[8] *Unio Dissidentium* was one of the heretical works brought over from the Continent via the illicit book trade of the secret 'Christian Brethren' in the late 1520's,[9] and it was banned by Bishop Tunstall in 1526[10] and by the English Church authorities in 1531–2.[11] A priest such as Rede would hardly have been popular in Furness, and his opinions must have annoyed the people and made them alive to the threat of heresy, which worried the northern rebels so much.[12]

---

[1] L. & P., vii, 1368.   [2] L. & P., xii(1), 841. See below, Chapter Seven.
[3] L. & P., vii, 923, xviii. Opposition to religious policies usually led to refusal to pay taxes; this certainly happened during the Pilgrimage of Grace (L. & P., xii(1), 21, 67, 789 ii).
[4] L. & P., xi, 67.   [5] L. & P., xii(1), 842.   [6] L. & P., vi, 287.
[7] W. A. Clebsch, *England's Earliest Protestants*, 75–6.
[8] J. Strype, *Ecclesiastical Memorials*, i(1), 118.   [9] ibid., i(2), 64–5.
[10] ibid., i(1), 254.   [11] Wilkins, *Concilia*, iii, 717–21.
[12] e.g. L. & P., xi, 892, i; Strype, op. cit., 1(2), 266.

But there is a mass of evidence which shows that it was more particularly the suppression of the lesser houses which really annoyed the commons of the north. The mobs restored the canons of Cartmel and Conishead, and the Lancashire rebels must have had some contact with Sawley, which was also restored,[1] while they were in contact with the houses of Whalley and Furness.[2] Whenever the authorities moved against one of the houses, the commons immediately rose to its defence. In the south, however, the priories of Holland and Burscough found no rebels to champion them, though even there the Earl of Derby thought pulling down the lead and bells of Burscough was too risky 'in this busy world',[3] and the people were murmuring for their wages.[4] The rebellion was far more serious in the north-east and north-west of the county, where the religious houses appear still to have been popular, and where they certainly played an important part in local life. Aske's picture of the importance of the monasteries in the life of the North[5] may be overdrawn, but there is a solid basis of fact for Lancashire for most of the points he made.

Aske objected to the Act of Suppression, firstly 'because the abbeys in the north parts gave great alms to poor men'.[6] Savine argued that the average over England for monastic charities was about $2\frac{1}{2}\%$ of the gross annual income,[7] based on the tax-free alms, as given in the 1535 *Valor*, which the houses were bound to give by foundation. Westminster Abbey gave only 2·7%, Fountains 1·7%, and St. Werburgh's at Chester only 1·3%.[8] The comparable figure for the seven independent Lancashire houses, however, is three times the national average, 7·6%, even including only 'compulsory' alms. If all the known charitable activities of these houses for which costs are available are included,[9] the result is an even more commendable 10·8%, of gross annual income. In charity at least, Aske was right, and the Lancashire houses certainly deserved to be popular for their activities in this sphere. In 1535 Whalley was allowed £116/18/10d. in tax-free alms,[10] given in doles at Christmas and on Maundy Thursday, and in keeping twenty-four poor men in the house; this was an amazing 21% of the income of £551/4/6d. gross.[11] Cockersand, a much poorer house, was allowed £18/13/4d.,[12] in doles at the Nativity of the Virgin Mary and on Maundy Thursday, 8% of its gross income. In 1536 the house also had fifteen 'poor aged and impotent men found daily at bread and board', at a cost of another £22/7/4d.,[13]

---

[1] Though in Yorks, Sawley was only just over the county border.
[2] For all this, see below, Chapters Six and Seven.
[3] L. & P., xi, 1118.
[4] L. & P., xii(1), 348.
[5] 'Aske's Examination', E.H.R., v, 561–2.
[6] ibid.
[7] Savine, *English Monasteries on the Eve of Dissolution*, 239.
[8] G. W. O. Woodward, *The Dissolution of the Monasteries*, 22.
[9] Corrodies are excluded, as involving purchase.
[10] *Valor*, v, 230.
[11] ibid., 229.
[12] ibid., 261.
[13] P.R.O., DL43/5/4.

which must have been influenced by the house's original foundation as a hospital.[1] Furness was allowed only £11/10/od. in 1535,[2] in doles on St. Crispin's Day and on Maundy Thursday, a meagre 1·2% of its gross income, but the house also kept thirteen paupers at a cost of £21/13/4d. and gave weekly doles costing £12 a year to eight poor widows,[3] which were presumably not allowed for taxation purposes as not being compulsory, and this gives Furness the more respectable figure of 4·8% for its charity. Conishead was allowed £10/10/od. in tax-free alms[4] for doles on Maundy Thursday, or 8% of its gross income, but the house also gave another £1 in alms.[5] Cartmel was allowed only 6/8d. for compulsory alms,[6] for doles on Easter Sunday, but it gave another £12[7] in daily doles to seven poor men, giving a percentage for total alms of 10·7%. The performance of these north Lancashire houses was thus exceptionally good, and far above the national average. But again there is some difference between north and south, with the two independent southern houses being far less generous to the local people. Burscough gave £7 worth of grain, distributed weekly to the poor,[8] or 5½% of its gross income, but the two men who were also 'having living for term of life' were obviously corrodians by purchase.[9] Holland, admittedly a poor house, gave no tax-free alms in 1535,[10] and the only other known charitable activity of the Priory was two men 'aged and impotent kept of alms' in 1536.[11] Though their performance varied, the Lancashire monasteries were clearly much more generous than those in many other areas. In Essex, for example, the religious houses as a group gave little in charity;[12] Walden gave 2·5% of its income, while at St. John's the Prior alone was given an amount equivalent to two-thirds of the total charitable gifts of the house.[13]

Aske's second point[14] was that the monasteries had 'laudably served God', and after their suppression 'the divine service of Almighty God is much minished, great numbers of masses unsaid, and the blessed consecration of the Sacrament now not used and showed in those places'. This is obviously more difficult to document, but if their stock of ornaments and vestments is anything to judge by, the Lancashire monasteries must have provided colourful and splendid services which the local people would be sorry to lose. Even Holland, one of the poorer houses, had nine sets of vestments, three copes, and a relic of St. Thomas of Canterbury.[15] Burscough had nineteen sets of vestments, as well as three old ones, six copes which the Earl of Derby had given, fifteen old copes, four chalices, four

[1] Colvin, *White Canons*, 143.
[2] *Valor*, v, 270.
[3] ibid.; P.R.O., SC12/9/73.
[4] *Valor*, v, 271; P.R.O., DL43/5/2, f. 10.
[5] *Valor*, v, 271.
[6] ibid., 272.
[7] ibid.
[8] *Valor*, v, 230.
[9] P.R.O., DL43/5/7, f. 4.
[10] *Valor*, v, 221.
[11] P.R.O., DL43/5/7, f. 5.
[12] Oxley, *The Reformation in Essex*, 53.
[13] ibid., 55, 56.
[14] E.H.R., v, 561.
[15] P.R.O., DL41/11/47.

crosses, two of them of silver, and a relic of the true Cross.[1] Cockersand's services were even more splendid, with twelve copes of red damask, and four other copes, a silver chalice, a gilt crozier, silver censers, and three organs,[2] a 'pair of organs' in the chancel, 'a pair of great organs' in the rood loft, and a 'pair of little organs' in the Lady Chapel. Whalley's services must have been the most sumptuous of all, with fifteen gilt chalices, a silver-gilt cross bearing images of Mary and St. John, and a gilt cross with the four Evangelists on it, two silver pastoral crooks, two mitres, one silver-gilt and heavily jewelled, all the necessary silver plate, and eighteen richly embroidered copes, one of 'Venice gold' with Lord Mounteagle's arms on it, one of cloth of gold, with the same arms, one with a picture of Christ on it, and another with a picture of St. Martin, and twenty-four vestments, thirteen for normal use, and eleven more elaborate, with pictures of the Crucifix, St. Michael, and the Trinity embroidered on them.[3] The services which these church goods would have helped to provide must have been a very real loss to the local people, even those with no theological interest who were not concerned with the cessation of the stream of masses which the abbeys provided. This must have been especially true at Cartmel, where the priory church was also the parish church, and where the people were anxious to secure the 'suit of copes' which they said belonged to the parish, and a chalice, mass-books, vestments, and other things.[4] They were also very worried at the prospect of losing the Priory's relic of the Cross, for which they applied to the Duchy for permission to keep.[5] At Burscough the monastery buildings excited the feelings of the people so much that at one stage the Earl of Derby did not dare to strip off the lead from the roof for fear of provoking a riot.[6] At Cartmel and Holland there was probably little reduction in the number of services, since the churches were both allowed to stand for the use of the people;[7] in March 1537 the people of Holland petitioned the Earls of Derby and Sussex that the priory church should be made a chapel for their use, and this appears to have been granted.[8]

Aske argued that there was 'none hospitality now in those places kept', for which the monasteries had been particularly useful to 'strangers and baggers of corn as betwixt Yorkshire, Lancashire, Kendal, Westmorland, and the Bishopric'.[9] This again is difficult to prove, but the chronicles of houses in other areas show a constant stream of guests, and Lord Mounteagle was born while his mother was staying at Butley Priory.[10] At least in 1494, Cockersand had a guest-master[11] and visitors to Whalley could

---

[1] P.R.O., DL41/11/36. [2] P.R.O., DL43/5/4.
[3] The Earl of Sussex's inventory, printed Whitaker, i, 185–8; *Whalley Coucher*, 1255–65.
[4] P.R.O., DL41/12/11, Nos. 12, 13. [5] ibid., No. 21.
[6] L. & P., xi, 1118. [7] P.R.O., DL41/12/11, Nos. 10, 11.
[8] Dugdale, *Monasticon*, iv, 412. [9] i.e. Durham; E.H.R., v, 561–2.
[10] *Chronicle of Butley Priory*, ed. Dickens, 55.
[11] C.A.P., ii, 122.

E

expect to be well fed, as two-thirds of the Abbey's income was spent on food and drink for the monks and their guests.[1] According to Aske, 'the said Abbeys was one [*sic*] of the beauties of this realm to all men and to strangers passing through the same',[2] and the sight of such architectural splendour being thrown down must have offended many. Cartmel Church is still very attractive, and the ruins of Whalley and Furness remained impressive for centuries. In the years before the Reformation, a new West Tower of magnificent proportions was added at Furness,[3] and the last Abbot of Whalley built a Lady Chapel which was so admired that when, in 1532, the people of Burnley had their church repaired they chose the two masons whom Paslew had employed, and stipulated that eighteen buttresses were to be added to the church, 'every buttress having a funnel upon the top according to the fashion of the funnels upon the new chapel of our Lady at Whalley'.[4] Architectural splendour may not have been enough to drive the north of Lancashire to revolt, but it would certainly provide another weighty reason for resistance to the suppression.

Aske thought that the monasteries had 'all gentlemen much succoured in their needs with money',[5] and if by this he meant that fees from monasteries were a useful source of extra income for hard-pressed gentry, he was certainly right. Furness, the most obvious example, paid 40/- each to five Furness J.P.'s, £6/13/4d. to Thomas Holcroft, fees to sixteen bailiffs, £6 to John Lambert for holding the sessions, £20 to Leonard Fawcett, 'generali receptori nostro', £10 to the Earl of Derby, and £6 to the Earl of Cumberland.[6] Whalley, in 1535, paid fees to eleven bailiffs, £5/6/8d. to the Earl of Derby as steward, and £5 each to Alexander Nowell and Richard Cromboke as sub-seneschals.[7] Of the smaller houses, Conishead paid six bailiffs and a steward,[8] Cartmel paid four bailiffs, £4 to an auditor, 33/4d. to John Standish for keeping the court, and 40/- to the Earl of Derby as steward.[9] More probably, however, Aske meant that the monasteries could be relied on for loans; this is less certain, though Cartmel certainly lent £20 and £10 to two local men, and at the suppression was a creditor to the tune of £63/9/od.[10] The Lancashire monasteries, in fact, appear to have acted as unofficial bankers for the area; when Sir John Husee bought the wardship of the young Lord Mounteagle in 1524, he placed £360 of the 1,200 marks purchase price to the King's use in the hands of the Abbot of Whalley,[11] and the Abbot of Furness acted as one of the late Lord Mounteagle's executors.[12] In 1520, when Sir Thomas Butler of Warrington wished to found a grammar

---

[1] See above, Chapter One; L.R.O., DDTo/B21.   [2] E.H.R., v, 562.
[3] Bouch and Jones, *Economic and Social History of the Lake Counties*, 30.
[4] Wallis, *History of the Church in Blackburnshire*, 143.   [5] E.H.R., v, 562.
[6] P.R.O., SC12/9/73; *Valor*, v, 270.   [7] *Valor*, v, 229.
[8] ibid., 271.   [9] ibid., 272.
[10] P.R.O., DL43/4/12, f. 2.   [11] L. & P., iv(1), 13.
[12] ibid., 2130.

school under his will, he 'delivered by indenture tripartite into the custody and keeping of the right reverend Father in God John, Abbot of Whalley, 500 marks in gold, safely to be kept to his use and to be disposed at his pleasure'.[1] Such services would obviously be missed.

Aske's point on the importance of the abbeys in the education of the children of the gentry[2] is certainly much exaggerated for Lancashire. There were no nunneries for the education of Lancashire girls, though in 1582 an old man who had been one of the scholars remembered that Furness Abbey had educated and boarded the children of its tenants,[3] and in 1536 Holland had two 'children at school' in the Priory.[4] The educational attainment of the monks themselves in the larger houses appears to have been good; about 1535 Furness paid £10 to its scholar at Oxford,[5] and Whalley also kept a scholar there; in 1521 the house paid £9/6/8d. towards the expenses of its scholar proceeding to the degree of B.A.,[6] had a scholar at Oxford in 1536,[7] and another in 1537.[8] Whalley appears to have possessed a library of some size, and seven of its books are still extant,[9] including a thirteenth-century French and Latin psalter, a fourteenth-century 'Life of Aildred', and several philosophical works, including a thirteenth-century Duns Scotus, and a thirteenth-century 'Compilacio de libris Aristotelis', while for lighter reading there was an edition of the 'Polychronicon'. The books appear to have been used by the monks, for, in 1478 at least, 8/- was spent on the repair of books.[10] Less is known of the intellectual possibilities at Furness, but it must have had a library of some kind since one book survives from it.[11] Cockersand was certainly well supplied with books; in 1536 it had a library with glazed windows, in which were fifty-two books which the Suppression Comissioners valued at only 5/-,[12] and another fifty-four books valued at 6/8d.; the fifty-four 'parchment books' in the choir were probably psalters and mass-books, but even the possession of so many of those is commendable. Only one of the Cockersand books survives, however, a thirteenth-century 'Theologica'.[13] Almost nothing is known for the smaller houses; even the inventories yield no information except that at Holland there were four old mass-books, two printed on paper, and two written on parchment.[14] But in the northern houses there was at least some intellectual activity, the ending of which would constitute some loss to the local community.

The substance of Aske's defence of the monasteries, then, can be con-

[1] Lancs Chantries, i, 57. [2] E.H.R., v, 562.
[3] Bouch & Jones, op. cit., 29. [4] P.R.O., DL43/5/7, f. 5.
[5] P.R.O., SC12/9/73. [6] Whitaker, i, 127.
[7] L. & P., xi, 23.
[8] L. & P., xii(1), 389; the references may, however, be to the same man. See below, Chapter Six.
[9] Ker, Medieval Libraries of Great Britain, 197. [10] Whitaker, i, 126.
[11] Ker, op. cit., 89. [12] P.R.O., DL43/5/4.
[13] Ker, op. cit., 52. [14] P.R.O., DL41/11/47.

firmed for Lancashire. Whatever their moral and spiritual condition, they still fulfilled useful functions in the life of the county, functions important enough to raise a rebellion when the houses were attacked. The common people judged the monks by their public acts, their services to the community, rather than their private behaviour; even a den of vice might be defended if it eased the lot of the poor. The government's argument that the monasteries were too evil to be allowed to continue would thus make little impact, especially in Lancashire, where the Commissioners' offer of redemption for a cash payment[1] made the financial motive for the Suppression obvious. This last must have been particularly galling, and may go far towards explaining why the Lancashire rebels were so eager to defend the monasteries.

Many men in the north of Lancashire must have taken the Pilgrims' oath out of resentment at the spoliation of the religious houses beside which they spent their lives, and many more must have taken it because of personal connections with the suppressed houses, or with those still standing, which must also have appeared to be threatened. When Furness was surveyed in June 1537, it was found to have 400 horsemen and 458 footsoldiers on its possessions in Lancashire, Cumberland, and Yorkshire,[2] and the Minister's Accounts show about 300 armed men on the Cartmel estates,[3] and an even larger number on Conishead's.[4] In addition, there must have been something over 2,000 customary tenants of the Lancashire houses,[5] and if only a fraction of the men bound to the monasteries turned out to defend them, they must have constituted a formidable force. The customs of Furness, as set out in 1509, stipulated that the tenants could be sworn only to the King and the Abbey's steward, that the tenants were not to take the part of any other in disputes against the monastery, and that they were each to provide a horse and armour when required.[6] Furness certainly had a force of liveried men in 1525,[7] and this seems to have remained in being until the suppression.[8]

In 1516 the local influence of Furness was so great that when Abbot Banke was cited to appear in the Duchy Court, a memorandum was added to the orders for the case that no gentlemen of the Abbot's 'fee, kin, or allied shall be put upon the jury, neither shall any of them be of the retinue of Lord Mounteagle',[9] who was steward of the house. Similarly, in a dispute in 1535–6, the plaintiff said he had to go to the Duchy Court as he could not sue the Prior of Cartmel at a common law court since he was a great man in Lancashire, 'greatly friended and favoured there'.[10] When Abbot Paslew was tried for treason, the Earl of Sussex was very

---

[1] See above, Chapter Four.
[2] P.R.O., SC11/376.
[3] P.R.O., DL29/2228.
[4] P.R.O., DL29/2273.
[5] Mason, *The Income, Administration, and Disposal of Monastic Lands in Lancashire*, 117.
[6] Beck, *Annales*, 303–5.
[7] ibid., 309.
[8] L. & P., xii(1), 632.
[9] *Duchy Pleadings*, i, 68–9.
[10] ibid., ii, 70.

relieved that the Abbot had pleaded guilty, 'else otherwise considering my Lord of Derby is steward of that house, so many gentlemen in these quarters the abbot's fee'd men, and others his friends . . . it would have been hard to find anything against him in these parts'.[1] If the personal influence of an abbot was dangerous at a treason trial, the effect of the suppression of a house must have been very serious. There would have been considerable sympathy for the ejected monks, most of whom were probably local men,[2] and many of them seem to have had relatives among the tenants of their house, so were probably born on monastery lands. At Furness, for example, about half the monks appear to have had relatives among the tenants—Abbot Pyle,[3] Brian Garner,[4] John Troughton,[5] Roger Preston,[6] Christopher Carre,[7] Anthony Plummer,[8] James Forster,[9] Christopher Massrudder,[10] William Barwick,[11] William Rigge,[12] William Forest,[13] Robert Kechyn,[14] Edward Blomer,[15] Michael Thornborough,[16] Henry Salley,[17] Roger Waller,[18] and Thomas Hartley.[19] Similar results have been found for the monks of both Whalley and Cockersand, by comparing the lists of monks we have with the lists of tenants in accounts. The same sort of picture would presumably emerge for the smaller houses, but no accounts are in print and to work through unindexed original accounts is impracticable.

Though it is difficult to penetrate the minds of common people, and find what their motives really were in 1536 when they rebelled, enough has been said on their probable motives and the usefulness of the monasteries to indicate that in Lancashire at least the origins of the Pilgrimage must be sought amongst religious ideas, and particularly opposition to the dissolution of the monasteries. It is also likely that the reason why the rebellion was confined almost entirely to the north of the county was not only that the bulk of the south was under the control of the Earl of Derby and gentry who remained loyal to the Crown, but mainly because the fall of the monasteries in the south of the county was a less serious event for the local people, since the houses had ceased to play a significant part in their lives. In Lancashire the monasteries were defended because of the great influence they wielded over the laity; there is thus a clear contrast between Lancashire and another area of religious reaction, Wales, where there was no resistance to the Suppression because the religious houses were already largely controlled by the laity.[20]

[1] L. & P., xii(1), 630; Beck, *Annales*, 343–4.
[2] Of 121 known monks in the seven independent houses, only twelve did not have fairly common local names.
[3] *Furness Coucher*, 593, 597.   [4] ibid., 602.   [5] ibid., 610, 665, 666, 668, etc.
[6] ibid., 685.   [7] ibid., 647, 648.   [8] ibid., 616.
[9] ibid., 647, 648.   [10] ibid., 641.   [11] ibid., 682, etc.
[12] ibid., 682, 683, 616, etc.   [13] ibid., 632, 680.   [14] ibid., 610, 622.
[15] ibid., 682, 683.   [16] ibid., 630.   [17] ibid., 641.
[18] ibid., 641, 674.   [19] ibid., 602.
[20] G. Williams, *The Welsh Church from Conquest to Reformation*, 405–9.

It would be unwise to assume that the rebels who defended the monasteries did so only for strictly religious reasons, or that they were all committed to the old religion and the claims of the papacy. But the monasteries, as social institutions, had obviously played an important part in local life. The Pilgrims, perhaps, were defending not so much religious houses, but ways of thought and behaviour, a whole social pattern and ethos, which they felt were threatened by the great changes of the 1530's. The old religion, to which Protestantism and later reformed Catholicism were almost equally alien, was a necessary part of the life which the rebels wished to preserve.[1]

[1] Dr. C. S. L. Davies' article 'The Pilgrimage of Grace Reconsidered' (*Past and Present*, Vol. 41, December 1968) appeared while this work was in page proof, but his conclusions on the relative importance of religious and other factors in the origins of the rebellion agree with my own view. I wish to thank Dr. W. H. Chaloner for drawing my attention to this article.

CHAPTER SIX

THE DEFENCE OF THE MONASTERIES: THE PILGRIMAGE OF GRACE

THE last of the smaller houses in Lancashire, Conishead, was suppressed in mid-September.[1] Preparations for rebellion began too soon after for the attack on the monasteries not to have been a major cause. On October 10th Lord Darcy instructed his kinsman, Sir Arthur, to tell the King that the people of Lancashire were buying up arms.[2] Six days later Darcy's servant, Thomas Gryce, wrote to inform him that Lancashire was very restless, and that arms were still being purchased,[3] and Darcy passed this news on to the King, with the advice that a postal organisation should be set up so that they could keep in touch with events.[4] The Earl of Derby appears to have begun preparations against the rebels even before receiving orders from the King; he sent to York for arms in the first week of October,[5] and one of his relations reported to Darcy that although there was much support for the rebel cause in Lancashire, the Earl was preparing to serve the King.[6]

Henry's first instructions were dispatched on October 10th, when it still seemed that the main threat would come from Lincolnshire.[7] Derby was informed of the Lincolnshire rebellion, and the steps which were being taken for its repression, but, the King added, 'the events of such enterprises' being uncertain, and 'minding to be in such awaredness as for such chances shall be requisite and necessary', it was thought wise that Derby should put his forces in readiness in case the rebellion should spread northwards.[8] The Earl received this letter on October 14th, and immediately dispatched a circular to the local gentry informing them of the King's commands, and asking them to prepare their men to serve under him when the King ordered it.[9]

By this time the rebellion in Lincolnshire had ceased to be the main fear, and the government's attention had switched to the rising in Yorkshire. On October 15th the King wrote again to Derby, with the news that parts of Yorkshire had risen, and that the Earl of Shrewsbury had been put in charge of an army to oppose the rebels.[10] Derby was ordered, with the Earls of Rutland and Huntingdon, to prepare his forces and march to meet the main army, while leaving a force behind in case Lancashire should become involved.[11] Despite his initial eagerness to serve the King,

---

[1] P.R.O., DL29/158/26.   [2] L. & P., xi, 563.   [3] ibid., 678.
[4] ibid., 692.   [5] ibid., 678.   [6] ibid., 635.
[7] ibid., 634; *Corresp.*, 18–19.   [8] ibid.   [9] L. & P., xi, 703; *Corresp.*, 19–20.
[10] L. & P., xi, 719; *Corresp.*, 22–24.   [11] ibid.

Derby appears to have been in no hurry to obey his commands; when he received the letter, he wrote to Shrewsbury, enclosing a copy of the King's letter, and asked for instructions.[1] The Earl was certainly not eager to become involved in any fighting; he stressed his 'little power', and pointed out that the people of the county were 'very poor and of small ability', while his main concern was that Shrewsbury should 'remember their conduct money' and appoint a place where his men could collect their wages on their arrival in Yorkshire.[2] Although Derby did prepare another circular to the gentry,[3] this had not been dispatched when the King's next letter arrived on the 23rd.[4]

These orders, however, were soon out of date, for the north of Lancashire was soon involved in the Pilgrimage, and turned to the defence of the religious houses. On October 12th the monks of Sawley, a Cistercian house just over the Yorkshire border, were restored to their monastery,[5] and Lancashire men must have been involved in the incident. The idea of restoring the monks spread rapidly, and the canons of Conishead must have been restored a day or two after the Sawley monks, for by October 16th they were together in their house. On that day they wrote to William Collins, the bailiff of Kendal, who was one of the rebel leaders, to ask him to proclaim that all those who favoured the house should give it succour, and with the request that he himself would send help to save the priory's goods.[6] The convent was concerned to prevent the farmers of the house from taking over the monastic property, and this clearly implied that the monks intended to remain in their house. The commons restored the neighbouring priory of Cartmel soon after, and Collins seems to have played some part in this. It was alleged later that Collins wrote to the convent urging them to re-enter their monastery,[7] and they needed little encouragement, for they were all back in their house well before October 30th, when the Prior, who had fled, reached Derby at Preston.[8] The ex-monks must have been together in the vicinity of their houses to have been ready to be restored, and there must be a suspicion that, at least in the case of Conishead, they had been urging the commons to help them and defy the King.

These events made the King's orders and the Earl of Derby's preparations completely inappropriate. Henry wrote again to Derby on October 20th with the news that Sawley had been restored and that the Lancashire borders were in revolt.[9] The previous instructions were cancelled, and

[1] L. & P., xi, 719; Corresp., 26.   [2] ibid.
[3] ibid.; Corresp., 26-7.   [4] L. & P., xi, 856; Corresp., 32-3.
[5] L. & P., xi, 784.
[6] L. & P., Add., 1112; xii(1), 1089. Collins was apparently a friend of the house, and had bought wool at its suppression (P.R.O., DL29/158/26).
[7] L. & P., xii(1), 965, No. 2.
[8] L. & P., xi, 947, No. 2, ii; Corresp., 43-7. Derby was at Preston on the 30th (ibid., 38).
[9] L. & P., xi, 806; Corresp., 28-31.

instead the Earl was ordered to gather his forces and march against the rebels on the borders, 'and incontinently to cause them like traitors to be executed there'.[1] The government considered that the ejected monks were to blame for the insurrection, and Derby was ordered to arrest the Abbot and monks of Sawley, and 'without any manner of delay, in their monks' apparel, cause them to be hanged up as most errant traitors and movers of insurrection and sedition'.[2] At this stage, the government obviously anticipated that forceful and decisive action would easily crush the rebellion, and with the same letter, the King sent Derby a commission to give him the authority necessary to bring the rising to a speedy conclusion. The Earl was given power over all the King's subjects in Lancashire, and commanded to move against 'divers seditious persons in the parts of Lancashire and thereabouts'.[3]

Derby was delighted with this commission, and told one of his relations, with obvious pride, that none of his ancestors had ever had anything like it.[4] Thomas Stanley pointed out that the commission had only been given so that he would support Cromwell and others; this comment angered Derby.[5] The Earl was a typical conservative northern nobleman, and had as much reason as others to support the rebels; he was steward of five Lancashire monasteries,[6] and he was in debt to the Crown.[7] The government was far from sure of Derby's loyalty, and Cromwell seems to have kept a spy in the Earl's household.[8] Among Derby's servants, Cromwell was as hated as he was among the rebels; the spy reported to the Lord Privy Seal that 'or your lordship should be there as they would have you to be, I had liefer to be in Jerusalem to come home upon my bare feet'.[9] But Derby seems to have judged that loyalty would pay higher dividends than rebellion, as his reaction to the commission indicates, and though he was hardly enthusiastic in the King's cause, he did not turn to the rebels.

In fact, the Earl could hardly have been slower to obey the King's urgent commands. The instructions of October 20th ordered that 'gathering all your force together, and calling unto you all the gentlemen of the county thereabouts, you shall immediately upon the sight hereof proceed with the same to the repression of the said rebellion'.[10] Derby received the King's letter on the evening of October 23rd, and held a meeting of the local gentry next morning to form a plan of campaign.[11] But the decision was that Derby's force would not set out until the following Saturday, the 28th, and that the gentry would not meet him until the Tuesday after, the 31st, at Whalley.[12] Thus the earliest date on which Derby could reach Sawley was November 1st, nine days after receiving the King's urgent command. The Earl did at least make his preparations thoroughly. After

---

[1] ibid. [2] ibid. [3] ibid., 27–8.
[4] L. & P., xi, 807. [5] ibid. [6] Valor, v, 223, 229, 270, 272, 305.
[7] L. & P., Add., 1222. [8] L. & P., xi, 859. [9] ibid.
[10] L. & P., xi, 806; Corresp., 28–31. [11] L. & P., xi, 856; Corresp., 32–3.
[12] ibid.; Corresp., 35–6.

the meeting of October 24th, he spread word that he intended to move in a different direction than Sawley, so that the rebels could not make plans to resist him,[1] and on the following day he sent out a circular letter to the Lancashire gentry with the order that they should all meet him, with such armed men as they could muster, at Whalley the following Tuesday.[2] Knowing the reluctance of the people to serve, he pointed out that he had already asked the King for their payment.[3] At the same time, Derby wrote to Abbot Paslew of Whalley to tell him that he intended to be at the Abbey on the evening of the 30th, and to command him to be ready to do the King's service.[4] It is likely that Derby was aware of the government's mistrust of him, since he wrote immediately to the King,[5] Cromwell,[6] and the Earl of Sussex,[7] to report what he had done.

Unfortunately for Derby, there occurred at this time an incident which must have increased the government's doubts on his loyalty. One of his servants was captured by rebels while on business in Yorkshire, and forced to take the rebel oath. The servant was given a letter to deliver to the Earl, but on receiving the letter Derby passed it on to the King unopened.[8] The message was from Aske, the rebel leader in Yorkshire, and it must have been a request to join the rebellion, since at the same time Derby's servant was given a copy of the rebel oath, with instructions to spread the oath on his way back to the Earl, 'to the intent to stir the country of Lancashire to take their part'.[9]

While Derby was making his dilatory preparations, eastern Lancashire was becoming yet more involved in the Pilgrimage. The situation in the county at this point was very serious; Thomas Stanley reported to Lord Darcy that while Derby and Mounteagle made their preparations, the commons were rising in response to the summons of the rebel leaders, for all the people supported the rebels, and if a quarter of the county rebelled, the rest would follow.[10] On October 21st, Nicholas Tempest, who lived a few miles over the Yorkshire border, was forced to take the rebel oath by a force of about a thousand men; they captured his son, and threatened to murder the boy if his father did not join them.[11] Despite this inauspicious beginning to his association with the rebels, Tempest seems already to have been in strong sympathy with their aims, and, as he said, within three hours he was 'in earnest in the commons' causes'.[12] On the 22nd, Tempest, Sir Stephen Hammerton, who had also been sworn, and about 300 rebels, held a meeting at Manubent, about nine miles inside Yorkshire, and made their plans for the following day.[13] The next day, Monday 23rd, Hammer-

[1] L. & P., xi, 856; Corresp., 35–6.   [2] ibid.
[3] ibid.   [4] L. & P., xi, 872, iii.
[5] L. & P., xi, 856; Corresp., 32–3.   [6] L. & P., xi, 857; Corresp., 33.
[7] Corresp., 34.   [8] L. & P., xi, 858; Corresp., 34–5.
[9] 'Aske's Examination', E.H.R., v, 560.   [10] L. & P., xi, 807.
[11] L. & P., xii(1), 1020; Y.A.J., xi, 251.   [12] L. & P., xii(1), 518.
[13] From original deposition, Y.A.J., xi, 252.

ton marched into Lancashire with a force of rebels, and swore Colne and Burnley to the Pilgrim cause.[1] Tempest went with three or four hundred rebels to Whalley, to swear the commons there, and, though this was not mentioned in their plans, they seem to have decided to swear the monks of Whalley at the same time. Paslew and his monks, though they must have been in sympathy with the rebel aims, were more concerned to preserve their own house, which, they must have felt, would best be achieved by avoiding all contact with the Pilgrimage. They therefore refused to allow the rebels to enter the Abbey, and kept the gates closed, but after two hours the insurgents threatened to burn the Abbey's barns and corn, and the monks admitted them. Abbot Paslew and eight of his monks then took the rebel oath.[2] Tempest's account of this, however, may have been designed to conceal the real attitude of the monks to the rising; it seems surprising that the monks had to be threatened, especially as Tempest knew the Abbot well, was Paslew's deputy-steward for Blackburn and Accrington in 1526,[3] and had acted as an arbitrator in a dispute involving the Abbot in 1533.[4]

Three or four days later, the rebels heard of Derby's intention of marching into the area and ejecting the monks of Sawley.[5] It seems likely that when he received Derby's letter of the 25th[6] Abbot Paslew, who was the only man in eastern Lancashire to know the Earl's real plans, warned his fellow abbot at Sawley. The Abbot of Sawley then wrote to Hammerton and the rebel leaders in east Yorkshire asking for help, as it was feared that Derby would burn down Whalley Abbey and the Tempests' house at Bashall, as well as attacking Sawley.[7] Hammerton and Nicholas Tempest then wrote to the other rebel leaders to ask for asistance, and held a meeting at Manubent to decide how they could stop Derby.[8] The Earl's intentions caused concern even in the north of the county, where it was feared that an attack on the commons in the east would lead to the subverting of the 'good and laudable customs of the country', for 'if our said brethren be subdued, they are like to go forward to the utter undoing of the commonwealth'.[9] The eastern rebels had asked for assistance, and 'for the aid and assistance of your faith and holy Church, and for the reformation of such abbeys and monasteries now dissolved and suppressed without any just cause', it was commanded that the people of the north should muster on Stoke Green, near to Hawkshead church, to receive their instructions.[10] The rebellion had begun in an attempt to restore the houses which had been suppressed, and now the rebels were preparing to defend the monasteries again.

As a result of these meetings, a rebel order was issued, which com-

[1] Y.A.J., xi, 253.
[2] ibid.
[3] *Duchy Pleadings*, i, 130.
[4] P.R.O., E315/237, f. 3.
[5] Y.A.J., xi, 255-6.
[6] L. & P., xi, 872, iii.
[7] Y.A.J., xi, 255-6.
[8] ibid.
[9] L. & P., xi, 892, ii; *Corresp.*, 49.
[10] ibid.

manded all males over the age of sixteen to meet on the following Monday, October 30th, on Clitheroe Moor, which was about two miles from Whalley Abbey.[1] The same order forbade anyone to assist the Earl of Derby, or anyone else not sworn to the commonwealth.[2] It was planned that Hammerton would take one part of the border forces and Tempest the other, and that they should march down opposite sides of the Ribble, raising the people as they went, so that a force could assemble at Clitheroe and attack Derby when he arrived.[3] Until now the rebellion in Lancashire had been widespread, but with little violence; but it looked as if resistance to the rebels by Derby would bring a confrontation between the two sides.

But by this time Aske and the Yorkshire leaders had made their preliminary agreement with the King's lieutenant, the Duke of Norfolk, and a truce had been arranged at Doncaster.[4] The threat of a pitched battle between Derby and the Lancashire rebels thus caused great consternation among the rebel leaders, for they were hoping to gain the main points of their programme by negotiation with Norfolk. At Pontefract, Aske received news of Derby's preparations and the intention of the rebels of west Yorkshire and north and east Lancashire of resisting him.[5] He therefore wrote to the commons on the borders, informed them of the 'order taken at Doncaster', and instructed them 'how they should meddle in no condition with the said Earl [Derby], although he invaded them, but to withdraw them to the mountains and straits, except he raised fire'.[6] He then got Darcy to write to the Earl of Shrewsbury and ask him, for the sake of the Doncaster meeting and their hopes of peace, to write to Derby and order him not to attack the rebels.[7] Darcy wrote to the Earl as he was asked,[8] and this must have been on October 27th, since on the next day Shrewsbury received Darcy's letter, wrote to Derby forbidding him to attack and ordering him to disband his forces,[9] and then wrote back to Darcy, with a copy of his letter to Derby[10] and a request that Darcy would hold back the commons.[11]

As he had planned, Derby was at Preston on Monday October 30th, ready to set out for Whalley, when Berwick, the herald, arrived with Shrewsbury's letter.[12] The Earl then disbanded his forces, as ordered, and returned to his house at Lathom, reported what had happened to the King,[13] and sent out another circular to the gentry so that they too would disband their forces.[14] As Darcy reported to Shrewsbury, Aske had written to the Lancashire and Craven rebels ordering them to disband,[15] but

[1] L. & P., xi, 892, ii; *Corresp.*, 51–2.
[2] ibid.
[3] Y.A.J., xi, 255–6.
[4] Dodds, *The Pilgrimage of Grace*, i, 264–9.
[5] L. & P., xii(1), 6; E.H.R., v, 338.
[6] ibid.
[7] ibid.
[8] L. & P., xi, 1046, 1096.
[9] L. & P., xi, 901; *Corresp.*, 36–7.
[10] L. & P., xii(1), 1089.
[11] L. & P., xi, 900.
[12] L. & P., xi, 947; *Corresp.*, 38–43.
[13] ibid.
[14] L. & P., xi, 922; *Corresp.*, 37–8.
[15] L. & P., xi, 912.

apparently the letter did not reach them in time.[1] As had been planned, the rebels marched to Clitheroe Moor, where, said Hammerton, they heard that Derby had disbanded his forces.[2] The commons therefore also went home, but a few of the gentry in the party went on to Whalley Abbey.[3] Derby's account of this was that the rebels took Whalley Abbey, and then went home after that, on hearing that Derby would not attack them.[4] Though there seems little reason why the rebels should need to 'take' the Abbey, since the monks had already submitted to the oath, unless the convent was still anxious to avoid involvement, there is a strong suspicion that Derby's version may be correct. Aske later tried to defend the Lancashire rebels by saying that their actions at Whalley had taken place before his letter reached them,[5] but there would have been no need for such a defence if the Lancashire rebels had not been involved in some act of violence.

The King, of course, knew nothing of all this, and thought that Derby was still vacillating before moving against Sawley. On October 28th, Henry wrote, angrily, acknowledging the Earl's two letters of the 24th,[6] and ordering him to set out at once against the monks of Sawley, and hang them and the rebel leaders.[7] On the same day, letters were dispatched to the local gentry who were acting with Derby, Sir Roger Bradshawe,[8] Sir Thomas Langton,[9] and Sir William Leyland,[10] to thank them for raising their forces to help Derby, and to ask them to continue to do so. The government appears to have been worried about the loyalty of the Lancashire gentry, and took great care to shower them with thanks. Two days after this, Cromwell wrote to Sir Thomas Butler, a prominent gentleman in the south of Lancashire, to send him more letters of thanks for distribution.[11] Cromwell took advantage of the opportunity for a piece of propaganda which he must have hoped would encourage the Lancashire gentry to remain faithful to the King, and he pointed out that the gentry would do well to support his policies, which were designed to assist those who worked hard. From Butler, a man he could trust, Cromwell asked for vigilance, 'now in this quesy time'.[12]

When he arrived back at Lathom after the Whalley affair, Derby wrote at once to the King to report what had happened; obviously the King's letter of the 28th had arrived, for the Earl was very anxious to prove the energy of his efforts on the King's behalf. If there had been a battle, Derby asserted, 'the traitors so assembled should finally have had an overthrow and been vanquished',[13] but Darcy had reported to Shrewsbury that, on the contrary, the intervention of Aske and the Earl had saved Derby's

[1] E.H.R., v, 338. [2] L. & P., xii(1), 1034; Y.A.J., xi, 259. [3] ibid.
[4] L. & P., xi, 947; Corresp., 38-43. [5] E.H.R., v, 338.
[6] L. & P., xi, 856, 858. [7] ibid., 894. [8] ibid., 895.
[9] ibid., 896. [10] ibid., 897.
[11] L. & P., xi, 919; Merriman, Letters, ii, No. 16. [12] ibid.
[13] L. & P., xi, 947; Corresp., 38-43.

life.[1] With this letter Derby sent to the King certain 'false and feigned letters and devices' which the rebels had spread 'abroad amongst your subjects by setting them on church doors and otherwise'.[2] These 'letters and devices' were rebel orders and items of propaganda, some of which have already been noted, which indicate the religious orientation of this part of the Pilgrimage. A rebel manifesto declared that the faith was 'piteously and abominably confounded', by 'certain heretics in our time', who were 'not shaming in open preaching to blaspheme the honour of our Lord God, working most cruelly by spoiling and suppression of holy places, as abbeys, churches, and minsters of the same'.[3] It is plain that at least the rebels thought the monasteries had fulfilled important religious functions, and it was ordered that all men of over sixteen years should 'be in readiness to aid us in maintaining of the said faith of Christ and his Church'.[4] A rebel summons to muster spoke of 'the reformation of such abbeys and monasteries now dissolved and suppressed' as the main aim of the Pilgrimage, together with the defence of 'our faith so sore decayed'.[5]

The constantly recurring theme in all rebel statements was 'the love ye bear to God, his faith, and Church militant',[6] which was held to be sufficient reason for supporting the insurrection. To 'expulse and suppress all heretics and their opinions'[7] was held to be one element in the policy of the rebels, and the most important of the others was the defence of the religious houses. This was the theme most stressed by the Lancashire rebels, in their actions as well as their propaganda, and the Yorkshire order, which was put up on the door of York Minister, was circulated in Lancashire.[8] This order proclaimed that all the dispossessed religious were to 'enter into their houses again', and were 'there to do divine service as the King's bedemen, to such time as our petition be granted'.[9] As their cause was that of God's Church, the rebels clearly expected it to prevail, and they had sufficient faith in the religion and sincerity of the King to assume that he would grant their petitions. The extent to which the northern insurgents were out of step with the people in the south is indicated by their attitude to the new policies; the King's new advisers, those responsible for the royal programme, were 'heretics'[10] and men of 'villein blood',[11] who were said to have 'procured and purposed against the commonwealth certain acts of law under the colour of Parliament, which, put in execution, the estate of Poverty can no longer bear nor suffer'.[12] The new legislation was, of course, only possible because Crom-

[1] L. & P., xi, 928.
[2] L. & P., xi, 947; *Corresp.*, 38–43.
[3] L. & P., xi, 892; *Corresp.*, 47–8.
[4] ibid.
[5] L. & P., xi, 892; *Corresp.*, 49.
[6] L. & P., xi, 892, No. 2; *Corresp.*, 51–2.
[7] ibid.
[8] E.H.R., v, 335; L. & P., xi, 784, ii; *Corresp.*, 51.
[9] E.H.R., v, 335; L. & P., xi, 784, ii; *Corresp.*, 51.
[10] L. & P., xi, 892; *Corresp.*, 47–8.
[11] L. & P., xi, 892; *Corresp.*, 51–2.
[12] L. & P., xi, 892; *Corresp.*, 47–8.

well and the others were able to take advantage of the prevailing anti-
clericalism of London and large parts of the south. This spirit was entirely
foreign to the rebels, who could only blame it on heresy and the King's
use of upstart councillors, who were thought to be aiming at the destruction of both Church and commonwealth, by taxes on baptisms, certain
items of food, and lands.[1]

In the same letter, Derby gave the government the first news it had had
of the risings in the north of Lancashire,[2] and enclosed certain articles
which explained what Derby knew of these events. A force of between
3,000 and 6,000 rebels from the north had occupied Lancaster at the end
of October, put the rebel oath to the citizens, and tried to force John
Standish, the mayor, to declare for the rebel cause.[3] Derby had sent two
of his servants to Lancaster to order the rebels to disband, but Atkinson,
the rebel leader, replied 'that they had a Pilgrimage to do for the Commonwealth, which they would accomplish or jeopard their lives to die in
that quarrel'.[4] These rebels, who were able to occupy the administrative
centre of the county without resistance, had no need to obey the Earl's
order, and refused to threaten their position by agreeing to Derby's
challenge to a pitched battle.[5] Further north, too, the Pilgrims had been
successful and unchallenged; they had chased Lord Mounteagle and Sir
Marmaduke Tunstall, both powerful men, out of their homes[6] as well as
Sir Robert Bellingham, many of Derby's tenants and servants, and his
deputy at Furness, William Fitton.[7] Derby also passed on the first news of
the restoration of the canons of Cartmel,[8] and reported that the other
trouble-spot, the eastern border with Yorkshire, could not be trusted, 'for
the most part of them show themselves to be rebels'.[9] For all Derby's
protestations of strength in the letter, he had to admit that these defections
meant that his own power was 'minished, and the traitors strength thereby
the more increased'.[10] Though Derby was able to maintain order in south
Lancashire, north of the Ribble his authority had collapsed almost
completely.

There now followed a lull in the recorded events of the Pilgrimage, but
the surviving correspondence indicates that the rebel strength in no way
abated. November, a quiet month for the Pilgrimage, was taken up with
the rebel Council at York, Norfolk's negotiations with the Yorkshire
leaders, and the preparation of the first pardons.[11] The authorities were
therefore most concerned to maintain vigilance and keep the rebels quiet

[1] *Corresp.*, 50.   [2] L. & P., xi, 947.   [3] ibid., No. 2, i; *Corresp.*, 43–7.
[4] ibid.   [5] ibid.
[6] L. & P., xi, 947, No. 2, vi. Tunstall's flight was a serious blow to the loyalists, as
he was constable of Lancaster Castle, as well as steward of Lonsdale (Somerville, op. cit.,
498, 501).
[7] L. & P., xi, 947, No. 2, iii & iv.   [8] ibid., No. 2, ii.
[9] ibid., No. 2, v.   [10] ibid.
[11] A. G. Dickens, 'Royal Pardons for the Pilgrimage of Grace', Y.A.J., xxxiii, 401–3;
Dodds, op. cit., 272–340.

while an attempt was made to defeat them with duplicity, and the rebel leaders were concerned not to break the truce so that their aims could be achieved by negotiation. The King replied to Derby's letter on the sixth of November, and showed no trust of the calm which had developed; Henry expected that a new insurrection might break out at any time, and so ordered Derby to keep his forces ready, and to send out spies to find 'how the people do now use themselves upon this retirement'.[1] The King also sent more letters of thanks to keep the gentry sweet, while reminding Derby that his interest lay on the government side, for his loyalty would 'bring forth from time to time such fruit as effects towards you as ye shall have good cause to think your labours therein well employed'.[2] Derby, however, had anticipated the King's requirements, and before receiving these new orders he had written to the local officials in the county to order them to form watches within their jurisdictions, and to arrest all suspicious persons and any who 'speak any unfitting or slanderous words by the King's Highness or by any of his most honourable Council'.[3]

There are hints, however, that although the Pilgrimage had lost its initial impetus, and the situation had settled down to an uneasy stalemate, the rebels in some areas were still active.[4] This was particularly true in Lancashire, where the rebellion remained largely self-contained and independent of the Yorkshire rising, which has attracted the attention of most historians. The separateness of the Lancashire revolt is indicated by the county's initial failure to comply with the Doncaster truce, and by the activity of the Lancashire commons in November, when most of Yorkshire was quiet. On November 6th the Earl of Cumberland reported to Fitzwilliam that the commons of Yorkshire, Cumberland, Durham, and most of Lancashire were up with gentry support, and were molesting those few who were not sworn to their cause.[5] His charges for Yorkshire, however, were inaccurate, for the Pilgrims there were quiet, and the charges of the Yorkshire moderates at this time centred on the north-west of England. On November 7th Sir Ralph Ellerker and Robert Bowes wrote to Darcy alleging that since his agreement with Norfolk, Aske had written into Cumberland, Westmorland, and Lancashire to provoke a new rising.[6] Darcy wrote back indignantly denying the charge, and enclosing a statement from Aske that he had not tried to provoke Lancashire and the other counties.[7] But there is evidence that at this time, or at least soon after, Aske had been encouraging Lancashire. By November 27th, Derby had found, and passed on to the King, a letter written by Aske to Atkinson, the captain of the rebels in Kendal and northern Lancashire, which showed that Aske was trying to raise a new revolt.[8] For such a letter to

[1] L. & P., xi, 992; *Corresp.*, 52–5.   [2] ibid.
[3] L. & P., xi, 1010; *Corresp.*, 55–6.
[4] In Pontefract, Northumberland, Cumberland, and Westmorland—Dodds, *Pilgrimage of Grace*, i, 296–9.   [5] L. & P., xi, 993.
[6] L. & P., xi, 1009.   [7] ibid., 1046.   [8] L. & P., xi, 1178; *Corresp.*, 65–6.

have been in Henry's hands by the 27th, it must have been written, in Yorkshire, in the first half of the month. Further, this must be the letter from 'Mr. Captain in this our Pilgrimage' referred to by an unknown writer about this time.[1] The writer, who must be Atkinson, informed 'Cousin Towneley', who must be John Towneley, a prominent gentleman supporter of the rebels in north Lancashire, that Aske had written ordering that the commons of Lancashire were to be raised.[2] Atkinson was displeased with Towneley's brother, who must be Sir John, for refusing to be sworn to the cause, but he had taken care that the rest of Lancashire would not be so backward, and had sent out orders for the commons to rise in the Lancaster area, and now sent Towneley a copy of Aske's letter so that he too could raise his forces.[3] This reconstruction, if accurate, must cast some doubt on the sincerity and frankness with which Robert Aske has usually been credited.[4]

The government was rather more in touch with these events than was usually true, and on November 9th the King wrote to Lord Mounteagle with the order that he was to have all his friends, and such servants and tenants as had not been involved with the rebels, ready to serve under the Earl of Derby whenever necessary.[5] The next day, Henry wrote to Derby, enclosing a batch of letters addressed to various Lancashire and Cheshire gentry, which ordered them to be ready to serve under Derby, and with another ten letters with the addresses blank, for Derby to forward as he thought necessary.[6] The King thought that despite 'the great clemency which we have determined to show unto them', the people would still be swayed by the 'persuasion of divers and certain most detestable traitors inculcating and beating into their heads certain forged lies, feigned and most untrue tales and surmises'.[7] A new rebellion might therefore result, and Derby was ordered to have his forces ready to proceed against the rebels at an hour's notice, either to move against any new insurrection in Lancashire, or join the Earl of Shrewsbury to combat any rising elsewhere.[8]

The rebels in the north were indeed active and, as Sir Richard Houghton reported to Derby, the men of Dent, Sedburgh, and northern Lancashire were preparing to march through the county and attack the houses of those gentry who did not support them.[9] Derby was sure the rebels would not dare to do this, though he was probably putting on a brave face, and ordered Houghton to send out spies and keep the Earl informed, and if the rebels did attack he and the other gentry in the area were to raise what forces they could and harry the rebels until Derby could arrive with a larger force.[10] Derby had also heard that the rebels of Kendal intended

---

[1] L. & P., xi, 804.   [2] ibid.   [3] ibid.
[4] e.g. by Dom David Knowles, *Religious Orders*, iii, 334–5.   [5] L. & P., xi, 1232.
[6] L. & P., xi, 1022, 1031; *Corresp.*, 56–8, 58.
[7] L. & P., xi, 1031; *Corresp.*, 56–8.
[8] ibid.   [9] L. & P., xi, 1060; *Corresp.*, 59–60.   [10] ibid.

F

to swear Furness and Cartmel to the Pilgrimage, and to levy corn and money to pay the expenses of the insurrection.[1] He therefore wrote to the gentry of Furness to command them that if the rebels rose again in Lancashire north of the Sands they were to assemble their own forces and serve under William Fitton, Derby's deputy in Furness, and move against the commons.[2] The Earl appears to have expected the rebels to be successful, for he warned the gentry that if the rebel forces pressed on to Lancaster and Preston, they were to follow them, harrying their rear, while Derby's forces moved towards them to give battle; he also warned them to tell the people of Furness that they were not bound by any oaths against God and the King which they made to the rebels.[3]

For though he maintained a bluff and arrogant exterior, Derby's position was very weak, and he knew it. He had completely lost control of his lands and tenants in the north and east of the county,[4] and this was common knowledge in Lancashire even among the loyalists.[5] The county was ablaze with rumours and seditious songs; Darcy received a copy of a rhyme which was circulating in the north-west, which he seems to have found amusing,[6] and a minstrel from Cartmel was going round singing a seditious song called 'Crummock' which remained popular even after the rebellion.[7] Even more serious, Derby's power was in doubt in the south; he was bound to the Suppression Commissioners to pull down the lead and bells of Burscough Priory, but he was afraid to do so and had to write to the Chancellor of the Duchy for permission to leave this a little longer as 'in this busy world' it would cause much discontent among the people.[8] The Earl was even losing control of his forces, who were becoming angry at their failure to receive payment; there was even a rumour in London that his men had mutinied for lack of pay.[9] He wrote to Cromwell on November 14th asking that those who had served the King under him should have their pay, as the county was bare of money and the people had been put to great cost.[10] The government was well aware of Derby's difficulties, for the King wrote to him before this plea had been received, promising payment and asking that a list should be drawn up of those who had been put to any expense.[11] The King wrote again in the same vein when he received Derby's letter,[12] and though the Earl spread word that payment would be made, the people thought they would never get their money.[13]

The real cause of Derby's weakness was that no-one trusted him. The rebels certainly expected his support; both Sir Thomas Percy[14] and Archbishop Lee[15] reported rumours among the Yorkshire Pilgrims that Derby

---

[1] L. & P., xi, 1092; Corresp., 61–2.   [2] ibid.   [3] ibid.
[4] L. & P., xi, 947, No. 2.   [5] L. & P., xi, 1253.
[6] L. & P., xi, 1086.   [7] L. & P., xiii(1), 1346, 1370.
[8] L. & P., xi, 1118.   [9] ibid., 1097.   [10] ibid., 1066.
[11] L. & P., xi, 1074; Corresp., 63–4.   [12] L. & P., xi, 1178.
[13] L. & P., xi, 1253.   [14] L. & P., xii(1), 393.   [15] ibid., 1022.

would join them. As early as 1534, Lord Darcy told Chapuys that the Earl
was strongly opposed to the King's policies.[1] Those close to Derby thought
that at least his men would refuse to fight the rebels,[2] while rumours that
Derby would never do anything active against the commons continued to
circulate. At the end of November, William Singleton, a servant of Sir
Richard Houghton, and three others, met Nicholas Tempest and told him
how Houghton and Sir Thomas Southworth were preparing to resist the
rebels, who were ready to enter Lancaster, Whalley, and even Manchester.[3] But Tempest thought there would be little they could do, for
Derby had, he alleged, informed Robert Aske that 'he would do little in
the matter when it should come to the point,' so the gentry 'had been
deceived of their trust in him'.[4] The same story came from a different
source soon after. On Christmas Eve, Sir Francis Bigod told his servant,
a Lancashire man, that he had seen Aske with a letter which, Aske said,
was from the Earl of Derby, 'and the same Aske showed me that my said
Lord of Derby would be with us in time of need'.[5] That the same thing
should be reported by two men whose only connection was that they were
both in close touch with Aske and in a good position to know the truth,
throws some considerable doubt on Derby's loyalty. Such rumours, naturally, made the government reluctant to trust Derby far; Cromwell had a
spy in the Earl's household,[6] and Fitzherbert seems to have been sent into
Lancashire after the rebellion not only to help with the prosecutions, but
to keep an eye on Derby. He certainly reported to Cromwell with obvious
relief that the Earl of Derby had been as loyal as any nobleman could be.[7]
Rumour, of course, exaggerated both Derby's connection with the rebels
and the authorities' attitude towards him; it was thought by some that
Derby had actually risen in support of the Pilgrimage and would be proclaimed a traitor[8] and others thought that he had been arrested and put
in the Tower.[9] Among the rebels, Derby was equally mistrusted, as it
became obvious that he would not fulfil the promises he was thought to
have made. It was said that Aske called him a 'false flattering boy' who
ran away from the commons, for when it came to the point he chose to
serve the King.[10] Among the rank and file of the rebels, the Earl was 'cried
traitor' because he did not support the rising.[11]

The truth of the matter is probably that Derby, like the Abbot of
Furness,[12] was not sure which side he ought to support, from interest or
principle, and so compromised by trying to retain the support of both
sides. From the evidence available, it seems quite clear that Derby made
some sort of promise to the rebel leaders, and he may even have acted upon
it, for he had never actually had to fight against the rebels in Lancashire,

[1] ibid., vii, 1206. [2] ibid., xii(1), 849, No. 8. [3] ibid., 518.
[4] ibid. [5] ibid., 678. [6] L. & P., xi, 859.
[7] L. & P., xii(1), 970. [8] L. & P., xii(1), 1212, No. 2.
[9] L. & P., xiii(2), 632. [10] L. & P., xii(1), 853.
[11] ibid., 578. [12] See below, Chapter Seven.

while he was always slow to execute the King's commands and often complained of the difficulty of raising forces and the need for payment.[1] Derby, in fact, was in a very difficult position; he must have had sympathy for the rebel aims, and his servants and tenants, especially in the north of Lancashire, usually supported the Pilgrimage. To make matters worse, the Earl had the greatest difficulty in obtaining instructions from the King's Commissioners, as his communications with them were constantly threatened by the rebels. In mid-November, a messenger carried a letter to Derby from the Earl of Rutland, and then returned with a letter from Derby to Fitzwilliam, but he was captured by the rebels and put in the stocks at Wakefield, and the rebels read his letter. When Derby was sent news of this, that letter too was intercepted.[2] But the King had given him a commission which gave him wide authority in Lancashire and Cheshire, with promises of reward for faithful service. Derby was probably emulating his ancestors in the Wars of the Roses, who had been able to enhance their power and status by playing a waiting game and then throwing in their lot with the winning side. He gave the government just enough support to ensure that if the Pilgrimage failed, he would be among those who benefited, while involving himself with the rebels just enough to be in a favourable position if the rebellion succeeded. The government, however little it trusted him, had no choice but to rely upon him, despite his poor reputation; a foreign observer called him 'a child in wisdom and half a fool'.[3] No-one could be spared from opposing the Yorkshire and Lincolnshire rebels to intervene in Lancashire, and Derby was the only man in the county capable, in power and prestige, of uniting the loyalist forces and, by his attitude, preventing the whole of the county from going over to the rebels. Lancashire was outside the sphere of action of the Council in the North, yet was too far north to be controlled from London; the government had no choice but to rely on Derby. Cromwell gambled on buying the Earl's loyalty with an extensive commission, and won.

On November 22nd the leaders of the Pilgrimage in Yorkshire held a council at York. It was decided that, in view of the movements in Lancashire and the likelihood that the commons of the county would muster again, if the commons of Lancashire mustered, then Craven, Dent, Sedburgh, and Lancashire north of the Sands would also muster to help them, and report to Aske the 'demeanour' of Lancashire.[4] This obviously confirms the impression that the rebels in Lancashire were acting independently of the leaders in Yorkshire, and even dictating, by their actions, what the leaders would have to do. The leaders certainly thought the Lancashire rising a movement apart, and, as Stapleton later confessed, it was argued at the York meeting that it was less important to observe the truce and meet the Duke of Norfolk again at Doncaster than it was to

---

[1] See above.
[3] L. & P., xiii(2), 732.
[2] L. & P., xi, 1042.
[4] L. & P., xi, 1135.

keep Lancashire and Cheshire favourable towards the Yorkshire leaders by supporting the risings in those counties.[1] But a more cautious view prevailed and, as Aske reported, the leaders, 'after much deceding into our articles, would not so generally join in their quarrel'.[2] It was, however, decided that the commons of Dent and Sedburgh should be allowed to stir Lancashire, since it was said that Cromwell had 'warranted that county for any rising'.[3]

At the York conference, lists were drawn up of those who were to be invited to attend the meeting with the Duke of Norfolk at Pontefract, and representatives were to be summoned from among those Lancashire gentry who had taken the rebels' part. One list mentioned John Houghton of Pendleton and John Towneley, Sir John's brother, with six of the best horsemen of the county in coats of plate,[4] but a fuller list named Richard Kirkby, Mr. Bardsey, Gervaise Middleham, Richard Newman, and six others for Furness, Michael Thornborough and three yeomen, Edward Manser, Thomas Croft, and two others for Cartmel, and John Houghton and John Towneley, with six or eight tall men, from the rest of Lancashire.[5] Apparently, the Yorkshire leaders also invited the Abbot of Whalley.[6] As far as is known, there were no leaders from Lancashire at the York meeting, though Nicholas Tempest and Sir Stephen Hammerton, who lived just over the Yorkshire border and were in contact with the rebels in the Whalley area, were there.[7] During the meeting, a message came from the Abbot of Sawley that the Lancashire–Yorkshire borders had risen again, and Tempest and Hammerton were sent back to take charge of the commons, who had risen to resist the Earl of Derby.[8]

There now followed a chain of events rather similar to what had taken place in Lancashire at the end of October, when the Yorkshire leaders had to intervene to prevent a confrontation between the Lancashire rebels and the Earl of Derby, which would have disrupted peace negotiations with Norfolk. After the King's orders of November 10th,[9] Derby had been mustering his forces ready to move when he received orders to do so, but the commons were so ready to fight that they interpreted this as a challenge. The Abbot of Sawley reported this,[10] and Aske wrote immediately to Darcy with a request that he should write to Shrewsbury so that Derby could be stopped; the commons could not be kept in order for fear of being overrun, and unless something was done new trouble would break out and disturb the negotiations.[11] Darcy received the letter on the same day, and passed on the message to the Earl of Shrewsbury at once, with the warning that if Derby made any move the Lancashire borders could not be held

[1] L. & P., xii(1), 392.
[2] L. & P., xi, 901; E.H.R., v, 339.
[3] ibid.
[4] L. & P., xi, 1155, No. 1.
[5] L. & P., xi, 1155, No. 2.
[6] L. & P., xii(1), 853.
[7] Y.A.J., xi, 261.
[8] ibid.
[9] L. & P., xi, 1031; Corresp., 56–8.
[10] Y.A.J., xi, 261.
[11] L. & P., xi, 1134.

back.[1] Shrewsbury wrote to Derby on the 24th, ordering him not to assemble forces until ordered to do so,[2] and then reported what he had done to Darcy, with the comment 'for surely, my lord, there shall nothing be done contrary to the appointment taken between my Lord of Norfolk, me, you, and others at our last meeting at Doncaster'.[3] Once again, events in Lancashire had almost disrupted the Yorkshire settlement, but by the time Tempest and Hammerton reached the north-west border of Lancashire after the York meeting, the commons had calmed down again.[4] Aske's intervention had again prevented a confrontation between Derby and the Lancashire rebels.

On November 27th the King wrote to Derby on the complaints of the Lancashire loyalists that they had not yet been paid their expenses for mustering against the rebels and marching against Sawley and Whalley.[5] The Earl was to draw up a list of those who had helped him so that they could be paid, and the government's fears were indicated by the King's comment that payment would be made so that the loyalists would again be prepared to help in the event of further troubles.[6] Henry's ministers certainly anticipated more trouble from Lancashire, for Derby had just sent them the letter from Aske to Atkinson which showed the rebel leaders wished to keep Lancashire active,[7] and Derby was given orders to counter their efforts. He was to have his forces ready to act against any insurrection, send a report to the King of the forces he could count on, send out spies to find the inclination of the people, and arrest all those known to be spreading sedition.[8]

Henry's concern for Lancashire was certainly justified, for the rebellion, which had been a stalemate with the King's forces for some time in other parts of the north, was still spreading in Lancashire. At Chorley, on the night of the 28th, John Piper, a minstrel, and two others, wearing armour and with their faces blackened, went around the township swearing men to the rebel cause, and Percival Saunders, William Charnock, Laurence Whitell, Robert Bankes, and Thurstan Collins all took the oath; they said later that it was only through fear that they did so, but this would be a natural defence and was not necessarily true.[9] It is quite clear that perhaps the majority of the commons in the north of the county, where the larger monasteries were situated and where the religious houses had played a more important part in community life, supported the rebellion. The extent of support for the rebels in the south is more difficult to gauge, and though there seems to have been an underlying current of sympathy, as incidents such as this, the reluctance of Derby's forces to fight, and the hatred of Cromwell in Derby's household, indicate, there was little open

[1] L. & P., xi, 1140; ibid., xii(1), 1089.   [2] L. & P., xi, 1154.
[3] ibid., 1153.   [4] Y.A.J., xi, 261.   [5] L. & P., xi, 1178.
[6] ibid.   [7] ibid.; see above.   [8] L. & P., xi, 1178.
[9] L. & P., xi, 1230; Corresp., 70–5.

support or action for the Pilgrims. The power of the Earl of Derby in the south of the county, and the greater density of gentry population must have been important factors, but the contrast with the north indicates that the small size, worse behaviour, and less charity of the south Lancashire monasteries were also significant.

Throughout all this time the canons of Cartmel and Conishead continued unmolested in their houses. No-one made any move to eject them, and the government was very poorly informed on what they were doing. There is no evidence that the authorities ever knew that Conishead had been restored until the revolt had collapsed and depositions were being taken, and the King only knew of the restoration of Cartmel because the ex-prior had refused to return to his monastery and had fled to the Earl of Derby.[1] As no reports were made, the evidence on the restored houses is very scant, and comes only from confessions made after the rebellion. We know nothing about the month of November, and only isolated incidents emerge later; this, however, must lead to the conclusion that the canons continued in their normal religious life, much as they had done until the Suppression. Their position, though, was very uncertain, and the first recorded incident after the restoration was an attempt to regularise the position of Cartmel and Conishead.

On December 2nd,[2] William Collins, the bailiff of Kendal, was at York, where he met John Dakyn, the Vicar-General of the Archdeaconry of Richmond.[3] Collins asked Dakyn if, in view of the promise that Norfolk was thought to have made that the religious could return to their houses, he would 'write also to the priors of Conishead and Cartmel, seeing ye be their visitor, and give them your counsel what is best for them to do'.[4] Collins said that all the canons of Cartmel had returned, 'except the foolish prior'.[5] Dakyn appears to have been reluctant to commit himself, for it was not until eight days later[6] that he wrote to the priors of the two houses that, by the King's consent, all religious persons should re-enter their suppressed houses, until further settlement was made by Parliament. He encouraged them to do so, and trusted that their houses would stand for ever.[7] Dakyn then gave the letter to Collins, who took it with him to Kendal, and then sent it on by another messenger.[8] It was thus thought that Norfolk had promised that the monks could remain in their houses as an interim measure, and it is probable that he did indeed make this promise, for he had written to the King on October 25th, urging him not to take too seriously the promises he might make to the rebel leaders, for he would not feel that his honour made their fulfilment necessary.[9]

[1] L. & P., xi, 947, No. 2, ii.
[2] 'The Saturday before Lady Day'—this must refer to the Conception, Friday, 8th.
[3] L. & P., xii(1), 878.   [4] L. & P., xii(1), 914.   [5] ibid., 787.
[6] 'The Saturday or Sunday after the Conception'—the letter shows it was Sunday.
[7] L. & P., xi, 1279; ibid., xii(1), 787.
[8] ibid., 914.   [9] L. & P., xi, 864.

Certainly the authorities were very eager to deny that the Duke had ever made such a promise, and Sussex was later instructed to tell the people of Lancashire that Norfolk had only promised to intercede with the King on the monks' behalf.[1] Dakyn's letter seems to have had little effect, unless it raised the morale of the monks, for all the canons of Conishead were already back, and the prior of Cartmel seems not to have returned even after Dakyn had written, for he was not tried with the others.[2]

We know nothing more of the canons until December 22nd, when Clarencieux Herald proclaimed the royal pardon at Kendal. Some of the farmers of monastic demesnes, which must mean those of Cartmel and Conishead, the only houses in the area which had been restored, complained that the monks who had returned were using the corn which the Suppressors had granted to them, so the herald proclaimed that no-one should be disturbed in possession of lands or tithes.[3] The settlement which the rebel leaders had decided upon, and which had circulated in Lancashire,[4] was that the farmers were to provide the monks with their needs, that what was used by the monks should be written down so that the farmers could be compensated, and that the farmers were not to be disturbed in their tenure. The farmers, it seems, were unwilling to obey this ruling, and there was no reason why they should, for it was only a demand by the rebels. Two monks of Cartmel, who were there when the herald made his proclamation, asked that the order should be written down, but the herald was in a hurry, or else reluctant to commit himself, so Collins, the bailiff, wrote for the canons as follows: 'Neighbours of Cartmel, so it is that the King's Herald hath made proclamation here that every man, pain of high treason, should suffer everything, as farms, tithes, and such other, to be in like stay and order concerning possessions as they were in time of the last meeting at Doncaster, except ye will of your charity help the brethren there somewhat toward their board, till my Lord of Norfolk come again and make further order therein'.[5]

After this, the canons must have lived off the charity of their supporters, as the Abbot and monks of Sawley, who were sent an ox, mutton, and two or three geese by Nicholas Tempest had been doing.[6] But the canons and the local people seem to have tired of this arrangement, while the farmers were taking the profits of the old monastery lands, and about the middle of February[7] the canons and husbandmen of Cartmel prevented the King's farmer, Thomas Holcroft, from taking the priory corn, and the same sort of thing seems to have taken place at Conishead.[8] Nothing more is known of the monks until all the canons except the prior, and sixteen husband-

---

[1] L. & P., xii(1), 302. [2] P.R.O., PL26/13/6.
[3] L. & P., xii(1), 914. [4] E.H.R., v, 335; L. & P., xi, 784, ii.
[5] L. & P., xii(1), 914. [6] ibid., 1014.
[7] Collins said both eight weeks after the proclamation and eight weeks after the letter to Cartmel and Conishead.
[8] L. & P., xii(1), 914.

men, of Cartmel, were tried for treason at Lancaster in March 1537.[1] The government apparently intended to try the canons of Conishead, and it was thought that the rebellion in Lancashire was begun by the letter the convent wrote to Collins asking for help.[2] A list of those to be prosecuted included, among the known leaders of the rebellion such as Aske, Darcy, and Bigod, 'the whole convent of Conishead', but this entry was later crossed out.[3] It must have been found that there was no evidence to convict the Conishead canons of treason after the issue of the royal pardon, and they were allowed to leave their monastery in peace.

In December 1536 the main negotiations between Norfolk and the leaders of the Yorkshire rebels on the issue of a full pardon without exceptions took place. On December 2nd the King issued instructions to Norfolk and Fitzwilliam on the conduct of the negotiations,[4] and it is clear from these that the government had realised it could not defeat the rebels by military action and hoped to outwit them and break the rebellion by stealth. The emissaries were told to make only vague promises, and if the rebels were not satisfied with these they were to break off the talks for twenty days and during that time write secretly to the Earl of Derby to tell him to put the loyalist forces of Lancashire and Cheshire in arms, and similarly to other supporters of the King, so that the rebels could be held down until the King arrived with an army from the south. Norfolk was to try to persuade the rebels to accept a pardon with exceptions, in the hope of dividing the moderates from the extremists, but he was given a full pardon with instructions not to issue it. If the leaders refused to accept a pardon with exceptions, Norfolk was to pretend to send to London for a full pardon, and then show the pardon, which he already had, but without officially issuing it.[5] The hope was that the Pilgrimage would collapse when it was thought that the King had issued a full pardon, while the King could then proceed against any he wished to except from pardon. The plan, however, broke down; Norfolk went beyond his instructions, and produced the full pardon soon after negotiations began at Pontefract.[6] A full pardon was drawn up on December 9th, which included 'such other the King's subjects inhabited in the town of Lancaster and elsewhere by north in the shire of Lancaster', made no mention of exceptions, and covered all offences committed up to the day of proclamation.[7]

But the Lancashire rebels, independent as ever, took little notice of the negotiations; rebel activity continued throughout December, and into 1537. On December 3rd Lord Mounteagle wrote to Henry VIII to report that, after the King's letter of November 9th,[8] he had gathered all the

---

[1] P.R.O., PL26/13/6.
[2] L. & P., xii(1), 849, No. 29.
[3] L. & P., xii(1), 1088.
[4] L. & P., xi, 1227; State Papers, i, 511–18.
[5] ibid.
[6] Dickens, 'Royal Pardons for the Pilgrimage of Grace', Y.A.J., xxxiii, 404.
[7] L. & P., xi, 1276; Dickens, art. cit., 405–8; Hughes & Larkin, Tudor Royal Proclamations, 246–7.
[8] L. & P., xi, 1232.

forces he could trust, and excluded those who had been sworn to the rebels.[1] Some of the rebels said they had only been sworn by intimidation, and were now willing to serve the King, and Mounteagle wished to know what he should do.[2] Clearly those who had joined the rebels from fear, or from an initial burst of enthusiasm, were now falling away as the rebellion did not achieve any substantial concessions from the government, but this did not mean that the rebellion was collapsing, for the hard core of committed rebels showed no sign of weakening, and were as active as ever. In the same letter Mounteagle reported that the rebels in the extreme north of the county and the Kendal area were as lively as ever, and they had been interfering with his bailiffs and preventing the collection of rents.[3] Mounteagle had apprehended a vicar who had spoken out against the King and in support of the rebels, and bound him over to appear before the Council on a surety of £200.[4] The only case known of a vicar supporting the rebels openly is that of Ralph Lynney, the Vicar of Blackburn, who, according to a witness 'did say, if the commons come again to Lancashire he would bear the cross before them, and God speed them well in their journey'.[5] There is no evidence that he ever did appear before the Council, but he was later arrested by the Earl of Sussex and imprisoned for a short time in Lancaster Castle.[6]

The Earl of Derby sent his first full report for some time to the King on December 5th, enclosing a list of those gentlemen, with their forces, who had served under him; the force totalled 7,811.[7] In the event of a new confrontation, Derby thought he would be able to raise 3,000 horsemen in Lancashire, but all north of Lancaster, and the Whalley area in the east of the county, was sworn to the rebels. In the face of this danger, the Earl was looking out for seditious persons, and sent up the depositions on the Chorley affair,[8] but Piper, the minstrel, could not be found. As for the inclinations of the people, Derby trusted the gentry, on the whole, but had considerable doubts on the loyalty of the commons. He had heard that Sir John Towneley, whose brother was a prominent rebel supporter, and Sir James Layburne were much with the commons, and it was said that both had been sworn, Layburne over a month ago.[9] The extent of gentry support for the commons is difficult to assess, as there is little evidence on the matter. Derby's list of those who supported him includes most of the gentry from the south of Lancashire, but only Lord Mounteagle and Sir Marmaduke Tunstall, who both fled south from the rebels, from the north.[10] The most obvious omission is Sir John Towneley, one of the greatest of the northern gentry, who took no part in the attack on the monasteries or the chantries, and was later a vigorous conservative.

---

[1] L. & P., xi, 1232.   [2] ibid.   [3] ibid.   [4] ibid.
[5] L. & P., xii(1), 853.   [6] See below, Chapter Seven.
[7] L. & P., xi, 1251, ii.   [8] ibid., 1230.
[9] ibid., 1251, i.   [10] ibid., ii.

Sir John Towneley was said, probably in November,[1] to have refused to take the oath, although he was 'very near that time',[2] but he may have been sworn later, or supported the commons without committing himself to the oath. Aske later suggested Sir John to the King as one with influence over the rebels who could help to 'stay the country' after the rising,[3] and his brother was certainly a rebel supporter.[4] Sir James Layburne, though he later testified against the commons[5] and took depositions against the canons of Cartmel,[6] was said by William Collins to be a supporter of the Pilgrimage,[7] as was Richard Duckett,[8] who had leased one of the rectories belonging to Conishead.[9] Though, from Derby's list of those who had assisted him, and Cumberland's view that the north-Lancashire rebels had gentry support,[10] it is clear that there were many more, the names of only a few other Lancashire gentlemen known to have supported the Pilgrimage can be found. Thomas Catterall and Nicholas Bannester were with the commons at Doncaster and Pontefract,[11] Michael Thornborough, Richard Kirkby, and John Houghton were summoned to the rebel council,[12] and Nicholas Tempest, said to have been among the 'first captains that came into Lancashire',[13] lived only just over the Yorkshire border. After the rebellion was over, the government seems to have borne no grudges; Layburne and Kirkby were among the seven local men appointed to the Commission for the Peace in Furness in March 1538.[14] Although the absence of clear evidence makes the conclusion only tenuous, it seems that the Pilgrimage in Lancashire was different again from that in Yorkshire, in that, like the revolt in Cumberland and Westmorland,[15] it was predominantly a movement of the commons; Derby certainly thought this was so.[16] This, in a sense, made the rebellion even more dangerous in Lancashire, as it meant there was no more responsible force to control the impetuous commons, and this was why the rebels in the county took so little notice of the Yorkshire leaders' negotiations with the government, ignored the truces, and even continued their activities after the issue of the pardon.

After reporting to the King, Derby wrote on the same day to Cromwell, to give a brief summary of the report he had sent in to Henry, and thank the Lord Privy Seal for his kindness.[17] The Earl, as ever, was anxious to keep on the right side of Cromwell, especially as the arrears on his debt to the King were piling up and he was unable to make any payments.[18]

[1] See above,   [2] L. & P., xi, 804.   [3] E.H.R., v, 344.
[4] L. & P., xi, 1155; ibid., 804.   [5] L. & P., xii(1), 671, No. 2, iii.
[6] L. & P., xii(1), 965, No. 2.   [7] ibid., 914.
[8] ibid.   [9] P.R.O., DL41/11/59, fos. 7 & 12.
[10] L. & P., xi, 993.
[11] L. & P., xii(1), 853. Both were Lancashire J.P.'s, Watson, art. cit., Appendix A.
[12] L. & P., xi, 1155.   [13] ibid., xii(1), 632.
[14] ibid., xiii(1), 646, g. 31.
[15] Dodds, The Pilgrimage of Grace, i, 192, 225.   [16] L. & P., xi, 1251.
[17] L. & P., xi, 1252.   [18] L. & P., Add., 1222.

Derby's position in Lancashire was still very awkward; at one point it was thought that he had been attacked by his own men, who were mutinous for want of pay,[1] and they had still not been paid early in December. At that point Sir Thomas Butler took matters into his own hands, and to keep the men quiet he paid his forces out of his own pocket.[2] He also announced that all those with payments due should present their bills to the Earl of Derby, who would get them their money, but it was thought by the people that they would never be paid.[3]

The royal pardon was drawn up on December 9th, and on the same day a warrant was issued to Audley, the Lord Chancellor, for the issue of free individual pardons for those who sued for them.[4] On December 22nd the pardon was proclaimed at Kendal,[5] and then at Lancaster on the 31st.[6] Although doubts as to its validity were a major cause of the Hallam–Bigod rising,[7] the proclamation of the pardon meant the collapse of the rebellion in Yorkshire, and the government was able to arrest the ringleaders under the fiction that this was done for offences committed after the pardon. But the pardon seems to have had little effect in Lancashire; the Yorkshire rebels dispersed, but those in Lancashire, especially the extreme north, continued their activities. Derby clearly thought that the danger in Lancashire was as great as ever, and he spent Christmas repairing the walls of Lathom and preparing his artillery in case of more trouble.[8] Lord Mounteagle went to Derby to warn him that the commons of Blackburnshire, Kendal, and Craven were ready to rise if anyone tried to eject the monks of Sawley.[9]

In the north of Lancashire, the situation was even worse from the government's point of view. In the middle of January, when the Kendal rebels were still a dangerous force, the commons of the parish of Heysham in Lancashire were going around swearing men to support the Kendal rebels,[10] and those who refused found a larger band returning next day to force them to swear.[11] At the beginning of February one Edmund Lawrence called together the parishioners of Warton to discuss the order they had received to assemble at Kendal, and he at least was resolved to keep to the oath he had sworn.[12] On February 12th the 'Captain of Poverty', presumably Atkinson,[13] wrote to the Constable of Melling telling of the disasters which had befallen the Westmorland rebels, and adding that '. . . we desire you for aid and help, according to your oaths, and as ye will have help of us if your cause require, as God forbid, and this Tuesday[14]

---

[1] L. & P., xi, 1097.   [2] ibid., 1253.   [3] ibid.
[4] L. & P., xi, 1276, i. & ii.   [5] L. & P., xii(1), 914.
[6] ibid., xi, 1392.   [7] ibid., xii(1), 201.   [8] ibid., 7.
[9] ibid.   [10] L. & P., xii(1), 671, No. 2, ii.
[11] ibid.   [12] ibid., 671.
[13] L. & P., xi, 947; xii(1), 914. It is possible, however, that the writers were two priests, Robert Dodgeson and Thomas Whytton, who were said to have tried to raise Lancashire again (L. & P., xii(1), 849).   [14] February 13th.

we command you every one to be at Kendal afore eight of the clock, or we are like to be destroyed.'[1]

The north Lancashire rebellion ended not through content at the issue of the pardon, or the preliminary settlement agreed to with Norfolk, but with the failure of the Carlisle rising, and the terrible vengeance taken there by Norfolk.[2] The extent of Lancashire's involvement in the Carlisle affair is not known, but summonses such as the one to Melling and the earlier one to Warton must have evoked some response. Probably at least a few of the rebels at Carlisle and Kendal were Lancashire men, and Norfolk wrote to Derby and Mounteagle to ask them to capture those who had been at Carlisle who fled into Lancashire.[3] At least one man was caught in Lancashire after fleeing from Carlisle; William Barrett, a tanner from Craven, was caught spreading sedition in Manchester,[4] and was hanged in chains.[5]

In Lancashire the rebellion collapsed from fear, and the resentments which had caused rebellion were not appeased. The conservatism of the county was not broken, for the rebels merely stopped operations without being defeated, and except for the ten husbandmen of Cartmel all those who were executed were monks.[6] The executions of the monks, and especially the Duke of Norfolk's executions at Carlisle, produced a fear of violence which kept Lancashire out of all the other religious revolts of the sixteenth century, but the reactionary movement remained as strong as ever. Lancashire remained a danger-spot until the arrival of the royal Commission to try the rebel leaders at the end of February, and Sir Thomas Butler reported that even in the south the people were still very corrupted, murmuring for the pay they had not yet received, and if the rebellion broke out again they might join this time.[7] Butler, whose knowledge was confined to the south of the county, had thought the rebellion dangerous enough, but he had not known the full extent of the threat. He reported to Cromwell, 'I do think your lordship shall have a marvellous certificate of the said Sir Richard Houghton, ye shall see thereby that the country was in much more danger than I thought it had been, he knows more than I know therein'.[8]

The Pilgrimage failed, as much as for anything else, because the King, though he could not defeat it, refused to give in to the rebels' demands. It must have become clear that despite its strength, the rebellion would achieve nothing, and after that it was only north of the Sands, where there were Cartmel and Conishead to defend, and in the east, where Whalley and Sawley were threatened, that the rebels remained active. The fact that the rebellion only continued in the areas where the religious houses were

---

[1] L. & P., xii(1), 411, printed in full, Dodds, op. cit., ii, 113.
[2] ibid., ii, 118–21.   [3] L. & P., xii(1), 478.   [4] ibid., 520.
[5] ibid., 632.   [6] P.R.O., PL26/13/6.
[7] L. & P., xii(1), 348.   [8] ibid.

important is yet more evidence of the role the monasteries played in provoking the Pilgrimage of Grace. But even in these areas the rebels and
their supporters lost their confidence as the Pilgrimage collapsed elsewhere. On January 1st the Abbot and convent of Whalley granted a
pension of ten marks to Cromwell,[1] and that this should have been granted
at such a late date must have been due to fears of what might happen when
the royal vengeance began. On February 10th William Rede, a baker
from Oxford, was arrested at Wotton on his way south, and examined at
Kenilworth; his evidence revealed a complete failure of confidence on the
part of Abbot Paslew of Whalley.[2] Rede deposed that he had been at
Whalley, and intended to go to Oxford, so he asked Paslew if he wished
any letters to be taken to the Abbey's scholar at Oxford. Paslew gave him
a letter for the scholar, and another for the Abbot of Hailes, John Clitheroe,
who had been a monk of Whalley.[3] Clitheroe was to be given the message
that Paslew was 'sore stopped and acrazed', and to be asked when he
would next be visiting Lancashire, 'for I would be glad to see him ere I
departed out of this world, seeing I brought him up here as a child'.[4]
Paslew was clearly very agitated, and though little is known of his involvement in the rebellion, he had been sufficiently implicated to anticipate
disaster by this time. Rede also took a letter to the Abbey's scholar at
Oxford, from the proctor of Blackburn, which is probably the letter
calendared in the *Letters and Papers*.[5] This is the only known letter from
Ralph Lynney, until recently the proctor of Blackburn,[6] which might
fit the circumstances, and it is difficult to explain how it would come to
be in the state archives unless it was the letter taken from Rede.[7] In the
calendar, the letter is dated 1536, although no year is given in the original
document, but the time, early January, is when Rede would have
been at Whalley. Lynney's chamber had been broken into, and two silver
pieces had been taken, and Lynney wanted advice on what to do.[8] Clearly
this particular letter had nothing to do with the Pilgrimage, unless the
robbery is thought indicative of the confused state of the area. What
happened to the two letters Paslew sent is not clear, and their contents can
only be guessed. The letter to Clitheroe probably repeated the message
which had been given to Rede,[9] but the letter to the scholar is more
difficult to explain. One possible explanation emerges from the identifica-
tion of the scholar given by Lynney's letter, addressed to 'Edward Manchester, scholar of Whalley'.[10] Manchester had taken his B.D. at Oxford
just over six months before, and seems to have remained in the University
after this,[11] but some time between the beginning of January, when the
Lynney letter was written, and February 2nd, the date of his institution,

---

[1] Whitaker, i, 108.
[2] L. & P., xii(1), 389.
[3] Whitaker, i, 114.
[4] L. & P., xii(1), 389.
[5] L. & P., x, 23.
[6] *Valor*, v, 229.
[7] L. & P., xii(1), 389.
[8] L. & P., x, 23.
[9] L. & P., xii(1), 389.
[10] L. & P., x, 23.
[11] Wood, *Athenae*, ii, 103.

Manchester returned to Whalley, Robert Parish, the vicar of Whalley, resigned, and Manchester was instituted in his place on the presentation of Whalley Abbey.[1] It therefore seems likely that Paslew's letter to him was a summons back to Whalley so that he could be made vicar. This again is an indication of Paslew's anticipation of disaster, for he must have wished to settle the Abbey's most highly qualified monk, and one who could not be accused of involvement in the Pilgrimage, in the vicarage, in case the Abbey was suppressed, so that he could use his patronage to provide for his brethren.[2] As far as Whalley was concerned at least, the Pilgrimage was over, and all that was left was insulate the monks of the house against the retribution which Paslew saw would follow.

[1] Lich. R.O, B/A/I, Reg. Lee, f. 36.
[2] See below, Chapter Nine.

CHAPTER SEVEN

THE AFTERMATH OF THE PILGRIMAGE:
THE ATTACK ON WHALLEY AND FURNESS

THE intimate connection between the Lancashire monasteries and the Pilgrimage is shown by the 'cleaning-up' operation the government conducted after the failure of the rebellion, which was designed not so much to punish those who could be convicted of treason, but to break the influence of the religious houses in the county. The Earl of Sussex's expedition into Lancashire was above all a stage in the suppression of the Lancashire monasteries, and the destruction of their power. Late in December 1536, the government compiled a 'Device made by the King's Highness and his Council for the perfect establishment of the North Parts',[1] which included the decision that the Earl of Sussex was to join the Earl of Derby in Lancashire, and there put those parts not infected by the late rebellion on a war footing. The leading gentlemen of Cheshire were to be ordered to assist the Earls, who were to report how many men they could assemble, and the King would send virtuous and learned men into those parts of Lancashire still not as quiet as the King would wish, who would teach the people God's word, ignorance of which had been the major cause of the rebellion.[2] It is not known whether the preachers were ever sent, but the first part of the instruction, which anticipated battle against the remaining rebels, was never necessary.

By January 1537 it must have been clear that the Pilgrimage would collapse of its own accord, and no military operation, such as that mounted in Westmorland, would be necessary. When the King issued his instructions to Sussex, the Earl was ordered first to take the submissions of the ex-rebels, and it was clearly expected that there would be no resistance.[3] The two Earls were to call together all the important men who had supported the rebels, reprove them for their disloyalty, and administer the oath of fidelity to them. They were then to put the oath to the commons, punishing those who refused to take it, and arresting the leaders and those who had been in any contact with the Yorkshire leaders, while those guilty of unlawful assembly or pillage after the pardon were 'incontinently to be justified'. The Earls were to collect the King's rents, and try to stop those who had caused disquiet among the people by undue enclosures.[4]

This procedure against the ex-rebels was but a small part of the mission, and the most important part, to which the most detailed discussion was given, concerned the attack on the monasteries. The instructions pointed

[1] L. & P., xi, 1410, No. 3. [2] ibid.
[3] L. & P., xii(1), 302. [4] ibid.

out that some monks ejected under the 1536 Act had returned to their houses, while others, whose houses had not been suppressed, had kept their monasteries with unseemly force, hoping to force the King 'to relinquish his right in such monasteries, whereunto by law he is justly entitled'.[1] When the county was quiet, the Earls were to eject those monks and force them to go to other houses, or else arrest them as vagabonds, and restore the lessees of the dissolved houses to their possessions. If it was argued that Norfolk had promised at Doncaster that the monks could remain until a Parliament decided their future, the Earls were to say that Norfolk had only said that he would ask the King if they could stay, and no promise had been given.[2]

Derby and Sussex were also given detailed instructions for propaganda against the monks; it must have been thought that the religious of Lancashire had too great an influence on the people, and this influence was to be broken. It was to be pointed out that the monks, by refusing to go elsewhere, were breaking their vows of obedience and poverty. The remainder of the document is not merely an argument against the monks involved in the rebellion, but a concerted attempt to ensure that the people were turned against all the religious. While the King risked life and treasure to defend the people, the monks were warm and snug in their cloister, and though they could not fight for the King in war, they had decided that they could fight against him in rebellion. While the husbandman and artificer had to work in all weathers, the monks were assured of a comfortable life.[3] These comments were obviously calculated to make the Lancashire monks unpopular, and their necessity is a tribute to the importance of the religious in Lancashire society.

The importance the government attached to the influence of the houses is shown by the fact that these instructions were further refined, and Wriothesley drew up a more elaborate argument against the monks of Lancashire,[4] presumably at Cromwell's instigation. This second document was a powerful statement of the government's case against the religious, elaborating some of the charges made in the preamble to the Act of Suppression, and adding new ones. 'For first,' it was asked, 'how can he call himself wilfully poor that will not live but as they list himself?' and what obedience is there in those who presume to direct the actions of their prince? The monks, therefore, were to be accused of failing to live up to their vows, and it was to be pointed out that they had become enemies of the commonwealth and devourers of the labour of others. The monks had become so powerful and exempt from the laws that no prince could live as freely as they, while 'they have declared at the late rebellion that they might fight against their prince and country'.[5] The monks were no longer poor, as they ought to be, but were richer even than the King, who used

[1] ibid.   [2] ibid.   [3] ibid.   [4] L. & P., xii(1), App. I.
[5] ibid.

G

his wealth to care for his subjects, and they had gained their wealth not
from work, as the people had to do, but under the cloak of holiness they
had scraped together wealth at the expense of the King and other noble
men. After building up this case against the monks, the government gave
the people an incentive to support the attack on the houses, with the final
comment that if the lands of the monks were taken, the King would not
need to trouble his people with taxes.[1] When the authorities were going to
such trouble to turn the people against the monks, there can be no doubt
that the role of the religious houses in the origins and the course of the
Pilgrimage was substantial, or that an attack on the monasteries was the
main aim of Sussex's mission.

From the reports sent in by Derby, Mounteagle, Butler, and others, the
King and his ministers already had a large body of evidence upon which
they could proceed against the rebel leaders and the monks. But they still
had only part of the story, and knew nothing of, for example, the restoration of Conishead, and the role of Furness in the Pilgrimage. The process
of gathering information began even before Sussex set out for Lancashire,
and on February 1st a number of letters were ordered to be sent to Lancashire gentry who were thought to have information.[2] These letters must
have been written immediately, for they had been delivered to Sir Thomas
Butler in Lancashire by the 6th, and he forwarded them.[3] Clearly the
matter of evidence was thought very important, for most of the gentry sent
their replies in to Butler immediately, and one intended to go up to
London to make a personal report.[4] The main task of gathering testi-
monies was, however, left to the royal Commission which was sent into
Lancashire.

Late in February the King's Commissioners for the pacification of the
county, the punishment of the rebel leaders, and the attack on the
monasteries began to assemble. The Earl of Sussex, accompanied by Sir
Antony Fitzherbert, one of the royal justices, arrived at Warrington on the
26th,[5] and the next day Derby and most of the others arrived.[6] They held
a meeting at the Friary, where Sussex explained the King's instructions
to his colleagues, the Commissioners formulated their plans,[7] and the long
process of taking depositions was begun, with evidence from William
Singleton on his discussion with Nicholas Tempest,[8] from two Cheshire
men who had been in Yorkshire at the time of the rebellion,[9] and from
the bailiff of Warrington on the attitude of the people in the south.[10] The
next day, Wednesday the 28th, was market day at Warrington, when it
was expected that many people from the surrounding areas would be in
the town, so it was proclaimed that the Commissioners would take bills of

[1] L. & P., xii(1), App. 1.   [2] ibid., 785.   [3] ibid., 348.
[4] ibid.   [5] L. & P., xii(1), 520.   [6] ibid.
[7] ibid.   [8] ibid., 518.   [9] L. & P., xi, 1253.
[10] ibid.

complaint for all offences against the King's subjects, and that the officers would put the oath of loyalty.[1] Most of the neighbouring gentry took the oath, and about 1,000 of the commons, and though all who took the oath were very eager to do so, some refused it.[2] The Commissioners also examined one William Barrett, a tanner from Craven, who had been at Carlisle during the troubles there; he had been spreading rumours in Manchester that the Duke of Norfolk had been taking a tax of 6/8d. or an ox on every plough, and 6/8d. for every christening or burial,[3] a rumour which had been circulating in the county for some time.[4]

The Commissioners moved on to Manchester on March 1st, and there took the oaths of the gentry, and then the commons on the 2nd and 3rd.[5] They went on to Preston on Sunday 4th,[6] to continue their work there. The next day, Sir Thomas Butler, Richard Halsall,[7] and Thomas Burgoyne took the deposition of John Smith, Bigod's servant, who told them of the letter Derby was said to have written to Aske; Smith said he had repented of his connection with the rebels when Butler put the oath of loyalty to the King to him at Warrington.[8] It is probable that Sussex and some of the other Commissioners then went on to Whalley, to collect evidence for the assizes at Lancaster, for a household was established for the Earl at Whalley Abbey on March 6th.[9]

On Friday 9th, the trial was held at Lancaster of those who were thought to have been the ringleaders in the rebellion. Abbot Paslew of Whalley, William Haydock and John Estgate, two of his monks, Richard Estgate and Henry Banaster, both of Sawley, were all charged with treason, though Banaster had not been captured.[10] John Estgate was acquitted, but the other three present were found guilty; Paslew pleaded guilty on all five counts on which he was charged.[11] The Abbot was executed at Lancaster the next day,[12] Haydock was hanged at Whalley on the following Monday,[13] and despite his protestations of innocence[14] Richard Estgate had been executed by March 17th.[15] At the same time as the Whalley and Sawley monks, also before Sussex, Derby, and their Commission, nine of the canons of Cartmel, only six of whom were present, and sixteen husbandmen of Cartmel, thirteen of whom were present, were also tried.[16] Two of the canons and three of the local men were acquitted, and four of the canons and ten of the husbandmen were hanged.[17]

On March 11th, the day after Paslew's execution, Sussex reported to

[1] L. & P., xii(1), 520.   [2] ibid.   [3] ibid.
[4] Corresp., 50.   [5] L. & P., xii(1), 520.   [6] ibid.
[7] He was acting as attorney to the Commissioners—L. & P., xii(1), 781.
[8] L. & P., xii(1), 578; see above.   [9] P.R.O., SC6/1797, m. 18d.
[10] P.R.O., PL26/13/6; printed in full, Wallis, 'Narrative of the Indictment of the Traitors of Whalley and Cartmel', Chetham Miscellanies, V, 13–15.
[11] ibid.
[12] B.M. Cotton MS. Vesp. D., xvii, f. 16; Wallis, art. cit., 16.
[13] ibid.   [14] P.R.O., PL26/13/6.
[15] L. & P., xii(1), 632.   [16] P.R.O., PL26/13/6.   [17] ibid.

Cromwell from Lancaster. As he had promised, he had executed the traitorous monks, though he thought that the successful accomplishment of the Whalley affair was 'the ordinance of Almighty God', for the Abbot was so wealthy and powerful that conviction would have been difficult had he not pleaded guilty. The execution, Sussex thought, 'shall be a spectacle and terror to all other corrupt minds hereafter'. Turning to less encouraging matters, he reported the evidence of Bigod's servant[1] and Sir Richard Houghton's servants,[2] which indicated that Derby may have had dealings with the rebel leaders, 'Albeit I think the same is not true.' But as Bigod had been taken 'the King's Highness may have commodity . . . to know the certainty.'[3] Sussex, apparently, was anxious for instructions on what he should do next, for on the same day he wrote to Wriothesley, Cromwell's secretary, asking him to ensure that the bearer of his letter to Cromwell should be sent back with orders as soon as possible.[4]

The next few days were taken up by the examination of further witnesses, and Sussex was clearly not satisfied that he had punished all those responsible for the seriousness of the rebellion in Lancashire. On the 14th the deposition of Alexander Richardson revealed events which the Commissioners had not yet begun to investigate. He reported, probably at Lancaster, that the monks of Furness had been acting as recruiting agents for the rebels, and had given them money, while at least one of the monks, Henry Salley, had been speaking out against the royal supremacy.[5] Examinations taken by two local J.P.'s in the north of the county revealed that the commons in that area had been more active in the rebel cause than had been thought, and that they had sent representatives to the meetings of the Yorkshire rebels.[6]

On the 17th,[7] Sussex reported his proceedings to the Duke of Norfolk, telling him of the executions, and warning him that three of the Cartmel canons[8] had escaped and were thought to be in the Kendal area. Barrett, the tanner who had been spreading false rumours,[9] was to be hanged in chains in Manchester, with John Stones, from Bethom in Westmorland, who had helped to swear the people of Warton in Lancashire to the rebel cause.[10] The Commissioners had put the oath of loyalty to the people of Lancaster, who were all sorry for their offences. According to Sussex, the principal offenders in Lancashire were Atkinson, who had led the com-

[1] L. & P., xii(1), 578.   [2] ibid., 518.
[3] ibid., 630; printed in full, Beck, Annales, 343-4.
[4] L. & P., xii(1), 631.   [5] ibid., 652.
[6] L. & P., xii(1), 671, i–iii.
[7] L. & P., xii(1), 632 gives the date as 11th or 17th, but it must be the latter as by the 11th the execution of Haydock, which is reported, had not taken place—see above—and the statements referred to were not taken until 17th (L. & P., xii(1), 671).
[8] Sussex gives Eskrigge, Ridley, and the late sub-prior—the last is a mistake for Thomas Person (P.R.O., PL26/13/6). Eskrigge was sub-prior (P.R.O., DL43/4/12, f. 1).
[9] L. & P., xii(1), 520.   [10] L. & P., xii(1), 671, 2, ii.

mons in Lancaster,[1] Collins, the bailiff of Kendal who had played an important part in the restoration of the monks,[2] one Robinson, a liveried retainer of the Abbot of Furness, and Nicholas Tempest, who had been so prominent in the Whalley affair.[3] Sussex, lastly, was looking out for those who had not yet been captured.[4]

On the same day the King sent Sussex and Derby the instructions which had been requested. They were thanked for their diligence, and for their arrangements for keeping the goods of Whalley.[5] As 'it should seem there remaineth very few therein that were meet to remain and continue in such an incorporation', it had been decided to dissolve the Abbey and take it into the King's hands, using the attainder of the Abbot as a pretext.[6] The Crown lawyers had apparently developed the doctrine that not only was a community, as a corporation, subject to the feudal law and so to the law of escheat, but that the treason of the head of the corporation, the abbot, constituted valid grounds for seizure.[7] The government was obviously worried that the monks of Whalley might stir up sedition if allowed out into the world, and thought 'it cannot be wholesome for our commonwealth to permit them to wander abroad', so the Earls of Sussex and Derby were to 'move them to enter into other houses' and to 'frame them to that point, that they may enter into other places', while meanwhile the Earls were to 'lie in a good wait of the monks, that they conspire not to the brewing of any inconvenience'. Finally, an ex-soldier whom they had sent up for questioning was 'for an example more worthy to suffer than the rest', having worn the King's coat, so he was sent back to them for execution.[8]

It seems to have taken the Earls a few more days to complete matters at Lancaster, and Sussex replied to these instructions in a letter to Cromwell from Preston four days later, on his way to Whalley.[9] Sussex asked for the King's letters to put the monks of Whalley in other houses, but as the people of Lancashire were now 'as obedient, faithful, and dreadful subjects, and as quiet, as any other generally within this realm', he hoped to be finished in the area within a week. But Sussex was rather optimistic; his investigations at Lancaster had revealed the extent of the involvement of the extreme north of the county in the rebellion, which he had not yet dealt with. With this letter he sent the letter from the 'Captain of Poverty' to the Constable of Melling,[10] and told Cromwell that the monks of Furness 'have been of as evil hearts and minds as any other'. Lastly, Cromwell,

---

[1] ibid., 914. [2] ibid., 965, No. 2; ibid., 787; ibid., 914.
[3] ibid., 1020. [4] ibid., 632.
[5] This proves Sussex had been at Whalley before the Lancaster trials—see above.
[6] L. & P., xii(1), 668; State Papers, i, 540.
[7] On this, see Knowles, Religious Orders, iii, 332.
[8] L. & P., xii(1), 668; State Papers, i, 540.
[9] L. & P., xii(1), 695; printed in full, Beck, Annales, 344.
[10] L. & P., xii(1), 411.

in a letter which has not survived, had asked for Richard Estgate's statement, but the Commissioners had been unable to get anything from him
either before or after his condemnation, except that Nicholas Tempest 'at
the first was one of their great favourers'.[1]

Sussex and part of the Commission then went on to Whalley; they were
certainly there by the 24th, when they took an inventory of the goods of
the Abbey. This was signed by Sussex, Fitzherbert, the justice, Leyland
and Farington, the two Lancashire knights who had played an important
part in the Suppression of the smaller monasteries, and John Claydon,[2] the
rector of Middleton. It must have been during the taking of the inventory[3]
that it was found that Abbot Paslew had been selling off the Abbey plate
for some time, and examinations were taken from the monks on the subject.[4] The Prior, Christopher Smith,[5] said the Abbey had had a gold cross,
which he thought the Abbot had sold two years before to pay debts, and a
gold chalice had also disappeared within the past twelve months. Richard
Cromboke, a servant of the house, said he was on his way back from
London about twelve months before when he met the Vicar of Blackburn,
Ralph Lynney,[6] who returned with him to London, and there Lynney
tried to sell a gold chalice, but could not agree on a price, though he did
sell some silver, and Cromboke thought the chalice was sold later. William
Whalley and Thomas Horowode[7] knew nothing, but John Henley[8] said
the Abbot had been selling off plate for six or seven years, since he took
his mitre. Laurence Forest[9] said a standing cup had been given to one of
the local gentry at Michaelmas, but James More[10] knew nothing.[11]

Sussex, as the King's instructions sent a few days later, on March 28th,[12]
showed, was expected to carry through the first stage of suppressing
Whalley, the supervision. Henry intended to send letters for putting the
monks of Whalley in other monasteries with his orders,[13] but it would also
be necessary to send three or four blank ones, as some of the houses were

[1] L. & P., xii(1), 695, Beck, op. cit., 344.
[2] *Valor*, v, 226—he was a considerable pluralist in the London area, and Master of
Attleborough College in Norfolk (V.C.H., v, 158)—perhaps one of those sent to preach
against rebellion (L. & P., xi, 1410, No. 3).
[3] L. & P., xii(1), 716; printed in full, *Whalley Coucher*, 1255-65.
[4] L. & P., xii(1), 621.
[5] F.O.R., 91; he was Commissary of the Abbey Court until 1529, *Whalley Act Book*, 125.
[6] V.C.H., vi, 241; also a monk of Whalley, Whitaker, i, 115; P.R.O., E315/237, f. 3.
Cromboke was sub-seneschal of the Abbey—*Valor*, v. 229.
[7] Both monks—F.O.R., 91.
[8] The only monk with a similar name is John Holden, F.O.R., 91.
[9] Monk, Whitaker, i, 114; receiver for Whalley rectory, *Valor*, v, 229.
[10] Monk—F.O.R., 91; last kitchener of Whalley, Whitaker, i, 188.
[11] L. & P., xii(1), 621.
[12] L. & P., xii(1), 706 dates this March 24th, but it is a reply to Sussex's letter of the
21st, ibid., 695, and another which has not survived, but was written after that of the 21st,
which would not have reached London in time for a reply on the 24th. Further, Sussex,
in his reply of April 6th, refers to it as the King's letter of the 28th—L. & P., xii(1),
840; printed, West, *Antiquities*, App. X, No. 5.
[13] But see below, Chapter Eight.

not able to take those who wished to go, 'as for that the house of Jervaulx is in some danger of suppression by like offence as hath been committed at Whalley'. Before the monks left, they were to be examined, and those who wished to have capacities, which would be sent by the next messenger,[1] should be given 'their bedding and chamber stuff, with such money as you shall, by your wisdoms, think meet'. But the evidence which could be obtained on the rebellion was not yet all in, and the Commissioners were to find out how the Vicar of Blackburn got hold of the copy of Norfolk's letter to Darcy, which they had sent up to London.[2]

Though the letter is apparently lost, Sussex must have written to the government about March 24th, reporting on his activities at Whalley, and enclosing the letter found in the Vicar of Blackburn's chamber.[3] On the King's orders,[4] Sussex recalled Lynney from Lancaster Castle,[5] where he must have been imprisoned when the letter was found. Sussex examined him at Whalley about April 9th, and sent the deposition to London with his report of that day.[6] The examination, unfortunately, has been lost, but the substance of what happened is clear from the other deposition Sussex sent at the same time, that of William Talbot.[7] Talbot received the Norfolk–Darcy letter from a servant of Aske, and delivered it to Abbot Paslew of Whalley, and also took to the Abbot a letter from Aske, which he thought was 'a summons to the convocation at Pomfret'.[8] Clearly Paslew passed the letter on to Ralph Lynney, the Vicar, who was a monk of the house[9] and whom he often trusted with delicate matters,[10] probably in an attempt to keep his communication with the rebel leaders secret. The letter was perhaps discovered following a search of Lynney's chamber, occasioned by the report that 'the vicar of Blackburn did say, if the commons come again to Lancashire he would bear the cross before them, and said God speed them well on their journey'.[11] But despite his involvement in the affair of the letter and his words in support of the commons, Lynney must have been released from prison and not molested further, for he remained at Blackburn as vicar until his resignation in 1555.[12] The government thought Paslew's connection with the rebel leaders more important, however, and in a summary of the main events of the Pilgrimage made by Cromwell's office, it was noted that 'Last Lent, Darcy sent a copy of Norfolk's letter to him to the Abbot of Whalley'.[13] This connection, the main lines of which are by no means clear, was probably the basis of one of the charges made against Paslew at the Lancaster trial, and two of the

---

[1] Some capacities issued April 1st, F.O.R., 91.
[2] L. & P., xii(1), 706; Beck, op. cit., 345–6.
[3] ibid.
[4] ibid.   [5] L. & P., xii(1), 878.
[6] ibid.
[7] L. & P., xii(1), 706; ibid., 853.
[8] ibid.
[9] P.R.O., E315/237, f. 3.
[10] e.g. the selling of the Abbey plate, L. & P., xii(1), 621.
[11] L. & P., xii(1), 853.
[12] V.C.H., vi, 240.
[13] L. & P., xii(1), 849.

counts were individual charges against him alone.[1] There was one more item concerning Whalley and the rebellion which, in the King's letter of the 28th, Sussex was instructed to settle. The Commissioners were to send up to London Richard Estgate of Sawley, as Sir Arthur Darcy now had new evidence against him which could prove enlightening.[2] This, however, Sussex and the others were unable to do, since Estgate had already been executed.[3]

The rest of the King's instructions concerned Furness, the disloyalty of which had only recently become apparent through the evidence of the bailiff of Dalton.[4] From this it seemed to the authorities that the Abbot and monks 'have not been of that truth towards us that to their duties appertained', and the Commissioners were to find 'the very truth of their proceedings', committing the guilty to prison.[5] Sussex set about this problem immediately, since he was eager to be finished in Lancashire and return to the King.[6] He summoned the Abbot and some of the monks of Furness to Whalley,[7] and a disconcerting picture emerged of the infidelity of one of the greatest houses in the north and its almost unanimous opposition to the Crown's religious policy.

Before the visitation of Layton and Legh, Abbot Pyle, according to two of his brethren, ordered that his monks were to tell the royal visitors nothing.[8] After the visitation, Friar Robert Legate was put into the house 'to read and preach to the brethren', but the monks would not allow Legate to lecture to them, and they ignored the visitors' Injunctions, failing to keep a schoolmaster or to distribute 'broken meat' to the poor.[9] Nothing is known of the Abbey over the next eight months, but when the rebellion began the monks were very soon involved. When Sawley was suppressed in April 1536[10] four of the monks were sent to Furness as transfers, but when Sawley was restored in October,[11] three of them returned, and Abbot Pyle tried to make the fourth go too, ejecting him from his chamber.[12] This was obviously interpreted as supporting the restoration of the monks of Sawley.

Late in October 1536, as the rebellion was spreading into the Furness area, Abbot Pyle told his monks that he would leave before the rebels arrived, as his presence would only cause trouble.[13] Before leaving he

---

[1] P.R.O., PL26/13/6.   [2] L. & P., xii(1), 706.
[3] ibid., 632.   [4] ibid., 652.
[5] ibid., 706; printed in full, Beck, *Annales*, 345–6.
[6] L. & P., xii(1), 706; ibid., 695.
[7] Sussex did not go to Furness until after Pyle surrendered the Abbey at Whalley on April 9th—ibid., 840, 832—but the depositions had already been taken by then, and two monks sent to prison—ibid., 840.
[8] ibid., 841, Nos. 3 & 4.   [9] ibid., 841, Nos. 2 & 4.
[10] Woodward, 'The Exemption from Suppression of Certain Yorks Priories', E.H.R., lxxvi, 390.
[11] L. & P., xi, 784.   [12] L. & P., xii(1), 841, Nos. 3 & 4.
[13] ibid., No. 3, ii.

appears to have encouraged the brethren to do what they could with the commons, while he did what he could with the King,[1] and he then fled to the Earl of Derby,[2] arriving at Lathom some time before November 1st.[3] Pyle's major concern was the future of his monastery, and while his monks were to secure the support of the rebels, he hoped to preserve the reputation of the Abbey with the King. His double-dealing was clearly indicated in a letter he was said to have written to Furness from Lathom; he said that he had taken a way to be sure of both King and commons, and he praised the conduct of the monks, 'for that their conversation was like men of religion'.[4]

After Pyle's departure, most of the monks turned to open support of the rebellion, in word and action. On October 30th, or 31st,[5] Michael Hammerton, the cellarer, Christopher Whalley, or Brown, John Broughton, and William Rigge, monks, with the agreement of the others, went out to meet the rebels at Swartmore, and took them either £20 or £23/6/8d. as a donation to the rebel cause.[6] The monks then marched with the rebels to Dalton, where, on the 31st, Prior Garner and John Green, another of the monks, called out the tenants of Dalton, Stanke, and Waney, commanding them, on pain of the destruction of their houses, to appear before the rebels in their arms and armour, ready to join the Pilgrimage.[7] The monks of Furness were open in their support of the rebels, showing none of the caution their brothers at Whalley had, and when the tenants of the Abbey asked for advice, the monks' reply was, 'Agree with them, as we have done.' They encouraged both rebels and tenants in their cause, saying, 'Now must they stick to it, or else never, for if they sit down both you and Holy Church is [sic] undone, and if they lack company we will go with them, and live and die to defend their most godly Pilgrimage.'[8] It seems the monks were not acting merely from fear of the rebels, or even in obedience to their Abbot's orders, but were sincere in their support for the rebel cause. After this the opinions which the government most feared, and against which the 1534 Treasons Act[9] had been passed, were rife in the Abbey.

On November 9th[10] John Green, one of those who had been vociferous in support of the Pilgrims, expressed opinions on the independence of the Church, and said that the King would never give them another abbot, but they would choose their own.[11] About this time, for he had returned before some of the later offences, Abbot Pyle went back to his monastery, and on

[1] ibid., 841, Nos. 1 & 4; ibid., 849, No. 24.   [2] ibid., 841, No. 3, ii.
[3] L. & P., xi, 947, No. 2.
[4] L. & P., xii(1), 652; ibid., 841, No. 4.
[5] On either All-hallows Eve or the day before.
[6] L. & P., xii(1), 652; ibid., 841, Nos. 2, 3, & 3, ii.
[7] L. & P., xii(1), 652; ibid., 841, Nos. 2, 3 & 4.
[8] ibid., 841, Nos. 2 & 3.   [9] 26 Henry VIII, c. 13.
[10] The Friday after St. Martin's Day.   [11] L. & P., xii(1), 841, No. 3.

his return the monks forced him to sign certain articles, presumably in favour of the rebels, and the monks were so friendly towards the commons that, so Pyle reported, he did not dare to enter the church alone after dark.[1] As well as those monks who had actually been involved with the rebels, others seem to have supported their aims, and William Forest, Matthew Kirkby, and Richard Martindale spoke out in their favour.[2] Some time before Christmas, John Harrington, John Broughton, and others were circulating a prophecy that 'in England shall be slain the decorate rose in his mother's belly', which they interpreted to mean that the King would be murdered by a priest, for the Church was the King's mother.[3] Abbot Paslew knew of the prophecy, though he failed to report it to the government, so it must have been common knowledge in the Abbey.[4] Soon after this,[5] Henry Salley, another of the monks, apparently of very conservative views, was saying that 'there should be no lay knave head of the Church',[6] or, in the version which the Abbot heard, that it was never a good world since 'secular men and knaves rule upon us, and the King made head of the Church'.[7] Abbot Pyle knew this was treason, but had no wish to endanger his house, and failed to report it;[8] he was said to have silenced Salley only so that Friar Legate would not report the incident to the authorities,[9] and he caused the whole matter to be kept quiet.[10] Incidents of this kind seem to have been common in the Abbey at this time, and we have reports of a number of others over the next month. John Broughton was saying that the King was not rightful heir to the throne, since his father only became king by the sword,[11] and also that the Bishop of Rome was unjustly put down, and within three years all would be changed and the new laws annulled.[12] The one priest of reformist views in the community was Friar Legate, but his opinions only made him unpopular with the others. On one occasion, he preached in favour of the King's laws, but afterwards Henry Salley said to two other monks that it was a wonder that God did not call down a vengeance upon them all, on Friar Legate for his preaching and on the monks for their listening.[13]

In view of the preparations being made for the royal Commission, led by Sussex, to sit in Lancashire, Pyle must have been getting very worried by the middle of February, 1537, for the words and actions of his monks seemed likely to bring the royal vengeance down on the Abbey. On February 18th,[14] Thomas Holcroft, who was in the confidence of the Earl

---

[1] L. & P., xii(1), 841, No. 3, ii.   [2] ibid.
[3] ibid., Nos. 3 & 4.   [4] ibid., Nos. 3, ii, & 4.
[5] Probably after December 31st, when the pardon was proclaimed at Lancaster; the other events can definitely be dated before the pardon, but as two monks were imprisoned, probably Salley and Broughton, for offences after the pardon, their statements must have been made after the pardon.
[6] L. & P., xii(1), 652.   [7] ibid., 841, No. 3, ii.
[8] ibid., Nos. 3 & 4.   [9] ibid., No. 3.   [10] L. & P., xii(1), 842.
[11] ibid., 841, Nos. 3, ii, & 3.   [12] ibid., Nos. 3 & 4.   [13] L. & P., xii(1), 842.
[14] The First Sunday in Lent.

of Derby and the government, was at Furness, and his visit shattered Pyle's nerves completely. After Holcroft had gone, the Abbot commanded his monks to obey the Injunctions of Layton and Legh, though he had released them from obedience to the orders in advance.[1] This action caused great discontent, for the monks were in no mood to be reformed at this late date; Pyle, however, sent Prior Garner to the brethren on the following day, to promise them favour if they stood by him.[2] The Abbot's new enthusiasm for reform, Legate said, was only the result of his fear that Holcroft would report the condition of the house to the Council.[3] It is also likely that Pyle intimidated the monks, for by March 13th Legate, who had been very forthcoming on the affairs of the Abbey before, refused to tell the bailiff of Dalton anything of what he thought might happen to Henry Salley.[4]

When it became clear, by the end of March, that Sussex and Derby would investigate Furness' involvement in the rebellion, Pyle did his best to ensure that as little of the story as possible would come out. He threatened Friar Legate once again, and also the bailiff of Dalton, with vengeance if any complaint should be laid against him;[5] he was presumably not aware that Richardson, the bailiff, had already made a statement to the Commissioners at Lancaster on March 14th.[6] When Pyle was summoned to appear before Sussex at Whalley, early in April, he called together his monks in the Chapter House at Furness, and commanded them that they 'should not meddle with them [the King's Lieutenants] nor showing anything at all to them', and 'if he might know any of them all to tell anything out of the Chapter House after that day, by Him that made him, he should go to prison, and never come out so long as he was abbot'.[7]

But all Pyle's precautions came to nothing when his monks were summoned before the Commissioners, who were able to build up evidence by taking advantage of the division which had characterised the convent for so long.[8] The depositions indicate that Prior Garner, John Green, Michael Hammerton, Christopher Brown, or Whalley, William Rigge, Matthew Kirkby, William Forest, Richard Martindale, and of course John Broughton and Henry Salley, supported the rebels.[9] Against these, the Abbot said that John Thornton, Thomas Settle, and James Forster took the King's part,[10] while Christopher Massrudder,[11] Roger Waller, the Vicar of Dalton,[12] and of course Friar Legate,[13] gave evidence against the others,

[1] L. & P., xii(1), 841, No. 3.   [2] ibid.   [3] ibid.
[4] L. & P., xii(1), 652.   [5] ibid., 841, No. 3.   [6] L. & P., xii(1), 652.
[7] ibid., 842.   [8] See above, Chapter One.
[9] L. & P., xii(1), 652; ibid., 841, Nos. 1–4.
[10] ibid., 841, No. 3, ii.
[11] The 'Christopher Masse' & the 'Christopher Rudde' of L. & P., xii(1), 841, No. 4 were the same man; 'Massrudder' in ibid., No. 1, 'Maschod' in the surrender, D.K.R., App. 2, 21, and 'Christopher Mashorder' in F.O.R., 97.
[12] *Valor*, v, 272; V.C.H., viii, 316; he was a monk of the house, F.O.R., 97; L. & P., xii(1), 841, No. 2.   [13] L. & P., xii(1), 841, No. 3.

and Anthony Plummer had passed on information to Legate,[1] so these were probably also loyal to the King. Pyle's hopes that the failings of the house might be kept secret could only be fulfilled if the monks remained united, but only division was possible in such a company, and the Commissioners were able to extract the evidence on which this account of the involvement of Furness in the rebellion has been based.

The Earl of Sussex, on the basis of his investigations, committed two of the monks to prison.[2] These must have been Henry Salley and John Broughton. Assuming that 'Christopher Whalley' and 'Christopher Brown' are the same man,[3] that Thomas Hartley was away at Urswick,[4] and that James Proctor was away at the benefice for which he had been granted a dispensation,[5] only Salley and Broughton, of those resident, did not sign the surrender or receive capacities.[6] As Sussex reported the imprisonment on April 6th,[7] and the surrender was not signed until April 9th,[8] the two who were imprisoned would not have been present to sign, while their failure to receive capacities can be explained by their imprisonment. Further, the offences of Salley and Broughton are the only ones which cannot definitely be dated before the pardon, while Sussex reported that those he imprisoned were the only ones guilty of offences before the pardon.[9] Conversely, if these two were the ones imprisoned, their offences can be dated after December 31st, when the pardon was proclaimed at Lancaster.[10]

Despite the King's orders of March 28th,[11] the Earl of Sussex was unable to commit the Abbot, or more than two of his monks, to prison.[12] Furness, therefore, could not be seized as attainted land, as Whalley had been, but Sussex was able to take advantage of Pyle's eagerness to save his own skin now that his house was in trouble. Sussex, anxious to please the King, considered how the monks could be got to leave their house, and again summoned Abbot Pyle to Whalley.[13] The Commissioners were unable to get any more information from Pyle which could be used to dissolve the house, but he was obviously very frightened, and Sussex took advantage of this to suggest a voluntary surrender, 'which thing so opened to the Abbot fairly, we found him of a very facile and ready mind to follow my advice in that behalf'.[14] The Abbot, therefore, made out a form of surrender to the King, 'knowing the mis-order and evil lives, both unto God and our Prince, of the brethren of the said monastery', and testifying to his willing-

---

[1] L. & P., xii(1), 841. No. 3.   [2] L. & P., xii(1), 840.
[3] cf. L. & P., xii(1), 841, No. 3, with 3, ii.
[4] F.O.R., 53; V.C.H., viii, 337.   [5] F.O.R., 21.
[6] D.K.R., viii, App. 2, 21; F.O.R., 97.   [7] L. & P., xii(1), 840.
[8] L. & P., xii(1), 880.
[9] ibid., 840; printed West, op. cit., App. X, No. 5.
[10] L. & P., xi, 1392.   [11] L. & P., xii(1), 706.
[12] ibid., 840.
[13] ibid., printed West, op. cit., App. X, No. 5.
[14] L. & P., xii(1), 840; West, loc. cit.

ness to certify to his action as directed.[1] The Earl then sent Sir Thomas
Butler, Sir John Byron, and Sir Richard Houghton on from Whalley to
Furness, to 'take into their hands, rule and governance, the said house, to
the use of your Highness, and to see that the monks and servants of the
same be kept in a due order, and nothing embezzled'.[2] They were to look
after matters until Sussex received the King's approval of what had been
done at Whalley, and so could go on to Furness himself. But that night Sir
Antony Fitzherbert arrived,[3] and he realised Pyle's surrender would not
stand legally, and that the house would have to be officially surrendered by
the Abbot and convent on a proper deed.[4] Fitzherbert then drew up such
a deed, a copy of which Sussex sent to the King next day.[5] This was as
doubtful as a legal expedient as the confiscation of Whalley, with its
assumption that a convent could surrender the rights of a corporation of
which the monks were but the living representatives.[6]

All this was reported to the King by Sussex in his letter of April 6th from
Whalley.[7] Everything had now been completed at Whalley, except that
the Commissioners awaited the King's letters for sending the monks into
other houses. The capacities for those who wished to leave religion had
presumably arrived by this time,[8] and the first batch of fourteen monks
for whom capacities had been issued was dispatched. The monks were
given 33/4d., and the prior £3/6/8d.[9] and those who had no capacities as
yet appear to have remained at Whalley.[10] Sussex reported that the Prior
of Whalley was an old man, who asked permission to remain at Whalley
as a chantry-priest in the parish church,[11] and the King granted the request in his next letter.[12] In the same letter, Sussex asked what was to be
done with the monks of Furness, of whom there were about thirty-three,
and if the King wishes would he send letters for them to go to other
houses.[13]

Sussex remained at Whalley at least until April 9th, supervising the
winding-up of the monastery. On that day he wrote to Nicholas Tempest
ordering him to return the chalice which the people of Billington and
Dinkley had bought for the monastery, and which the Abbot had lent to
him.[14] Tempest may thus still have been at liberty, though he was in the

[1] L. & P., xii(1), 832; West, op. cit., App. X, No. 4.
[2] L. & P., xii(1), 840.
[3] Probably he had been clearing up at Lancaster, holding the Assize with Sir John
Porte (P.R.O., PL25/13). Fitzherbert was Chief Justice at Lancaster, and Porte was
Second Justice (Somerville, op. cit., 470, 473).
[4] L. & P., xii(1), 840.
[5] Probably B.M. Cotton, Cleo. E. iv, 245, a corrected draft—L. & P., xii(1), 903.
[6] G. W. O. Woodward, *The Dissolution of the Monasteries*, 101.
[7] L. & P., xii(1), 840.
[8] F.O.R., 97; L. & P., xii(1), 706—the first fourteen were issued April 1st.
[9] P.R.O., E315/427, fos. 10-11.   [10] See below, Chapter Eight.
[11] L. & P., xii(1), 840.   [12] ibid., 896.
[13] L. & P., xii(1), 840.
[14] ibid., 879.

Tower by April 23rd, when he was questioned by Layton, Legh, Tregonwell, and Ap Rice.[1] Also on the 9th, Sussex wrote to Cromwell reporting on his activities, and telling him that a letter from Collins, the bailiff of Kendal, had been found at Conishead, and another from Conishead to Collins.[2] Even at this late stage evidence was still being collected, and it was on the 9th that Sussex sent up the depositions of the Vicar of Blackburn,[3] and William Talbot[4] on the letter from Norfolk to Darcy.[5]

The Earl of Sussex may have gone on to Furness from Whalley later on April 9th, since his signature appears on the surrender of that date.[6] But it is more likely that the surrender was taken by Butler, Byron, and Houghton, who also signed the document, and who had been sent on to Furness on the 5th,[7] and that the signatures of Sussex, Fitzherbert, Tunstall, and Claydon, were added when they went on to Furness from Whalley.[8] All that remained for Sussex and his Commission now, after Furness had been surrendered to the King by the Abbot and twenty-nine monks,[9] was to carry through the 'supervision' process of the Suppression of the house. Instructions on this were dispatched from London on April 11th.[10] The Commissioners were to make an inventory of the goods and valuables of the Abbey, and put them in safe-keeping until the arrival of suppression officials. The monks who wished to transfer were to be sent to other houses,[11] and capacities for the others would be issued by the Lord Chancellor.[12] The final problems such as the money and belongings to be given to the monks were left to the Earl's discretion, for the King knew he would look to the Crown's profit, and 'yet rid the said monks in such honest sort as all parties shall be therewith contented'.[13] This, however, was exactly what Sussex was unable to do, and the whole episode of the Pilgrimage and its aftermath ended, as it had begun, with angry and discontented monks.

Sussex was still in Lancashire on April 18th, when Fitzherbert wrote to Cromwell to make a final report on the proceedings of the two Earls in the county.[14] There is no record of any further activities by the Commission after this date, although the household which had been maintained at Whalley since March 6th remained in being until June 27th,[15] when it was dissolved by the Augmentations officials. Burgoyne and Dawtrey received

[1] L. & P., xii(1), 1014.
[2] L. & P., xii(1), 878; L. & P., Add. 1112.
[3] L. & P., xii(1), 878.
[4] ibid.; ibid., 853.
[5] ibid., 878.
[6] ibid., 880.
[7] ibid.; ibid., 840.
[8] L. & P., xii(1), 880, 878.
[9] Printed in full, West, *Antiquities*, App. X, No. 7.
[10] L. & P., xii(1), 896.
[11] See below, Chapter Eight.
[12] Capacities for twenty-nine Furness monks were issued on May 10th, F.O.R., 97, assuming that 'Holmo Cultram' is a mistake in the register; perhaps this was intended to be a note that capacities were needed for Holme Cultram, and there was no monk of that name, or any like it, at Furness.
[13] L. & P., xii(1), 896.
[14] ibid., 970.
[15] P.R.O., SC6/1797, m. 17d.

expenses for attending Sussex from February until April,[1] and Richard Halsall claimed expenses for attending the Commission as attorney for seven weeks,[2] roughly the period between the arrival of Sussex in Lancashire and April 18th. It is therefore likely that the Earl left the county soon after the 18th, leaving it, as Fitzherbert reported, faithful and true, with the griefs and causes of the people satisfied, and the shire likely to be well behaved for many years to come.[3] This optimistic picture, however, was far from accurate, and though Lancashire was not involved in another rebellion in the sixteenth century, it remained dogged in its conservative opposition to reformist policies. Only six weeks after Sussex left, a bill was pinned to the door of Shap, a religious house only twelve miles from Furness, which said that if the people would rise and go into Lancashire, they would find a captain with money ready to lead them.[4] The spirit of the Pilgrimage had not been crushed.

[1] P.R.O., DL29/2313, m. 13.
[3] ibid., 970.
[2] L. & P., xii(1), 781.
[4] L. & P., xii(2), 206.

CHAPTER EIGHT

THE SUPPRESSION OF THE
GREATER HOUSES

WHEN the Earl of Sussex left Whalley, the demesnes were committed to the charge of John Braddyll, and the impropriated rectories were farmed out for a year to those gentlemen who had assisted Sussex on his Commission.[1] Braddyll was a local gentleman of rising aspirations who was a servant to Thomas Holcroft,[2] who was in turn a servant of the Earl of Derby,[3] so it was perhaps at their intercession that he gained his position. It was originally intended that Whalley should go to the Duchy,[4] but this decision was reversed and as attainted land it passed to the General Surveyors.[5] It was therefore surveyed, with Bridlington, Jervaulx, Reading, and the other attainted abbeys,[6] by Richard Pollard, one of the General Surveyors. Pollard was at Whalley at the end of June and the early part of July; he surveyed the demesnes and granges, dating his survey June 29th.[7] He reported to Thomas Cromwell ten days later that he had let the lands until Michaelmas to the poor tenants, and granted out the tithes till Christmas, when the farmers were to yield their account for the year.[8] Though Pollard was rather more helpful to the poor than the Duchy officials had been, his other policies led to some difficulty, since late in July Sir Alexander Radcliffe complained to Cromwell that though he had been promised the farm of Eccles rectory, this had now been granted to Sir William Leyland by Pollard.[9]

Some of the Whalley monks may have remained in residence for some time after Sussex had gone, probably those who wished to transfer to other houses, for the Earl was awaiting the arrival of letters of authorisation to send the monks to other monasteries before his departure.[10] A list of the houses to which the monks wished to go had been sent to London by Sussex,[11] but it was found that 'some of the houses mentioned in your bill of their names be not well able to receive the number set upon them', especially as Jervaulx was likely to be suppressed.[12] All vacant places in the larger monasteries of England must by now have been filled by monks transferred from smaller houses suppressed under the Act of Dissolution. The draft of the King's letter to Sussex of March 28th[13] shows that it was

[1] P.R.O., SC6/1797, m. 17–18.   [2] *Lancs. & Ches. Wills*, ii, 106 ff.
[3] *Corresp.*, 10.   [4] L. & P., xii(1), 896.
[5] L. & P., xiii(2), 1195, iv.   [6] Richardson, *Court of Augmentations*, 276.
[7] Printed *Whalley Coucher*, 1197–1254.   [8] L. & P., xii(2), 234.
[9] ibid., 344.
[10] L. & P., xii(1), 840; West, *Antiquities*, App. X, No. 6.
[11] L. & P., xii(1), 706; Beck, *Annales*, 345–6.   [12] ibid.   [13] ibid.

intended to send the transfer documents with that letter, but it must have been found impossible to find places for the Whalley monks. Sussex certainly did not receive the authorisations with the King's letter, and they had not arrived by the time of his last report to Henry from Whalley, on April 6th, when he said that all had been completed at the Abbey except that the monks were still awaiting their letters.[1] There is no evidence that the letters ever arrived, and a strong presumption that they never did; the monks had to be accommodated six months after the first suppressions, and if the need for places had forced the government to exempt houses from suppression even at that stage, the difficulty of finding vacancies must have become even greater.

Although the government had been determined not to allow the Whalley monks to leave the monastic order, and perhaps spread sedition,[2] there was now no choice. Indeed, the fact that they were sent into the world is a strong argument in favour of the point that there were now no vacant places in the larger houses. The group of fourteen monks for whom capacities were issued on April 1st[3] must have been those who originally elected to leave religion, but a further batch of three dispensations was issued on May 10th,[4] a month after the first group had left the Abbey.[5] A last group of four capacities was issued on October 10th,[6] six months after the official suppression of Whalley. Clearly the seven monks who received their capacities so late were the monks who elected to transfer, and for whom there was now no room. This interpretation is borne out by the fact that one of this group, Christopher Cromboke, managed to find a place at Byland, one of his Order's houses in Yorkshire, even though a dispensation had been issued for him, and he signed the surrender there,[7] and received another capacity on the suppression of Byland.[8]

There were also another four monks who did not receive capacities, besides Paslew and Haydock, who had been executed. Edward Manchester was definitely a monk of Whalley,[9] but he was at Oxford; he took his B.D. at St. Benedict's College in 1536,[10] reverted to his family name of Pedley, and returned to Whalley to take over the vicarage from Robert Parish, who was also a monk of the Abbey,[11] who seems to have resigned before the suppression of the house.[12] Ralph Lynney was a monk of Whalley,[13] who was receiver for Blackburn rectory in 1535,[14] and Vicar of Blackburn from 1536,[15] but he would be away at his vicarage, or may have still been in prison.[16] John Estgate, monk, was tried for treason,[17] but was

[1] L. & P., xii(1), 840; West, op. cit., App. X, No. 6.
[2] L. & P., xii(1), 668.   [3] F.O.R., 91.   [4] ibid., 96.
[5] See above, Chapter Seven.   [6] F.O.R., 110.
[7] D.K.R., viii, App. 2, 14.   [8] F.O.R., 181.
[9] L. & P., x, 23.   [10] Wood, Athenae, ii, 103.
[11] Whitaker, i, 114, F.O.R., 97.
[12] Lich. R.O., B/A/I, Reg. Lee, f. 36.   [13] P.R.O., E315/237, f. 3.
[14] Valor, v, 229.   [15] Lich. R.O., B/A/I, Reg. Lee, f. 35.
[16] L. & P., xii(1), 878.   [17] P.R.O., PL26/13/6.

H

acquitted, and asked to go to Neath in Glamorgan;[1] this would explain
why he was not given a capacity, for probably the government would do
its utmost to find a place for him at least, but there is no evidence that he
ever actually went to Neath, as he did not receive a capacity there when
the house was dissolved.[2] Laurence Forest is more difficult to explain; he
was definitely a monk,[3] and was Commissary of the Ecclesiastical Court
of Whalley from 1530 to 1536,[4] succeeding the Prior in the office, and was
the Abbey's receiver for Whalley rectory in 1535,[5] an office held only by
monks of the house. Though he was certainly alive when Sussex and his
colleagues were at Whalley, and at the house himself,[6] he did not receive a
capacity, and has not been traced to another house; he did not receive a
capacity recorded in the 'Faculty Office Register' at any other house, and
he did not sign the surrender of any other house. But the only explanation
of his failure to receive a capacity at Whalley is that he transferred; he
must therefore have gone to a house which fell by attainder, thus leaving
no surrender list, and does not have its capacities recorded.

The suppression of Furness is rather more fully documented. The
King's orders to Sussex stipulated that, as Furness belonged to the Duchy,
the Lord Admiral, as Chancellor, was to appoint the commissioners to
survey the house, and all the Abbey records were to be turned over to
them.[7] For some reason, probably the inter-departmental rivalry of the
Duchy and Augmentations, Furness was allotted to the new and specialised Court; it is possible that it was thought too great a risk to allow the
apparently harsher methods of the Duchy free rein again, but in any
case, Augmentations got Furness.[8] Furness had surrendered, and not, like
Whalley, fallen by attainder, and the monks were not felt to present the
same threat as those of Whalley. The Earl of Sussex, therefore, was not
instructed to press the monks to go to other houses, especially as the
example of Whalley had shown that other places were not available; he
was merely instructed to carry through the first process of suppression, the
supervision, finding out what the monks wished to do,[9] and putting the
muniments and valuables in safe keeping.[10] Some of the monks seem to
have asked to go to other houses, and Sussex asked the King on April 6th
for letters to send them to the houses of their choice.[11] But there is the same
sort of ambiguity in the situation as at Whalley. Abbot Pyle and twenty-
nine monks had signed the surrender on April 9th,[12] but although some of
them had asked for transfers, capacities were issued on May 10th for

---

[1] L. & P., xii(1), 706.   [2] F.O.R., 170.
[3] L. & P., xii(1), 621; Duchy Pleadings, ii, 38.
[4] Whalley Act Book, 129, 132, 141, 147, etc.
[5] Valor, v, 229.   [6] L. & P., xii(1), 621.
[7] ibid., 896.   [8] L. & P., xiii(2), 1195.
[9] L. & P., xii(1), 840.   [10] ibid., 896.
[11] ibid., 840.
[12] West, Antiquities, App. X, No. 7.

twenty-nine Furness monks and Friar Legate.[1] On April 11th the King's letter to Sussex said that letters were enclosed to send the monks to other houses,[2] but only two of the monks, Thomas Hornby and Michael Hammerton, and Abbot Pyle, who signed the surrender, did not have dispensations issued for them a month later, and so can be expected to have transferred. Either the letters were not dispatched, as happened at Whalley, or some of the monks changed their minds on transferring. Further, it is by no means certain that Hornby and Hammerton did go to other houses; they did not receive capacities at the suppression of any other house, nor did they sign the surrender of any house. But as for the other monks, it seems likely that no room could be found for them elsewhere, for they were still at Furness, and very disgruntled, early in July, two months after the house had been surrendered.[3]

On May 20th, 1537, a commission was issued to Robert Southwell, the Augmentations solicitor,[4] Sir James Layburne, Thomas Holcroft, and John Assheton, to survey and dissolve Furness Abbey.[5] They arrived at Furness on June 23rd, with the capacities issued on May 10th,[6] to find the monks very discontented, refusing the offer of 20/- each, as a reward, which Southwell thought they had agreed upon with the Earl of Sussex. They presented the Commissioners with a bill of complaints setting out their grievances, especially that they had only surrendered their house in the hope of having their condition improved by the King.[7] Southwell realised the danger of the situation, especially when the monks began murmuring that their surrender was 'rather compulsory than voluntary, and fetched out of them by a politic compulsion'.[8] The Commissioners managed to force a settlement on the monks in front of the local people, by threatening to withhold the capacities they had for them, without which they would be unable to find benefices, and thus persuaded them to agree to take a 'reward' of £2.[9] Southwell refused to give the monks any payment in lieu of wages, and out of their 'reward' they had to buy the clothes of a secular priest, without which they were not allowed to leave the Abbey.[10] The Furness monks, unlike those of all the other larger monasteries which fell by surrender, were not awarded an Augmentations pension; it must have been felt that their behaviour during the Pilgrimage of Grace, though insufficient evidence could be found for prosecution,

---

[1] F.O.R., 97. Though there were no capacities for the two mentioned, the number was kept at the twenty-nine of the surrender by the addition of capacities for two monks who now served benefices, and so would not be at the house to sign the surrender—Michael Thornborough at St. Michael's (V.C.H., vii, 265, see below, Chapter Nine) and Roger Waller at Dalton (*Valor*, v, 272).

[2] L. & P., xii(1), 896.
[3] L. & P., xii(2), 206.
[4] Richardson, op. cit., 42.
[5] P.R.O., SC11/376.
[6] L. & P., xii(2), 206; Beck, op. cit., 356 ff.
[7] ibid.
[8] ibid.
[9] L. & P., xii(2), 206; printed in full, Beck, *Annales*, 356–60.
[10] ibid.

did not entitle them to the royal bounty, so they were sent into the world on the same terms as the monks who had been ejected from the smaller houses nearly six months before. Indeed, their position was more serious than that of the earlier dispossessed religious, for they now had much less chance of securing clerical employment.[1] Southwell, however, was able to make the monks accept their fate by threatening them with the 'goodly experiments that hangeth on each side of York, some in rochets and some in cowls', but to ensure that there would be no trouble he wrote to the gentry of the surrounding area to ask them to keep watch on the ex-monks.[2] The monks were then dispatched with their capacities.

After the departure of the monks, the Commissioners surveyed the lands of the Abbey 'by eye and measure, and not by credit', as Southwell said the 1536 Commissioners had done.[3] As seems to have been done by the surveyors for the Tenth in 1535, Southwell and his colleagues used one of the Abbey's rentals as the basis for their survey, since the figures correspond very closely, and inside the cover of the rental is a note in a different hand that the woods 'need to be well looked at', and that the office of water-bailiff is 'an honest man's living in that country'.[4] They sold off the cattle, first to the local poor and then to the hoards of southerners who had followed them,[5] in an attempt to avoid discontent among the poor and spoliation by the greedy, and sold 240 sheep to three local tenants.[6] The corn on the Abbey demesne was also sold off by the Commissioners.[7] Southwell suggested that small pieces of land should be let to the ex-servants of the house, who were now unemployed, and pleaded that the '72 tall fellows' should be allowed to keep their tenements on Beaumont Grange, to avoid the discontent caused by the high-handed actions of the 1536 Commissioners.[8] The Abbey muniments were packed up and dispatched to London; the receiver's account includes the item, 'paid, for the carriage of three packs of evidences and books of the lands and possessions of the late monastery to London, upon three horses, together with hemp and other packing needed for their safe carriage, £1/15/4d'.[9]

Though he was not named on the Commission, Sir John Lamplieu, a local gentleman who seems to have had some connection with Cromwell,[10] assisted Southwell and his colleagues in the suppression of Furness, at Cromwell's suggestion.[11] Southwell suggested to Cromwell that Lamplieu was a fit person to be put in charge of the site and lands of the Abbey, and for this purpose some of the buildings were left standing for Lamplieu

---

[1] See below, Chapter Nine.
[2] L. & P., xii(2), 206; Beck, loc. cit.
[3] ibid.; P.R.O., SC11/376.
[4] P.R.O., SC12/9/73.
[5] L. & P., xii(2), 206; Beck, loc. cit.
[6] P.R.O., DL29/2505.
[7] ibid.
[8] L. & P., xii(2), 206; Beck, loc. cit.
[9] P.R.O., DL29/2523; *Furness Coucher*, 660.
[10] e.g. L. & P., v, 1317, quoted Elton, *Tudor Revolution*, 428.
[11] L. & P., xii(2), 206; Beck, loc. cit.

to live in.¹ Cromwell was appointed chief steward of the suppressed monasteries north of the Trent,² and in December 1537 instructions were issued to Lamplieu to act as Cromwell's deputy at Furness.³ The deputy's major tasks were to maintain a force at Furness at all times, to maintain equitable justice, to ensure that the clergy preached the royal supremacy, to ensure that excessive fees were not taken, to keep all tenants armed and ready to do the King's service, and to prevent all unlawful assemblies.⁴ Clearly his function was to prevent any recurrence of the circumstances which had contributed to the involvement of the area in the Pilgrimage of Grace. Nothing is known of the effectiveness of Lamplieu's administration, but he began holding, with William Sandys and Thomas Carus, two local gentlemen, the court for the liberty of Furness soon after he took up residence.⁵ Southwell considered Furness a dangerous place,⁶ ostensibly because of the danger of enemy landings there, but the behaviour of the local people in the late rebellion must also have been in his mind. The Commissioners recommended that Peel Castle should be repaired and fortified 'with some small garrison and ordnance',⁷ and Lamplieu took up residence at Furness at the beginning of February 1538 with a force of seven soldiers,⁸ reporting to Cromwell the next month.⁹ Lamplieu's task was evidently thought important, since he was paid a fee of forty marks.¹⁰

Similar precautions were taken on the late Abbey's lands in Lonsdale, where Sir Marmaduke Tunstall was appointed Cromwell's deputy, with the same sort of instructions as were issued to Lamplieu; in particular, Tunstall was given detailed orders on treating the tenants well, taking only those payments which had been made to the Abbey, to avoid further trouble.¹¹ The ex-Abbot, Roger Pyle, was granted Dalton rectory,¹² in lieu of a pension of 100 marks, although he was not left in peaceful occupation for long; Cromwell tried to persuade him to make a lease of it soon after the grant, and when refusing Pyle had to offer the Lord Privy Seal 40/- not to press the point, with the promise of another £4 to follow.¹³ Except for this incident, the suppression of Furness was handled very carefully, and even the difficulties over Pyle's rectory were not the fault of the Augmentations men. Certainly the officials acted more tactfully than had the Duchy men in 1536; the monks were threatened,

---

¹ ibid.
² L. & P., xiv(1), 1355; though Cromwell's appointment is entered in the Augmentation Books under 1539, he had clearly been acting as steward for some time; Lamplieu's appointment is dated December 15th, 1537, and Tunstall must have been appointed about that time or even earlier—L. & P., xii(2), 1216 & xii(1), 881.
³ L. & P., xii(2), 1216. ⁴ ibid.
⁵ Furness Coucher, 664 ff. ⁶ L. & P., xii(2) 206; Beck, Annales, 356-60.
⁷ P.R.O., SC11/376. ⁸ P.R.O., DL29/2523; Furness Coucher, 659.
⁹ L. & P., xiii(1), 427. ¹⁰ P.R.O., DL29/2523; Furness Coucher, 659.
¹¹ L. & P., xii(1), 881. ¹² L. & P., xiii(1), 1520; Furness Coucher, 611.
¹³ L. & P., xiii(1), 67; printed in full, Beck, Annales, 366.

bought, and cajoled into acquiescence, they were given money, though admittedly not very much, even though they had been involved in the rebellion, the Abbot was suitably established, while provision was made for ex-servants, the local people were given pickings from the house, and the pensions granted by the Abbey, including one dated only a month before the suppression, were honoured.[1] In 1540 annuities totalling £126 were paid out from the profits of Furness,[2] even though Pyle had died early in that year and his rectory was no longer being deducted.[3]

The same care is apparent in the suppression of Cockersand, the last of the Lancashire houses, despite some underhand dealings on the part of the monks. Cockersand had been exempted from suppression by letters patent on December 19th, 1536,[4] but continuance was still uncertain, as it was only granted during the King's pleasure. It became clear towards the end of 1537, and certainly in 1538, with the flood of enforced surrenders,[5] that all the religious houses were in danger of dissolution.[6] The canons of Cockersand were therefore able to take advantage of their comparatively late suppression[7] to salvage what they could from their old home, and cushion themselves and their servants against the effects of dispossession. In 1538, therefore, Cockersand granted out a high proportion of its lands on long leases, usually for profitable entry-fines.[8] The lessees were usually local gentry and friends of the house, especially those who had recently given assistance. In September 1538, Sir Robert Hesketh was granted a sixty-one-year lease of certain lands and fisheries, as a reward for his payments towards the cost of repairs to the Abbey.[9] He was also granted a large portion of lands for ninety-nine years, on payment of a fine of twenty marks.[10] In June 1537 the Abbot of Cockersand entered into a bond for £40 with Sir Richard Houghton to appear to answer charges alleged against him.[11] Later in the same year, or early in 1538, a case was heard in the Duchy Court in which Houghton said the Abbot had possession of lands in Lancaster which belonged to the plaintiff,[12] and this was presumably the charge mentioned in the bond. But bonds of this kind were a typical Tudor device for making payments under cover;[13] possibly no offence took place, it was understood that the bond would be forfeit, and the £40 was paid to Houghton.

On the same day as Hesketh's grants, John Kechyn received a ninety-nine-year lease of two manors for a fine of £12;[14] Kechyn, whose family

[1] P.R.O., DL29/2523; *Furness Coucher*, 659–60.
[2] P.R.O., DL29/2525; Mason, op. cit., 135.
[3] P.R.O., DL29/2507; *Furness Coucher*, 653.
[4] L. & P., xi, 1417, printed in full, *Cock. Chart.*, 1087–1092.
[5] D.K.R., viii, App. 2, passim.   [6] Knowles, *Religious Orders*, iii, 351, 353.
[7] January 29th, 1539—L. & P., xiv(1), 163.
[8] *Cock. Chart.*, 1184–1200; Mason, op. cit., 135.   [9] *Cock. Chart.*, 1189.
[10] ibid.   [11] ibid., 1093–4.   [12] P.R.O., DL3/8, H.7.
[13] On this practice, see Elton, *Tudor Revolution*, 162.
[14] *Cock. Chart.*, 1200.

were tenants of the Abbey[1] was a trusted servant of the house, and acted as its receiver.[2] Later in the same month, Sir Thomas Langton paid a fine of 100 marks for a ninety-nine-year lease of the manor of Westhoughton,[3] and this lease was clearly to raise money by the large entry fine. Henry Audley, of St. Albans, who was possibly a relation of the Lord Chancellor, was granted a lease of the manor of Hutton in Leyland.[4] Thomas Burgoyne, who had been a member of the Duchy Commission which had surveyed Cockersand in 1536,[5] and must have been partly responsible for its exemption from suppression, especially by revaluing its income, was granted an eighty-one-year lease of Mitton rectory.[6] Three of the local gentlemen who had acted as guarantors for the payment of the redemption fine in 1536[7] were also rewarded; William Westby[8] and John Rigmaiden[9] were given ninety-nine-year leases, and John Standish was given a lease for seventy-nine years,[10] while the canons profited by the £10 entry fines charged for the two longer leases.

As well as these land grants to prominent men, and the entry fines which they received themselves, the canons also looked after their servants. Twenty-eight annuities, only three of which were dated before 1536, were granted out by the Abbey, most of them to servants; in 1539–40, the Augmentations receiver for Cockersand, John Kechyn, paid out £60 in annuities of this kind.[11] The corrodians of the house also received grants, with 20/– each being given to five of them.[12] In addition, Thomas Kellett, Vicar of Mitton, who was a canon of the house,[13] was granted a pension of twenty marks.[14] Although this is the only example of a grant made to one of the canons of the house, the convent must have taken care of its own interests; in particular, they raised £112 in entry fines[15] which they must have either spent on themselves or perhaps divided up. They were obviously much luckier than the monks dispossessed in 1536 or 1537, who had no warning and so were not able to take any precautions.

But when the Abbey was suppressed, the Augmentations officials must have had the example of 1536 at the back of their minds, to reinforce the policy of Augmentations, which was in any case less rigorous than Duchy practice, for all these grants except one of the leases and one of the annuities were allowed. One may be permitted to doubt if the land-hungry Duchy would have been so lenient. A complaint was made to Sir Richard Rich, the Chancellor of Augmentations,[16] and as a result Sir

---

[1] *Rentale de Cokersand*, Cheth. Soc., Vol. 57, 17.   [2] P.R.O., SC6/7304.
[3] *Cock. Chart.*, 1186–7.   [4] ibid., 1187–8.   [5] P.R.O., DL43/5/4.
[6] *Cock. Chart.*, 1184.   [7] P.R.O., DL41/11/49.   [8] *Cock. Chart.*, 1191–2.
[9] ibid., 1196–7.
[10] ibid., 1195. Standish was Mayor of Lancaster in 1536 (*Corresp.*, 43–7) and had been court steward for Cartmel (*Valor*, v, 272).
[11] P.R.O., SC6/7471, m. 3; Mason, op. cit., 135.   [12] ibid.
[13] C.A.P., ii, 120, 125, 127; *Duchy Pleadings*, i, 107.
[14] *Cock. Chart.*, 1185.
[15] ibid., 1186–7, 1189–92, 1196–7, 1200.   [16] P.R.O., E321/18/29.

Thomas Langton lost Westhoughton. Langton admitted that the usual addition of 100 hens had been left off his rent for the manor, leaving only £55/14/11½d. for him to pay;[1] this was probably done in return for his extremely high entry-fine. The other piece of chicanery which the officials would not allow was Kellett's pension; his dual position as vicar and canon must have emerged, and in any case the pension, double the amount most houses in Lancashire usually paid their vicars, was too high to escape suspicion. Whatever the reason, Kellett's grant was stopped.[2] The other grants escaped unchallenged, though only one of them was given official confirmation; in August 1540 Thomas Burgoyne was given a new lease of Mitton rectory.[3] It was the usual practice of Augmentations to confirm even those leases which had obviously been granted by the monks with an eye on the probable suppression of their houses;[4] this helped to allay the fears caused by secularisation.

Little is known of the actual surrender of Cockersand. The form of surrender was dated January 29th, 1539,[5] but the usual note that the document was confirmed by one of the Vicar-General's officials, Layton, Legh, Peter, London, or Tregonwell, on the same day, was not appended.[6] This probably means that the Cockersand surrender was more genuinely 'voluntary' than many of the others were, and the canons probably hoped to secure better treatment for themselves by taking the initiative and not waiting to be pushed into a surrender by the government. The Abbey was suppressed by Augmentations officials, and John Kechyn, the Abbey's receiver, was brought into help with the process.[7] He was made Augmentations particular receiver for the dissolved Abbey, already holding the same position for General Surveyors at Whalley,[8] and he rendered his first account for 1539–40.[9] No capacities for the canons are given in the 'Faculty Office Register', but they must have been issued, as by this time monks were not allowed to transfer. As they had surrendered to the King their rights as a corporation, and as they could have no choice of transfer, the canons of Cockersand, like those of the other houses dissolved at this time, were adjudged worthy of pensions. In March 1539 these were issued for the Abbot and twenty-one of the twenty-two canons who had signed the surrender,[10] the single omission being James Wainwright, who may have died since the end of January, or perhaps was the holder of a benefice which has not been traced. The three monks who certainly did

---

[1] P.R.O., E321/39/11; E315/93, f. 234v.
[2] *Cock. Chart.*, 1185.   [3] L. & P., xv, 1032.
[4] J. Youings, *Devon Monastic Lands: Calendar of Particulars for Grants, 1536–1558.* Devon and Cornwall Record Society, N.S. Vol. I, p. xii.
[5] D.K.R., viii, App. 2, 16.   [6] Rhymer, *Foedera*, xiv, 635.
[7] P.R.O., SC6/7470, m. 6.
[8] L. & P., xiii(1), 646, g. 50; P.R.O., SC6/7304.
[9] P.R.O., SC6/7471.
[10] L. & P., xiv(1), 1355; E315/233, f. 166; cf. D.K.R., viii, App. 2, 16.

hold benefices, Abraham Clitheroe, who was chantrist at Tunstall,[1] James Dugdale, the Vicar of Garstang,[2] and Thomas Kellett, who was Vicar of Mitton,[3] did not receive pensions. The first year's pensions to the canons cost Augmentations £147.[4] With the final pensioning off of the canons of Cockersand, the last of the regular communities disappeared from Lancashire.

[1] *Valor*, v, 260; P.R.O., DL43/5/4, f. 1; *Lancs Chantries*, ii, 233-4.
[2] *Valor*, v, 263; V.C.H., vii, 297.
[3] *Duchy Pleadings*, i, 107; *Cock. Chart.*, 1185.
[4] P.R.O., SC6/7471, m. 1.

CHAPTER NINE

THE DISPOSSESSED RELIGIOUS
AFTER THE SUPPRESSION

THERE has been some argument among scholars over what happened to the monks after their houses had been dissolved, or, as the problem is often called, the 'fate of the dispossessed religious', a rather melodramatic term which begs the questions at issue. To take the question of pensions first, a far smaller proportion of the Lancashire monks received pensions than in other parts of the country. Of the 119 monks known in the eight houses remaining to be dissolved after the mother houses had withdrawn the monks of Penwortham, Kersall, and Lytham, excluding those who were executed or are known to have fled, only thirty-three are known to have received pensions. These were the four priors and one quondam, of the houses dissolved under the 1536 Act,[1] Abbot Pyle of Furness,[2] four of the five canons of Hornby,[3] Christopher Cromboke, pensioned at Byland, and the Abbot and twenty-one canons of Cockersand.[4] The monks of Holland, Conishead, Cartmel, and Burscough, who were ejected under the 1536 Act, did not receive pensions, in common with all the other monks who left religion in that year. But although there was some justice in not paying pensions to these monks in other counties, as they were given a choice between continuing in religion at another house or taking a capacity and going into the world, as it could be argued that they had left the religious life of their own free will, it was unfair to the Lancashire monks who, as we have seen,[5] were forced into the world without any choice. The monks of Whalley, which fell by attainder, did not receive pensions, as a convent involved in treason could hardly expect compensation for loss of a house which, it was argued, had been forfeited to the King. For the monks of Furness, their failure to be pensioned was again unfair; the monks of all other houses which surrendered received pensions. All these, and Robert Derby of Hornby, did not receive pensions, and the total of 86 out of 119 Lancashire monks unpensioned compares very unfavourably with the figures of 168 unpensioned monks out of 597 found by Hodgett in the diocese of Lincoln.[6] The Lancashire proportion of pensioned to unpensioned of about 1 to 4 is the reverse of the ratio

---

[1] P.R.O., DL42/30, f. 185; DL29/2313, m. 8.   [2] L. & P., xiii(1), 520.
[3] Except for Derby, who left in 1536, the Hornby monks received pensions as canons of Croxton, to which they withdrew to surrender their house—see Chapter Three; L. & P., xiv(1), 1355, p. 598.
[4] L. & P., xiv(1), 1355, p. 602.   [5] See above, Chapter Four.
[6] Hodgett, 'The Unpensioned Ex-religious in Tudor England', J. Eccl. Hist., xiii, 201.

suggested by Hodgett as the national average.[1] The Lancashire monks were therefore much worse off, as a group, than those of other areas. This is partly due to the policy of the Duchy in not allowing, or perhaps being unable to arrange, transfers, and partly due to the involvement of the remaining Lancashire houses in the Pilgrimage of Grace. Baskerville, in seeking to minimise the number of unpensioned religious, points out that 'the monks of attainted abbeys like Whalley were expected to go elsewhere',[2] and so receive pensions on the suppression of their new homes, but, as has been shown,[3] there were no places for the Whalley monks who wished to go to other houses, and only one Whalley monk, Christopher Cromboke, was able to transfer, while the others still had no pensions.

Even those who received pensions were not very well off. The pensions were usually £5, and from this was deducted the clerical tenth, fees of 4d. in the £ to the receiver from whom they were collected, and the expense of collecting them.[4] Baskerville supposed[5] that £5 was an adequate pension, about the sum usually paid to a curate, but as Professor Dickens has pointed out,[6] all Baskerville's reference shows is that in 1538 £5/6/8d. was considered an inadequate payment for a priest to serve a cure.[7] The Lancashire pensioners, however, do appear to have been lucky in the payment of their pensions; when, in 1553, Commissioners in Lancashire enquired into arrears of monastic pensions, the ex-canons of Hornby and Cockersand appeared to swear that they had been paid up to date,[8] in which they were far luckier than their brethren in other counties, where the financial problems of Edward VI's reign had led to a cessation in the payment of pensions.[9]

As Mr. Hodgett found for the diocese of Lincoln,[10] the majority of the ex-monks settled near their former homes. It has already been shown that many of them were local men,[11] so this is hardly surprising, and it does not necessarily indicate any attachment to the sites of their monasteries. As so few of the Lancashire monks were pensioned, the voluminous Augmentation Office records are little use in tracing Lancashire ex-religious, leaving the problem of tracing those who left the county particularly serious. Only two of the Lancashire monks are known to have left the county after the Suppression, but this cannot be taken as a reliable estimate of the number who went elsewhere. William Halliday, the

[1] ibid.   [2] Baskerville, *English Monks and the Suppression*, 255.
[3] See above, Chapter Eight.
[4] Dickens, 'Edwardian Arrears in Augmentations Payments', E.H.R., lv, 415–16.
[5] Baskerville, op. cit., 256.
[6] Dickens, art. cit., 416.   [7] L. & P., xiii(1), 94.
[8] P.R.O., E101/76/17; Dickens, 'Edwardian Arrears in Augmentations Payments', 393, Prof. Dickens is surprised that so few appeared, and regards the Lancashire return as incomplete, forgetting that only these monks received pensions, and that the pensions to the four priors and the quondam were in any case paid by the Duchy.
[9] Dickens, art. cit., passim.
[10] L.R.S., Vol. 53, xi.   [11] See above, Chapter Five.

former prior of Hornby, who was in any case a Croxton canon and probably not a Lancashire man, died at Rothley in Leicestershire in 1555, and seems not to have found employment,[1] and Hugh Brown of Furness was a chaplain in Cambridgeshire in 1542.[2] Of the 119 monks known, excluding those of Penwortham, Kersall, and Lytham, and those who were executed or fled, forty-three have been traced as definitely in Lancashire or adjoining parishes after the fall of their houses. Even those unable to find employment appear to have stayed in the county as a rule, some of them turning to farming small tenements on land formerly held by their houses. Thus John Foster of Whalley had land there soon after the house was dissolved,[3] while Robert Parish, who resigned the vicarage of Whalley in 1537,[4] remained in the parish and died there in 1572.[5] Of the Burscough canons, William Aspinall died in Lancashire poor and unemployed in 1562.[6] Thomas Snell and Giles Bolland, or Taylor, were unbeneficed at Furness in 1542,[7] and do not seem to have obtained benefices later, while Matthew Kirkby of Furness, who did not obtain employment either, was involved in a property dispute at Furness in 1538,[8] and so seems to have held land.

But the most important factor affecting the future well-being of an ex-monk was whether or not he was able to find clerical employment. This was vital to an unpensioned monk, for if he remained unbeneficed he would have to turn to teaching, or work on the land, or depend on temporary clerical positions, or rely on the charity of his neighbours. It was almost as important to a pensioned monk, for his pension would hardly make life comfortable in the early years, and during the price-inflation it would rapidly become insufficient. Analysis of this problem is hindered by the scarcity of sources, especially for Lancashire with such a small proportion of pensioned monks. National records, especially the index to the Composition Books for First-Fruits,[9] have not been found to be useful, mainly because so few ex-monks left the county, and because many appointments were less official ones to curacies and chaplaincies. Local records produced much more useful information, especially as the 'Victoria County History' for Lancashire contains a workmanlike account of most of the presentations to Lancashire benefices, based on the institution records of the diocese of Chester. A number of lists of clergy after the Suppression are also in print, the reports of the chantry Commissioners,[10] and a list of clergy taken soon after the establishment of Chester diocese

[1] L.R.S., Vol. 53, 141.   [2] Beck, *Annales*, App. IX.
[3] *Whalley Coucher*, 1177.   [4] V.C.H., vi, 358.
[5] *Whalley Register*, 142.
[6] *Lancs & Ches. Wills and Inventories*, ii, 55.
[7] They appeared as witnesses in a case in that year—Beck, *Annales*, App. IX.
[8] *Furness Coucher*, 667.   [9] P.R.O., E334/1, 2.
[10] *History of the Chantries*, Reports of the Commissioners, ed. Raines, Cheth. Soc., O.S., Vols. 59 & 60.

in 1541.[1] In addition, a list for 1548 from the visitation Call Books,[2] and the first surviving Visitation Correction Book for the diocese,[3] though not in print, contain almost complete lists of the clergy in Lancashire.

The fate of the ex-monks of the three cells of Penwortham, Lytham, and Kersall, who were withdrawn to their mother houses after 1536 cannot be traced, as they could not be distinguished from their brethren in the suppression lists of the mother houses. In any case, most of them were probably not Lancashire men, and the numbers involved, probably only eight monks, would not materially affect the conclusions. There are five known ex-monks of the cell at Hornby, only three of whom were at the house at any one time, and three of these found positions in parishes in Lancashire. Robert Derby, who left the house in 1536,[4] was a chantry priest at Tunstall by 1548;[5] the rectory had been impropriated to Croxton Abbey,[6] the mother house of Hornby, so perhaps he was given the position by the Abbey when he left religion. John Fletcher and Thomas Edynstow, the two who had signed the surrender in 1538 at Croxton,[7] were also able to gain employment in one of the parishes held by the mother house, occurring as chaplains at Melling in 1548.[8] William Halliday, the former prior, as has been said, died in Leicestershire in 1555, and does not appear to have found employment,[9] but what happened to John Consyll, the last prior, is not known. The canons of Hornby, therefore, were lucky; they were able to take advantage of the impropriations their mother house had in Lancashire, while the two who stayed until 1538 also received pensions at Croxton.[10]

At Burscough, too, the monks were fortunate, mainly because of the impropriations of their house. Two of the seven known monks, Robert Madoke and Roger Mason, were vicars of impropriated benefices even before the Suppression, Madoke at Ormskirk[11] and Mason at Huyton,[12] and they both continued at their posts until their deaths, in 1538[13] and 1557,[14] respectively. Hugh Woodheaver also gained employment at Ormskirk, appearing as a chaplain in 1548[15] and 1554[16] though he had not been there in 1541.[17] Thus only three of the seven monks were left without either pension or position. At Holland, too, the monks were fortunate, although there the house was less well endowed with appropriated churches, and the monks had to look to other means; of the five monks, at least two gained employment. John Ainsdale had to wait until 1546,

[1] Lancs & Ches. Record Society, Vol. 31, Miscellanies No. 11, from C.R.O., EDV2/1.
[2] C.R.O., EDV2/4.   [3] C.R.O., EDV1/1, fos. 31–66v.
[4] See above, Chapter Three.   [5] *Lancs Chantries*, 232–3.
[6] V.C.H., viii, 228.   [7] D.K.R., viii, App. 2, 18.
[8] C.R.O., EDV2/4, f. 28. Both had disappeared by 1554—C.R.O., EDV1/1, f. 48v.
[9] L.R.S., Vol. 53, 141.   [10] L. & P., xiv(1), 1355, p. 598.
[11] *Valor*, v, 223.   [12] ibid., 222.
[13] V.C.H., iii, 244.   [14] ibid., 154; *Lancs & Ches. Wills*, 181.
[15] C.R.O., EDV2/4, f. 3.   [16] C.R.O., EDV1/1, f. 39.
[17] *Clergy List*, 16.

but then he obtained the vicarage of Childwall; in 1531 Holland granted
the next presentation to the Brereton family, but in 1540 they released
their right to the Ainsdales of Wallasey, who presumably hoped to place
John there, who must clearly have been a relation. John had to wait
rather longer than might have been expected, for though Robert Grieves
had held the benefice since 1514, he did not die until 1546, when Ainsdale
finally obtained his position.[1] James Smith of Holland was probably the
man who succeeded Mason as Vicar of Huyton in 1558,[2] though he may
have been the cleric of that name who was Vicar of Kirkham from 1542.[3]
The ex-prior of Holland may have been the Peter Prescot who held a
chantry at Ormskirk in 1548,[4] but this is, perhaps, unlikely as the same
man held the chantry in 1535,[5] before the Suppression. Some priors,
however, did hold benefices 'in commendam' with their priories,[6] and
if the prior and the chantrist were the same person, Prescot must have
been fairly well provided for, since he had a pension from the Duchy,[7]
and pensions were not usually cancelled unless the benefice had been
granted by the Crown.[8] The fact that a former monk of Holland secured
employment at Huyton, which had belonged to Burscough, while the Prior
may have held an Ormskirk chantry, indicates that some sort of arrangement had been made between the two houses, presumably as a safeguard
against the Suppression.

Of the northern houses, the canons of Cartmel are easy to trace, for
four were found guilty of treason and executed,[9] and three others fled
and could not be found.[10] One of these, Eskrigge, fled into Scotland and
became a monk at Holyrood Abbey.[11] The three remaining canons were
all well provided for; the ex-prior, Richard Preston, had his pension,[12]
and was also granted a lease of Cartmel rectory,[13] presumably as a reward
for his loyalty during the Pilgrimage. The other two did not have pensions, but they managed to find employment in the area. Thomas Briggs
became a chaplain at Ulverston,[14] where the rectory had been held by
Conishead,[15] and he must have married, since 'Janet Briggs, wife of Sir
Thomas', was buried at Cartmel in 1593.[16] Brian Willan became curate
of Cartmel some time between 1536 and 1548,[17] and remained there at
least until 1585,[18] two years after his wife died.[19] The Cartmel monks who
survived the rebellion certainly seem to have had no difficulty in accom-

[1] V.C.H., iii, 106.   [2] ibid., 154.
[3] ibid., vii, 147.
[4] Lancs Chantries, 103, 105; C.R.O., EDV2/4, f. 3.   [5] Valor, v, 223.
[6] e.g. the Prior of Lanercost also held the rectory of Halton—Valor, v, 267, 277.
[7] P.R.O., DL42/30, f. 185.   [8] L.R.S., Vol. 53, xvi.
[9] P.R.O., PL26/13/6.   [10] ibid., L. & P., xii(1), 632.
[11] L. & P., xv, 1405, 2, ii, misread as 'Arkwright' in L. & P.
[12] P.R.O., DL42/30, f. 185.   [13] V.C.H., viii, 262.
[14] C.R.O., EDV2/4, f. 30v.   [15] Valor, v, 271.
[16] Cartmel Reg., 135.   [17] C.R.O., EDV2/4, f. 30.
[18] Cartmel Reg., 132.   [19] ibid., 131.

modating themselves to the new conditions, and as Preston, the quondam, still held the farm of Cartmel at least in 1548,[1] they must have formed a small group of friendly colleagues and their life probably changed little. It must certainly have been through Preston that Willan secured his position at Cartmel.

At Conishead, the other Augustinian house north of the Sands, the ex-canons were less fortunate. Of the nine known canons, only two secured clerical employment, and one of these had a pension in any case. Thomas Lord, who had held the vicarage of Orton as prior,[2] retained the benefice, which had been impropriated to his house, after the fall of Conishead,[3] as well as his pension.[4] Christopher Poole may have been curate of Pennington before the Suppression, since it was appropriated to Conishead and was usually served by a canon of the house;[5] he was certainly curate there by 1548, and remained at least until 1562, when he seems to have absented himself from the visitation,[6] presumably to avoid subscribing to the Elizabethan settlement. No other Conishead religious found employment in a Lancashire benefice and, as far as is known, none secured a benefice elsewhere. George Cansforth, the quondam prior, who had resigned on a convent pension,[7] had a pension of £10 from the Duchy,[8] so he was provided for, while it is unreasonable to expect him to have been able to find a position as he was already sixty-eight by the time his house was suppressed.[9]

The next house to be dissolved was Whalley, the second richest of the Lancashire houses, which had four large impropriated parishes in the county,[10] with no less than twenty-five parochial chapelries within these areas, three in Blackburn, three in Eccles-Deane, four in Rochdale, and as many as fifteen in Whalley.[11] Such wide spiritual possessions meant that there were a large number of clerical appointments under the control of the house, so that the monks of the Abbey had a very good chance of securing employment. After the executions of Paslew and Haydock,[12] there were twenty-five known Whalley monks; of these Christopher Cromboke and probably John Estgate transferred to other houses, and have not been traced after that, leaving twenty-three monks in search of employment and without pensions. Of these, twelve were able to find employment within the Church, nine of them in parishes formerly held by the Abbey. When Whalley was suppressed, Christopher Smith, the former prior, asked the Earl of Sussex for permission to remain at Whalley and serve

---

[1] C.R.O., EDV2/4, f. 30.
[2] *Valor*, v, 295; F.O.R., 45.
[3] P.R.O., DL43/5/8.
[4] P.R.O., DL42/30, f. 185.
[5] V.C.H., viii, 341.   [6] ibid.
[7] P.R.O., DL41/11/59, f. 11.
[8] P.R.O., DL29/2313, m. 8.
[9] P.R.O., DL41/11/59, f. 11.
[10] The Abbey's income from them in 1521 was £592—Whitaker, i, 116—though in 1535 it was said to be £272—*Valor*, v, 227.
[11] Tupling, 'Pre-Reformation Parishes and Chapelries', Trans. L. & C. Antiq. Soc., Vol. 67, 12–16.
[12] L. & P., xii(1), 632.

one of the chapels in the parish church, and Sussex passed the request on
to the King.[1] Henry, generous for once in his life, agreed[2] and Sussex
granted Smith a chantry and an income of £6/14/4d., which was to be
paid at Christmas and Easter, as a survey of the lands soon after the
Suppression shows.[3] Smith was also able to collect a number of pieces of
land,[4] which must have left him quite comfortable until his death in
1539.[5] Thomas Horowode and John, or probably Thomas, Lawe, also
secured Whalley chantries;[6] Lawe also had some small plots of land,[7]
and he was buried at Whalley in 1558.[8] Other Whalley monks were also
accommodated within the parish, at the dependent chapels. John, more
probably Thomas, Holden, obtained the curacy of Haslingden chapel,[9]
where he appeared in 1541 and 1548, and which he retained until at
least 1554.[10] Richard Marstyn held the chantry at Burnley either at,
or soon after, the suppression of the Abbey,[11] but he had transferred out
of the parish to the chantry at Ribchester by 1541;[12] he seems to have
been quite happy with his new situation, and he married in 1558.[13]
Some of these must have owed their position to the Vicar of Whalley,
Edward Manchester, or Pedley, whose career has already been discussed.[14] The new vicar was presented by Whalley Abbey in 1537, on
the resignation of Robert Parish, also a monk of the house,[15] so this
must have been in January or February, when it was clear the house
was likely to be attacked. It must have been a calculated move, for
Parish had only been put into the vicarage in 1535,[16] and as he did not
die until 1572[17] his resignation cannot have been because of old age.
Either Parish was only given the vicarage while Pedley was at Oxford,
or Pedley was given the vicarage when it seemed likely the Abbey would
come under attack, so that control of it would not be lost through any
argument by the authorities that its vicar had been involved in the
Pilgrimage. The hope may have been that Pedley would use his new
position to provide for some of the monks when the house was dissolved;
in any case, he must have done this, and nine of the monks held positions
in his parish at one time or another. Pedley retained his position as vicar
until his death in 1558, when he was described in the parish register as
'Edwardus Pedley, vicarius ville de Whalley, et bacularius in divinitate
et egregius predicator'.[18]
    Ralph Lynney was promoted by the Abbot from receiver[19] to vicar of

[1] L. & P., xii(1), 840.   [2] ibid., 896.
[3] Whalley Coucher, 1184–90.   [4] ibid.; ibid., 1201, 1204.
[5] Whalley Reg., 105.   [6] Whitaker, i, 115.
[7] Whalley Coucher, 1177 & 1208.   [8] Whalley Reg., 126.
[9] Whitaker, i, 115.
[10] Clergy List, 18; Lancs Chantries, 265; C.R.O., EDVi/1, f. 36.
[11] V.C.H., vi, 452.   [12] Clergy List, 18.
[13] Whalley Reg., 87.   [14] See above, Chapter Eight.
[15] V.C.H., vi, 358.   [16] ibid.   [17] Whalley Reg., 142.
[18] Whalley Reg., 127.   [19] Valor, v, 229.

the impropriated church of Blackburn in 1536.[1] Despite some involvement in the rebellion,[2] he retained his position until 1555, when he
resigned on a pension[3] and went to act as private chaplain to Sir John
Byron,[4] a violently Catholic local gentleman.[5] Richard Wood was chaplain at Great Harwood in Blackburn parish at least in 1535;[6] he remained
there as curate at least until 1554,[7] and was buried at his chapel in 1560.[8]
It was presumably Lynney who secured Thomas Blackburn his appointment as chaplain at Blackburn some time before 1541,[9] but despite the
extent of the parish only these three found employment in it. Only three
ex-monks of Whalley found employment outside the Abbey's impropriated
benefices, which illustrates how important the spiritual possessions of a
house were for the future of its ejected members. James More, who had
been the Abbey's last kitchener,[10] obtained a curacy at Ribchester by
1548, and he was there again in 1554.[11] Ralph Catterall went just outside
the county to find his position, and was a chaplain at Ince in Chester
Deanery by 1541.[12] The last of the Whalley monks known to have found
clerical employment, John Chester, the former bursar,[13] was a stipendiary
priest at Leyland by 1541.[14] The ex-religious of Whalley, with twelve of
the twenty-three available for employment finding it, were extraordin-
arily lucky. Their house was dissolved six months after the smaller houses,
by which time almost all the vacant places in Lancashire parishes must
have been filled up by the monks ejected in 1536. Their success in finding
positions must be put down, therefore, to the large number of clerical
appointments under the control of the house within the impropriated
parishes. Others would not be quite so fortunate, and the monks' dependence on impropriated benefices is further demonstrated by the fact that
three, and probably four, of the twelve did not find positions after the
Suppression, but merely continued to hold positions to which they had
been appointed by the Abbot before the fall of the house.

The monks of Furness were among those who were not so lucky.
Though the Abbey had three impropriated rectories, these would not
go far to provide employment for a large house, especially as only two
chapels are known within these parishes, both of them in Dalton.[15] Abbot
Pyle was well provided for, with a lease of the rectory of Dalton,[16] which
he retained until his death.[17] This leaves thirty-eight known monks; of

[1] V.C.H., vi, 241.
[2] See above, Chapter Six.
[3] V.C.H., vi, 241.
[4] Whitaker, ii, 312.
[5] See his will, printed in *Lancs Chantries*, i, 14.
[6] *Valor*, v, 230.
[7] C.R.O. EDVI/1, f. 34.
[8] *Great Harwood Reg.*, 285.
[9] *Clergy List*, 18.
[10] Whitaker, i, 188.
[11] V.C.H., vii, 44; C.R.O., EDVI/1, f. 45v.
[12] *Clergy List*, 2.
[13] Whitaker, i, 114.
[14] *Clergy List*, 17.
[15] Tupling, art. cit., 12–16.
[16] West, *Antiquities*, 173; L. & P., xiii(2), 583.
[17] *Furness Coucher*, 653; *Richmond Wills*, Surtees Society, Vol. 26, 21.

I

these, Henry Salley and John Broughton were imprisoned,[1] Michael Hammerton and Thomas Hornby probably transferred,[2] and James Proctor had a dispensation to serve a cure in 1535,[3] and disappears after that. There were therefore thirty-three ex-monks of Furness, with no pensions, who needed employment; only six of these found positions, and four of these were merely continuing in benefices they had held before the Suppression.

Thomas Hartley was presented to the Abbey's church at Urswick in April 1536,[4] which he held until his death in 1547.[5] Roger Waller was Vicar of Dalton by 1535,[6] and he remained there probably until 1551.[7] In April 1537, just after the surrender of Furness, Edmund Stanford, Vicar of Millom, one of the Abbey's impropriated churches, in Cumberland, paid £4 for a special licence to continue to wear his habit under the dress of a secular priest;[8] he had been Vicar of Millom in 1535,[9] and he presumably continued there after the Suppression. The other Furness monk who retained a benefice after the Suppression was Richard Banke, who had given the Abbot so much trouble in 1533 and had been packed off to look after the Abbey's church in the Isle of Man;[10] he was paid a fee of £6/13/4d. for this by the Abbey,[11] and as Augmentations continued to pay this after the Abbey was dissolved,[12] presumably Banke continued to serve the cure. Only two monks of the house managed to secure new positions after the Suppression. Michael Thornborough was lucky enough to secure employment in the same year as his house was suppressed, and was presented to the vicarage of St. Michael's-on-Wyre by Battlefield College.[13] It is not clear why Battlefield should have presented him; though he received a capacity as a monk of Furness,[14] he was away when the surrender was signed,[15] so perhaps he had gone to Shrewsbury to persuade the College to present him to the vacant vicarage. The only other Furness monk to secure a clerical position was Hugh Brown, who was, in 1542 when he was called as a witness in the Proctor-Earl of Cumberland case,[16] a chaplain in Cambridgeshire.[17]

Furness is an apt illustration of the importance of impropriated benefices for the future of the monks. The impropriations a house held might be occupied by one of the religious, who would naturally retain the vicarage when his house was suppressed, and he might then be able to use his position to provide employment for fellow ex-religious if there were chaplaincies or chantries within the parish. Even if the impropriations

[1] See above, Chapter Seven.
[2] See above, Chapter Four.
[3] F.O.R., 21.
[4] F.O.R., 53.
[5] V.C.H., viii, 337.
[6] Valor, v, 272.
[7] V.C.H., viii, 316.
[8] F.O.R., 94.
[9] Valor, v, 267.
[10] See above, Chapter One.
[11] P.R.O., SC12/9/73.
[12] P.R.O., DL29/2523.
[13] V.C.H., vii, 265.
[14] F.O.R., 97.
[15] West, Antiquities, App. X, No. 7.
[16] See above, Chapter One.
[17] Beck, Annales, App. IX.

were not held by a monk of the monastery, the incumbent would probably be on good terms with the monks, and willing to help them when their positions were insecure. At Furness, four of the six monks able to find employment, did so in the impropriated benefices of the house, the three in England, and one in the Isle of Man. But six employed out of a total of thirty-three available is very poor, and shows how much more difficult it had become to find positions by 1537, after the vacancies had been filled up by the ejected religious of 1536. Half the monks of Whalley found employment because of the large number of chantries and chapels within its impropriated parishes, but the monks of Furness were less lucky because they had no such reserve of available positions, and there were few chapels within their parishes.

The monks of Cockersand, leaving religion in 1539, had the hardest time of all. Although they had pensions, there must have been a glut of clergy on the employment market by 1539, and few of them were able to find positions. Of the twenty-two monks pensioned,[1] only one found a position. In 1538 Cockersand granted the next presentation to their impropriated benefice of Garstang to John Kechyn,[2] an old friend and servant of the house.[3] Kechyn, naturally, would be willing to do what he could for the monks, by appointing one of them to the vicarage, and in view of the canons' obvious care for their future[4] it is quite likely that the presentation was granted so that one of the canons would be sure of an appointment when the house was surrendered. Thus in 1545, when the last incumbent finally died, Kechyn presented Richard Preston to the vicarage, where he remained until his death in 1559.[5] At least three other canons did not receive pensions, and this was because they were already beneficed; they continued to hold their positions after the Suppression. Abraham Clitheroe was cantarist at Thurland in 1535,[6] and was still there when the Commissioners surveyed Cockersand in 1536;[7] he retained his office, and was still there in 1548.[8] James Dugdale was Vicar of Garstang in 1535,[9] and remained so until his death in 1545.[10] Thomas Kellett, canon, was vicar of another of Cockersand's impropriations, Mitton in Yorkshire, in 1521–2,[11] and he retained his vicarage after the fall of Cockersand.[12]

Thus of the four Cockersand canons employed in clerical positions after the Suppression, three were merely continuing in positions they already held, and all four were accommodated in impropriations. The Augmentations officials seem to have followed the policy of not pensioning those canons with benefices, and as one other canon who signed the surrender,[13]

[1] L. & P., xiv(1), 1355.   [2] V.C.H., vii, 297.
[3] See above, Chapter Eight.   [4] ibid.
[5] V.C.H., vi, 297.   [6] Valor, v, 260.
[7] P.R.O., DL43/5/4, f. 1.   [8] Lancs Chantries, 233–4.
[9] Valor, v, 263.   [10] V.C.H., vii, 297.   [11] Duchy Pleadings, i, 107.
[12] Cock. Chart., 1185; B.I.Y., R/I/29, Reg. Holgate, f. 78v.
[13] Cock. Chart., 1153–4.

James Wainwright, was not pensioned, he too may have been beneficed. But he has not been traced to a benefice in national or local records, the possibility remains that he died between the surrender at the end of January[1] and the issue of pensions in the middle of March.[2] John Preston, who held the chantry of Middleton, to which the Abbey presented, in 1536[3] was pensioned,[4] so he must have lost the chantry by the Suppression, and he certainly did not hold it by 1548.[5]

Thus of twenty-six known canons of Cockersand, only four secured employment after the suppression of their house. The Cockersand monks were particularly unfortunate. Although they had their pensions, they were the last of the Lancashire monks to leave religion, and by the time they were on the employment market there could have been no vacancies at all. They were therefore entirely dependent on the Abbey's impropriations, but the house held only two rectories, Garstang and Mitton, both small,[6] and the presentation to two chantries. The positions in these benefices would not go far amongst twenty-six monks. The three monks who already had benefices, though they had no pensions, were much more fortunate than the others; of the twenty-three canons unbeneficed at the Suppression, only one ever found employment, and that was in one of the impropriations, for which an arrangement had been made. The difficulty of the clerical labour market by 1539 is shown by the fact that none of the monks were able to find employment outside the impropriated benefices of the Abbey.

Excluding all those who transferred, were executed, imprisoned, or fled, or had left their houses before they were suppressed, there were 108 Lancashire monks ejected from their houses and seeking employment, and young enough to expect to gain it; of these thirty-seven, or 34·1%, were able to find positions at some stage in their careers. But this average hides significant variations. Of the monks ejected in 1536 and available for employment, eleven out of twenty-two, exactly half, secured employment; the labour market must have been quite easy at this stage. Fifty-seven monks, who were not executed or imprisoned or allowed to go to other houses, were ejected from Furness and Whalley in 1537; of these, eighteen, or 31·6%, found employment.[7] This left thirty-one canons of Hornby and Cockersand, of whom only six, or 19·4%, found employment. These figures show how it became increasingly more difficult for the ex-religious to find employment as vacancies were filled, and even the large number of appointments within Whalley Abbey's impropriations did not prevent a sharp decline in the proportion who found posi-

[1] *Cock. Chart.*, 1153–4.
[2] L. & P., xiv(1), 1355.
[3] P.R.O., DL43/5/4, f. 1.
[4] L. & P., xiv(1), 1355.
[5] *Lancs Chantries*, i, 120.
[6] In 1535 the Abbey's revenue from these was only £45—*Valor*, v, 261.
[7] These figures include life-grants of rectories, where the new rector was resident, mong the positions obtained.

tions in the six months between the fall of the lesser houses and the suppression of Whalley and Furness.

The most significant figure is that for the proportion of unpensioned monks who were unable to find employment. There were seventy-nine unpensioned ex-monks available for employment, the monks of the four priories, Whalley, and Furness who survived and were young enough to expect employment, Derby of Hornby who left without a pension, and the four unpensioned monks of Cockersand; of these, thirty, or 37·9%, were able to find positions. This left 62·1% who could have worked, but were unable to find the opportunity, forty-nine monks who had no pensions and no employment. For them, life must have been hard, and many must have been entirely dependent on the charity of their neighbours. But although a large proportion of the Lancashire ex-monks were left without any known income, they were not nearly as badly off as those in other areas. Mr. Hodgett calculated[1] that in the diocese of Lincoln only eight out of 168 unpensioned ex-monks were able to find employment. The Lancashire monks were fortunate because of the comparatively small number of ex-religious in the county. There were probably about 130 monks in Lancashire in 1536,[2] including all eleven houses and cells, but in the diocese of Lincoln, which covered Lincoln, Leicester, Huntingdon, Bedford, Buckingham, and part of Hertfordshire,[3] there were 597 monks known to have left religion between 1536 and 1540.[4] Where the ex-monks formed a small part of the population, as they did in Lancashire, they would have a much better chance of finding employment. The Lancashire ex-monks also seem to have been more fortunate than their brethren over the country as a whole. Although the accuracy of his method of calculation must be doubted,[5] Mr. Hodgett suggested

[1] Hodgett, 'The Unpensioned Ex-religious', J. Eccl. Hist., xiii, 201–2.
[2] 132 left religion in all—two were at Cockersand only after 1536.
[3] L.R.S., Vol. 53, xi.   [4] Hodgett, art. cit., 201.
[5] The contrast between Lancashire and the rest of England and Wales is too glaring to be possible. Mr. Hodgett used the 'Faculty Office Register' to calculate the number of unpensioned religious, but he then assumes that all those who did not receive pensions were available for employment, comparing the number he found in employment with the number who received capacities. But not all monks would be available for positions—the aged monk at Holland was said to be too old even to go out into the world; at least one monk who had a capacity then went to another house and was eventually pensioned; most clearly of all, four of the nine canons of Cartmel were executed, and three others had to flee for their lives, so the two who did not receive capacities yet found employment represent 100% employment, and not two out of nine. Further, in using the Register, Mr. Hodgett omits those monks, of whom there were at least ten in Lancashire, who were already serving cures away from their houses, did not receive capacities because of their absence, yet who continued in employment after the Suppression—these men would make some difference to the picture. Lastly, Mr. Hodgett based his calculations on admittedly inadequate sources—art. cit., 196—but hazarded the opinion that more detailed study would make little difference to his conclusions—art. cit., 202—and this assumption must be seriously questioned. In treating the problem nationally Mr. Hodgett had to rely on sources which did not cover even all the rectories and vicarages adequately, and the host of chantries and chaplaincies were not represented at all in his calculations. Because of the size of the problem involved in tracing the fate of the ex-religious of all

that of 2,016 unpensioned male ex-religious, only about fifty found employment.[1] This figure includes the friars, but even if the nineteen known ex-friars of Lancashire,[2] only one of whom, John Carlisle of Warrington, found employment,[3] are included, thirty-one out of ninety-eight, or 31·6%, were able to find positions. Reliance on Hodgett's figures obscures the true picture, but this 31·6% is vastly greater than a suggested national figure of 2·4%, and even if more intensive study increases the average for the country as a whole, it still seems likely that the Lancashire monks will remain considerably better off.

Paradoxically, an unpensioned Lancashire monk may have stood a better chance of a reasonably comfortable future than a pensioned. There were thirty-one pensioned ex-monks available for employment, twenty-two Cockersand canons, four canons pensioned at Hornby, four priors, and Abbot Pyle;[4] of these, only seven, or 22·6% were able to find employment, compared with the 37·9% of the unpensioned able to find positions. This is in striking contrast to the figure of 52% of the pensioned religious in the diocese of Lincoln who were able to secure clerical positions.[5] The high Lincoln figure seems curious, for, as we have seen, employment became increasingly scarce as vacancies were filled up. In Lancashire the low proportion of pensioned monks later found in employment is certainly due to the fact that these monks left religion in 1538 and 1539, when there must already have been a surplus of clergy in the county.

If one factor in whether a monk was able to find a clerical position or not was the date of the suppression of his house, the other was the number of clerical appointments his house had controlled. Of the thirty-seven monks who have been traced in positions after the suppression of their monasteries, twenty-eight of these appointments were within parishes which had been impropriated to the convent of which each ex-monk had been a member. A further four appointments were in parishes where the advowson had been held by Lancashire monasteries other than the ex-monk's own, and in which some sort of arrangement is possible. Another one appointment was to a benefice held by a college in Shropshire, which is not far away. Thus, of the thirty-seven appointments, thirty-three were in parishes which had been impropriated to religious houses in the area. The importance of impropriations is illustrated by the case of the friars, though they are not included within the scope of this

England and Wales, Mr. Hodgett could not hope to do the detailed work required to give realistic results, and the present study shows that more intensive local study would materially affect his conclusions.
[1] Hodgett, 'The Unpensioned Ex-religious', J. Eccl. Hist., xiii, 201.
[2] Ten from Preston—F.O.R., 196—and nine from Warrington—F.O.R., 199.
[3] *History of Warrington Friary*, Chetham Miscellanies, IV, 71.
[4] Pyle is included because he was given a pension of 100 marks for which he was then given Dalton—L. & P., xiii(1), 1520; P.R.O., E315/232/11, f. 2.
[5] Hodgett, art. cit., 202.

essay. Friaries had no impropriations, and the friars were therefore entirely dependent on the good-will of outsiders for their future employment; only one of the nineteen who are known has been traced in clerical employment. Lastly, of the monks found in employment, eleven, and probably twelve, were merely continuing in positions in impropriations which they had held before the Suppression. If the Lancashire monks were not badly off after the Suppression, it was not because they were well pensioned or because the Crown provided for them, but because their monasteries had been well endowed with rectories and they were able to use this to cushion themselves against the worst effects of the Suppression, and save themselves from the poverty which befell the less fortunate of their brethren in other counties. Almost two-thirds of the Lancashire monks found themselves with neither pension nor benefice, but even this was a lower proportion than seems to have been true in other areas. It was perhaps only just that the monks should have been assimilated so much more easily into a society in which they had played such an important part.

CHAPTER TEN

THE PROFITS OF THE SUPPRESSION: THE NEW MONASTICS[1]

THE dissolution of the monasteries transferred a large block of land to the Crown, to the newly established Court of Augmentations and, in Lancashire, to the Duchy of Lancaster. The Duchy was an old-established government department, which had been administering its estates for the Crown since the Duchy lands passed to the royal house in 1399, and so was perhaps less likely to alienate lands than the new office. It has already been suggested that in 1536 the Duchy Commissioners were eager to secure as much land as possible, and thus augment the decreasing Duchy revenues.[2] When all the Lancashire monasteries suppressed after this date went to Augmentations or General Surveyors, the officials of the Duchy must have drawn attention to the increasing weakness of the Duchy as a complex of Crown estates, since in 1540 Furness was put under the Duchy organisation by Act of Parliament,[3] and the Act making the transfer expressed a determination to maintain the revenues of the department. The Duchy, therefore, would be unwilling to sell much of the recently acquired monastic land, and it was presumably the fact that the Duchy received about 40% of the monastic lands in Lancashire[4] which kept the sales of lands by 1558 down to 45%.[5] This is much lower than the 70% which Dr. Youings found for Devon,[6] and Dr. Savine's calculation that two-thirds of the secularised lands had been sold off by 1547.[7]

This does not mean, however, that the gentry of Lancashire were not able to acquire lands, for though a smaller proportion was sold in Lancashire than in other areas, much more of it than was usual went to local men. Thirty-four grants from the lands of the eleven religious houses have been studied;[8] these grants were made to twenty-three men, only nine of

---

[1] This chapter is not intended to be a detailed analysis of the technicalities and terms of sales and leases, or an exhaustive catalogue of grants, which would be more appropriate to a study of the monastic economy, and which have already been provided by R. J. Mason, *The Income, Administration, and Disposal of Monastic Land in Lancashire*, unpublished thesis, University of London, 1962. Instead, it attempts to provide an account of the men who replaced the monks as landlords, and of how they obtained their grants, by considering the grants, calendered in L. & P. and in C.P.R., Edward VI and Philip and Mary, from the lands of the Lancashire houses.

[2] See above, Chapter Four.   [3] 32 Henry VIII, c. 57.

[4] Mason, op. cit., 166.   [5] ibid., 146.

[6] 'The Terms of the Disposal of the Devon Monastic Lands, 1536–1558', E.H.R. Vol. 69 (1954), 37; *Devon Monastic Lands: Calendar of Particulars for Grants, 1536–1558*, Devon and Cornwall Record Soc., N.S. Vol. I, p. xx.

[7] In H.A.L. Fisher, *Political History of England*, v, App. 2.

[8] See Appendix B.

whom, often those with the smallest pieces of land, were not Lancashire men. Soon after the suppression of its parent house, the site and lands of the cell of Kersall were sold to Baldwin Willoughby, sewer of the King's Chamber.[1] A number of sales of Cockersand lands were made to outsiders, including Richard Steven[2] and Anthony Brown,[3] both members of the Household and so with considerable influence in Court circles. In May 1545 James Brown of London, a haberdasher, purchased the manor of Westhoughton, late of Cockersand,[4] of which he had already secured a lease.[5] Also from Cockersand, Laurence Rowsthorne, of Old Windsor in Berkshire, bought the manor of Hutton in March 1546.[6] John Benson, a Westmorland clothier, bought lands in Grasmere, which had belonged to Conishead, in January 1545.[7] These purchases, by established merchants, were probably for investment, but there were three cases in which lands from Lancashire houses were included in large speculative purchases by merchants of property all over the country. In March 1545 Henry Audley of St. Albans bought Humphreyhead in Cartmel,[8] Richard Pymonde, who had already made large purchases,[9] bought lands from Cockersand,[10] and a partnership between John Bellow of Grimsby and John Broxholme of London purchased Whalley lands in Wigan in November 1546.[11] Bellow and Broxholme were speculators on a considerable scale, and made four large purchases of widely scattered lands,[12] while Bellow was involved in another three purchases with different partners.[13] But the most fortunate man of all was Sir William Paget, an important Privy Councillor, who in 1547 was given a free grant of the sites and lands of the priories of Burscough and Conishead,[14] though soon after this he was given a licence to sell Conishead to John Machell, a London clothier.[15] Paget was the only man to receive a free grant of monastic lands in Lancashire, though Thomas and John Holcroft did receive reductions in the purchase price of their lands, as rewards for their services to the Crown. But the majority of the non-Lancashire grantees were either merchants seeking profits, or courtiers able to use their influence to obtain lands.

A similar picture emerges from a consideration of leases of monastic lands.[16] Twenty-two leases have been considered, and only five of these were made to non-Lancashire men. In 1542, after the cancellation of Sir

[1] L. & P., xv, 942, g. 102; Dugdale, *Monasticon*, v, 110.
[2] L. & P., xxi(2), 476, g. 55; D.K.R., x, App. 2, 277.
[3] C.P.R., Edward VI, iv, 168.
[4] L. & P., xx(1), 846, g. 76; D.K.R., ix, App. 2, 179.
[5] L. & P., xvii, 1258.
[6] L. & P., xxi(1), 504, g. 16; D.K.R., x, App. 2, 263.
[7] L. & P., xx(1), 1081, g. 6; D.K.R., x, App. 2, 170.
[8] L. & P., xx(1), 465, g. 99; D.K.R., ix, App. 2, 160.
[9] D.K.R., x, App. 2, 257.
[10] ibid.; L. & P., xix(2), 257, g. 48.
[11] L. & P., xxi(2), 476, g. 96.
[12] D.K.R., ix, App. 2, 168-70.
[13] ibid., 167-8, 170.
[14] P.R.O., DL42/23, fos. 10-12.
[15] C.P.R., Edward VI, i, 144.
[16] See Appendix C.

Thomas Langton's lease,[1] the manor of Westhoughton was farmed out to James Brown,[2] as has been said. Thomas Cromwell, Lord Privy Seal and the architect of the Suppression, was granted a lease of the site of Furness Abbey and its lands in Dalton in 1539,[3] but this did not last for long as Cromwell was executed in the following year. The lease was then given to Sir Thomas Curwen,[4] who, as a Cumberland J.P.[5] and a steward at Furness,[6] was almost a local man. The only other two leases given outside the county were minor matters, a fishery near Lancaster to John Aylyf, the King's surgeon,[7] and a small piece of land in Colton to John Booth of the royal household,[8] both from the lands of Furness.

This leaves forty grants or leases made to Lancashire men between the fall of the monasteries and the death of Mary. The benefits of the transfer were, however, concentrated in only a few hands; the seventeen leases were given to fourteen men, the twenty-three sales were to fourteen men, and the total benefits were divided between only twenty-four men. Assuming that they would not have made purchases or taken up leases unless these were, at least in the long term, financially rewarding, these men formed the select group which profited from the Suppression and replaced the monks as landlords.

The most important of the 'new monastics' was Thomas Holcroft, who secured four purchases and two leases from the lands of the Lancashire houses alone. When Cartmel was suppressed, Holcroft was given an immediate lease of the site and lands,[9] and four years later he bought the site and part of the lands from the Duchy,[10] though in 1545 he exchanged these with the King for lands in Cheshire from Vale Royal.[11] In March 1540 he was given a lease of Whalley's lands at Billington,[12] and he made two purchases of land from the Abbey, in May 1540,[13] and September 1546.[14] Finally, Holcroft bought Lytham Priory from Queen Mary in 1554.[15] Holcroft was more successful in acquiring lands than anyone else in Lancashire because he was in the best position to do so, with considerable influence in both local and governmental circles. He was a member of the Earl of Derby's unofficial local council in the 1530's,[16] and he began his career in London as an esquire of the body to the King, perhaps under Derby's patronage.[17] Henry VIII used Holcroft in Scottish affairs,[18] in

[1] See above, Chapter Eight.
[2] L. & P., xvii, 1258.
[3] L. & P., xv, 1032.
[4] ibid., xvi, 1500.
[5] ibid., 305, g. 29.
[6] R. Somerville, History of the Duchy of Lancaster, 510.
[7] L. & P., xiii(1), 1520.
[8] ibid.
[9] P.R.O., DL29/2228.
[10] L. & P., xvi, 305, g. 56.
[11] ibid., xx(2), 266, g. 1.
[12] L. & P., xv, 436, g. 68.
[13] ibid., 611, g. 31.
[14] ibid., xvi(2), 200, g. 1.
[15] C.P.R., Philip and Mary, i, 500-1.
[16] Corresp., 10.
[17] J. B. Watson, 'The Lancashire Gentry and the Public Service, 1529-1558', Trans. L. & C. Antiq. Soc., Vol. 73, 48.
[18] L. & P., xx(1), 857, 2.

which he was able to secure the patronage of the Earl of Hertford,[1] who, as Protector Somerset, later used him in the campaigns against the Scots.[2] The fall of Somerset involved Holcroft in momentary difficulties, and he was sent to the Tower,[3] but he was back in favour again when Mary became Queen, with the rank of Knight Marshall and an important part to play in the trials following Wyatt's rebellion.[4] A royal servant of such importance would have the influence necessary to secure grants, especially as Holcroft's involvement in the Lancashire Suppression[5] would have made him familiar both with monastic lands in the county and with the procedures of Augmentations and the Duchy. He was therefore able to obtain not only the property which has been mentioned, but also Vale Royal Abbey in Cheshire,[6] the friaries of Preston, Lancaster, and Warrington,[7] and a lease of the attainted land of Sir Stephen Hammerton.[8] Holcroft was not an 'average' new monastic of Lancashire, for his opportunities and achievements were greater than those of the others, but he illustrates, in a magnified form, the characteristics of most of the grantees; they were men with connections in Lancashire and at Court, who served the government in a host of minor capacities, and were able to use their positions and their knowledge for personal gain.

A lesser man, whose rise was equally spectacular, was John Braddyll. He began his career as a servant of Thomas Sherburne, who died in 1536 during his term of office as sheriff of the county.[9] After Sherburne's death, Braddyll, who throughout his life was always quick to spot a good opportunity, transferred himself to the service of Thomas Holcroft,[10] and acted as his deputy in the Duchy receivership for Lancashire and Cheshire.[11] In Holcroft's service, his advance was sure; he was made bailiff of Whalley when the house was suppressed,[12] he became a J.P. and was able to extend his influence in the county by frequent attendance at the quarter sessions,[13] and his new position enabled him to acquire considerable portions of land. Braddyll seems to have taken some time to accumulate capital, and his purchases did not begin until 1542, when he bought some of Whalley's land from Robert Holt.[14] As yet, he was not of sufficient stature and importance to secure grants directly from the government, and his next purchase was also from an earlier grantee, with more Whalley land from Richard Crimbleholme in May 1544.[15] Thereafter, Braddyll was able to make purchases from the government himself, with lands in Clayton, Downham, and Little Harwood from Whalley, and rents and services

[1] ibid., (2), 160.
[2] C.S.P.D., Addenda, 1547–65, 377, 379, 381–2, 383, 395; A.P.C., ii, 234, iii, 89.
[3] A.P.C., iv, 78, 82, 84.   [4] C.P.R., Philip and Mary, ii, 94; iii, 125.
[5] e.g. P.R.O., SC11/376.   [6] L. & P., xix(1), 278, g. 22.
[7] L. & P., xv, 831, g. 43; D.K.R., ix, App. 2, 230.
[8] L. & P., xvi, 305, g. 74.   [9] Watson, art. cit., 18.
[10] L. & C. Wills, ii, 106 f.   [11] Watson, art. cit., 25.
[12] L. & P., xvi, 611, g. 13.   [13] Watson, art. cit., Appendix A.
[14] L. & P., xvii, 361, g. 12.   [15] L. & P., xix(1), 610, g. 116.

from Cockersand in March 1545,[1] more Whalley lands in May of that year,[2] more rents in the Little Harwood area,[3] and finally, in partnership with Richard Assheton, the site and remaining lands of Whalley in 1553.[4] A partition was arranged between the two men, in which Assheton took the site and Braddyll the bulk of the lands.

Although he kept a sizeable block of lands, Braddyll seems to have learned the lesson of his own earlier purchases, that those who could not buy from the government might take smaller pieces of land from the grantees. He was therefore able to amass a not inconsiderable fortune, 'by reason of buying and selling of lands that I bought of King Henry VIII'.[5] His dealings were not confined to Lancashire monasteries, for he bought, and presumably resold, part of the Lancashire lands of Pontefract and lands in Kent and Yorkshire that had belonged to Thomas Wyatt and Stephen Hammerton,[6] a block of lands in Yorkshire which Kirkstall Abbey had held,[7] the Yorkshire lands of the order of St. John of Jerusalem,[8] and lands in Lancashire and Cheshire from Norton, Vale Royal, and Monkbretton.[9] Braddyll's traffickings give the impression that he was a grasping and unscrupulous speculator, but he seems to have been a quiet and inoffensive man, only rarely involved in litigation,[10] a pious and very old-fashioned Catholic,[11] a landlord who regarded his lands and wealth as a trust from God,[12] and, as far as a Lancashire gentleman ever could be, a man of some culture.[13]

John Kechyn made his gains not through the influence of patrons, as did Holcroft and Braddyll, but by the painstaking accumulation of a number of lesser, but strategically placed, offices, which enabled him to snap up lands. In 1501 his family was among the less important tenants of Cockersand Abbey,[14] and Kechyn was able to secure the position of receiver-general to the Abbey.[15] He assisted with the suppression of the house,[16] and his experience enabled him to acquire the receivership of Cockersand from Augmentations,[17] and that of Whalley from General Surveyors.[18] Few could have been in better positions for securing grants; he obtained a lease of Cockersand lands, and three from the lands of Whalley,[19] and in Septem-

[1] L. & P., xx(1), 465, g. 64; D.K.R., ix, App. 2, 174.
[2] ibid.; L. & P., xx(1), 846, g. 75.   [3] D.K.R., ix, App. 2, 174.
[4] C.P.R., Edward VI, v, 80–1; *Whalley Coucher*, 1175.
[5] *L. & C. Wills*, ii, 106 f.   [6] L. & P., xx(1), 465, g. 64.
[7] ibid., 846, g. 75.   [8] ibid., (2), 1383, g. 66.
[9] ibid.
[10] In 1554 (*Ducatus Lancastriae*, i, 275), and in 1560 (ibid., 232).
[11] *Lord Burghley's Map of Lancashire*, Catholic Record Society, Miscellanea, Vol. IV, 183; *L. & C. Wills*, ii, 106 f.
[12] ibid.
[13] In his will he left chronicles, statutes, and other books, including 'a great book made by Sir Thomas More, knight.' ibid.
[14] *Rentale de Cokersand*, Cheth. Soc., Vol. 57, 17.
[15] P.R.O., SC6/7304.   [16] ibid., SC6/7470.
[17] ibid.   [18] L. & P., xiii(1), 646, g. 50.
[19] L. & P., xviii(2), 107, g. 1; (1), 346, g. 21 & 22; 623, g. 79.

ber 1543 he bought the site of Cockersand and its lands in Garstang and Cockerham.[1] His new possessions became the foundation for a successful career; he became a J.P.,[2] a chantry commissioner,[3] and a parliamentary knight of the shire in 1545 and 1547.[4]

Thomas, Lord Mounteagle, head of a cadet branch of the Stanley family, qualified for rewards by both status and service. He had tried to keep the county quiet during the riots of 1535, though his own men had been involved,[5] and had assisted Derby against the Pilgrimage of Grace with a force of over 600 men.[6] When so many other northern lords had joined the rebels, this at least deserved some recognition. Mounteagle had been steward of the monasteries of Cockersand and Hornby,[7] which must have given him a thorough knowledge of the lands the religious houses possessed, so that he could choose which pieces he wished to acquire. At the suppression of Conishead he obtained a lease of the site and demesnes,[8] but he had to wait some time for more considerable gains. In November 1544, however, he bought the site and part of the lands of Hornby Priory in partnership with Henry Croft,[9] though soon after this he sold off some of the lands to Giles Bateson.[10] The original application for purchase had been made in Mounteagle's name only,[11] but the final grant was made to Mounteagle and Croft. This was the lord's first purchase, and it is possible that he expected to acquire the lands on highly favourable terms, only to find that prices were carefully calculated by officials eager to maximise receipts.[12] He may therefore have found the purchase price beyond his capability, and for this reason gone into partnership with Croft, who had been court steward of Hornby.[13] Mounteagle obviously learned his lesson, and when he bought up the rest of Hornby's lands in Melling in 1546, both the application[14] and the grant patent named Croft as his partner.[15]

Mounteagle, though a peer, was not wealthy,[16] and other Lancashire men were able to obtain as much land as he. Thurstan Tildesley, an important servant of the Earl of Derby,[17] had been an active loyalist during the Pilgrimage of Grace.[18] He had assisted with the Suppression, compiling a survey of Whalley soon after its fall,[19] and he clearly thought his services merited some recognition, for he asked Thomas Cromwell for a lease of

[1] ibid., xviii(2), 241, g. 2; D.K.R., x, App. 2, 224.
[2] Watson, art. cit., Appendix A.
[3] *Lancs Chantries*, i, 1; C.P.R., Edward VI, ii, 135.
[4] Watson, art. cit., 36.
[5] L. & P., viii, 984, 1046, 1108.
[6] L. & P., xi, 1251
[7] *Valor*, v, 261; iv, 151.
[8] P.R.O., DL29/2273.
[9] L. & P., xix(2), 690, g. 37.
[10] ibid., xx(1), 125, g. 31.
[11] D.K.R., x, App. 2, 241.
[12] J. Youings, E.H.R., lxix, 25–6.
[13] *Valor*, iv, 151.
[14] D.K.R., x, App. 2, 276.
[15] L. & P., xxi(1), 1383, g. 107.
[16] L. Stone, *The Crisis of the Aristocracy*, 760.
[17] L. & P., xiii(1), 406; xvi, 783. He was also Derby's deputy as Forester of Amounderness—Somerville, op. cit., 507.
[18] L. & P., xi, 1251.
[19] P.R.O., SC11/380.

Kersall Priory, in April 1538.[1] At this early stage, however, leases were only given to the especially favoured, but two years later he was able to buy part of the lands of Whalley;[2] we may assume that his survey of the Abbey possessions had helped with this. Tildesley did not make any further purchases from the government, although in February 1543 he bought Whalley lands in Rochdale from Robert Holt, an earlier grantee.[3] These new possessions made Tildesley a substantial gentleman in his own right; he became a J.P.[4] and went to Parliament in 1547 as a knight of the shire.[5]

The only real example of largely speculative purchases is that of Richard Crimbleholme, of whom, unfortunately, little is known. Crimbleholme, who lived in Dutton, bought lands in Blackburn, formerly of Whalley Abbey, in May 1543,[6] and in the following year he sold small plots of it in Wiswald to John Braddyll and Richard Cromboke, and in Witton to John Astley.[7] He did not confine his speculation to the lands of Lancashire houses, but purchased land in Dutton and Preston which had belonged to St. John of Jerusalem, and more land in Colne, formerly owned by Ponte-fract monastery.[8] He sold most of this in the following year, in eight small parcels, land in Marsden to John Braddyll and Henry Mankinholes, in Ribchester to Robert Byrley and Thomas Eccles, in Dutton to John Thrope, Richard Harrison, and Richard and Hugh Asshe, and in Preston to Sir Richard Houghton.[9] It is unlikely that Crimbleholme would have decided to sell and arranged so many sales in only fourteen months, and he must have bought the lands with the intention of selling them.

The other major grantees form a group of leading country gentlemen, whose influence in government circles was based not on the patronage of the great or tenure of office in land administration departments, but on fulfilling the normal functions of leaders of local society. John Holcroft, elder brother of the more successful Thomas, inherited the family estates, and so was less able to make a career in government,[10] but he bought the site of Holland Priory and its lands in Wigan, Holland, and Orrell in 1545,[11] part of which he sold to Sir Robert Worsley two years later.[12] His grant may have been due in part to his brother's influence, but John was quite able to look after his own interests and had achieved some import-ance in local affairs. He turned out to help Derby against the rebels in 1536,[13] he was twice sheriff of Lancashire and twice of Cheshire,[14] 'custos rotulorum' for Lancashire from 1547,[15] member of Parliament, chantry

[1] L. & P., xiii(1), 789.

[2] L. & P., xv, 942, g. 5.

[3] L. & P., xviii(1), 226, g. 1.

[4] Watson, art. cit., Appendix A.

[5] ibid., 36.

[6] L. & P., xviii(1), 623, g. 79.

[7] ibid., xix(1), 610, g, 116.

[8] ibid., xviii(1), 623, g. 79.

[9] ibid., xix(1), 610, g. 116.

[10] Watson, art. cit., 48.

[11] L. & P., xx(1), 846, g. 70; Dugdale, *Monasticon*, iv, 412; D.K.R., ix, App. 2, 229.

[12] L. & P., xxi(2), 777, g. 4.

[13] L. & P., xi, 1251.

[14] Watson, art. cit., 47; Somerville, *Duchy of Lancaster*, 463.

[15] C.P.R., Edward VI, i, 102.

commissioner,[1] joint receiver for Lenton Priory,[2] military officer, and a member of a number of local commissions.[3] A county leader of his standing could count on the influence necessary to secure land.

The same is true of Sir Richard Houghton, one of the most important landowners in the county, and a leading figure in local society. He was a member of the tenths commission in 1535,[4] a J.P.,[5] sheriff in 1540 and an M.P. in 1547, though he was unable to attend the House of Commons because of illness.[6] Houghton assisted Derby against the rebels in 1536,[7] helped in the collection of evidence afterwards,[8] and was a member of Sussex's commission for the suppression of Furness.[9] Thus Houghton had a reasonably safe expectation of such property as he could afford to purchase, and he began in June 1539 with a lease of the manor of Wheleton and other lands which had been held by Whalley Abbey.[10] After this, he must have pressed very strongly, for when the sale of lands began he was one of the first Lancashire men to obtain a grant, and in May 1540 he was able to purchase the lands he had already leased.[11] This was the only purchase of monastic land which Houghton made from the government, though in 1543 he bought land late of Preston Friary from Thomas Holcroft,[12] and in the following year Richard Crimbleholme sold him land in Preston which the order of St. John of Jerusalem had owned.[13]

Sir Alexander Radcliffe was also one of the earliest purchasers, and he secured a large grant of Whalley lands at Maunton in Eccles and at Romesgrove in July 1540,[14] though he immediately sold the Romesgrove portion to Andrew Barton.[15] Radcliffe had already tried to obtain the lease of Eccles rectory and lands in the parish, immediately after Whalley was suppressed, but John Pollard, the surveyor, had had other ideas;[16] it must have been Radcliffe's persistence which eventually brought dividends. Like Houghton, Radcliffe was a man of considerable, though local, importance; he was sheriff of Lancashire in 1523, 1528, 1538, and 1546, and of Cheshire in 1539,[17] butler in Lancashire and deputy bailiff of Salford hundred,[18] a member of the tenths commission in 1535,[19] and he served with his men under the Earl of Derby in 1536.[20]

The success of Thomas Holt was considerable under Henry VIII, but he failed to establish the fortunes of his family on a permanent footing. Holt, from Gristlehurst in Bury, was a member of the tenths commission,[21]

[1] L. & P., xxi(1), 302, g. 20.
[2] L. & P., xv, 282, g. 55.
[3] Watson, loc. cit.
[4] L. & P., viii, 149, g. 63.
[5] Watson, art. cit., Appendix A.
[6] ibid., 37.
[7] L. & P., xi, 1251.
[8] L. & P., xii(1), 785.
[9] ibid., 880.
[10] ibid., xiv(1), 1192, g. 15.
[11] L. & P., xv, 611, g. 11.
[12] ibid., xix(1), 241, g. 16.
[13] ibid., 610, g. 116.
[14] ibid., xv, 942, g. 4.
[15] ibid., g. 7.
[16] ibid., xii(2), 344.
[17] Watson, art. cit., 18; Somerville, *Duchy of Lancaster*, 462-3.
[18] Somerville, op. cit., 491, 503.
[19] L. & P., viii, 149, g. 63.
[20] L. & P., xi, 1251.
[21] L. & P., viii, 149, g. 63.

a J.P.,[1] and a captain in the county musters.[2] He was able to make very large purchases, beginning with the manor of Spotland in Rochdale and lands in Chadderton and Oldham, part of the estates of Whalley, in March 1542.[3] In the following year he made a massive purchase of lands, part of which he sold off to other gentlemen in 1544. Lands in Sefton, and the manors of Cronton and Staining, late of Whalley, were acquired in August 1543,[4] though Staining was sold to George Singleton,[5] and Holt also bought the manors of Counscough, Melling, Lydiate, and Forton, all from Cockersand,[6] of which he sold Counscough to Laurence Ireland.[7] His purchases were very large for a man of his standing, and he was probably following the common practice[8] of financing the purchase of land he wished to keep for himself by selling off the remainder to willing buyers.

Robert Holt of Stubley, a lesser man, followed a similar career, except that his lower status meant that he had to sell more of his purchases to enable himself to retain the rest. He too was a member of the tenths commission,[9] was a J.P.,[10] and turned out in 1536 against the rebels.[11] He purchased lands from Whalley in Clitheroe, Castleton in Rochdale, and Whalley in March 1542,[12] but he does not seem to have kept much of it, and he sold a large part within a year. In 1542 his purchasers were John Braddyll, Anthony Watson, Giles Colthurst, and Matthew Colthurst,[13] and in the next year Holt sold lands in Rochdale to Thurstan Tildesley and Laurence Asshawe.[14] Clearly, he too was financing his purchases out of capital gains.

In January 1543 the site, manor, and rectories of Penwortham Priory were sold to John Fleetwood,[15] who came from a Lancashire family which achieved considerable importance in local affairs later in the century, and led the Puritan attack on the Catholic gentry. Fleetwood was a lawyer who entered the service of Audley, the Lord Chancellor under Cromwell, and he used his influence with his master, Cromwell, and Richard Rich[16] to obtain a lease of Penwortham from Evesham Abbey in 1539.[17] The later sale of Penwortham by Augmentations must have been the result, too, of Fleetwood's position, and he was able to secure another grant in 1545,

[1] Watson, art. cit., Appendix A; L. & P., ix, 144.
[2] ibid., xix(2), App. 8.   [3] L. & P., xvii, 220, g. 74.
[4] L. & P., xviii(2), 107, g, 1; D.K.R., ix, App. 2, 230.
[5] L. & P., xix(1), 433, g. 10.   [6] L. & P., xviii(2), 107, g. 1.
[7] L. & P., xix(1), 443, g. 10.
[8] J. Youings, Devon Monastic Lands: Calendar of Particulars for Grants, xxii.
[9] L. & P., viii, 149, g. 63.   [10] Watson, art. cit., Appendix A.
[11] L. & P., xi, 1251.   [12] L. & P., xvii, 220, g. 75.
[13] L. & P., xvii, 361, g. 12; the last was presumably the Matthew Colthurst who was Augmentations auditor for south-west England—L. & P., xv, 540.
[14] L. & P., xviii(1), 226, g. 1.
[15] L. & P., xviii(1), 100, g. 18; Dugdale, Monasticon, iii, 421.
[16] L. & P., xi, 25.
[17] Dugdale, op. cit., iii, 418.

this time of property in Staffordshire.[1] But his connection with the county
at this stage was very tenuous, and he might almost be considered among
the non-Lancashire purchasers; certainly his grant owed nothing to influence in the county, but was exclusively a Court matter.

William Thornborough, of Hampsfield Hall, Lonsdale, succeeded to his
father's estates in 1544, took part in the invasion of Scotland in 1547, and
was knighted by Somerset.[2] In June 1545 Thornborough bought lands
which had belonged to Conishead Priory, though they were in fact in
Westmorland, in Kirkby Lonsdale and Kirkby Kendal.[3] Nothing is
known of his earlier career, but it seems likely that he had been involved
in some form of government or military service, which enabled him to
obtain his monastic lands. The last of the monastic grantees, William
Eccleston, is also a dim figure; in 1543 he bought, from Augmentations,
land in Kirkham which had once belonged to Cockersand Abbey,[4] of
which his family were tenants.[5] Eccleston was a J.P.,[6] but seems to have
taken little interest in local affairs, except that he was involved in a small
number of property disputes.[7] It cannot be thought that such an unim-
portant figure in the county would have much influence in governmental
circles, and it may be that his application was for land which no-one else
wanted, at a time when the government was eager to sell lands.

In addition to those who purchased lands, there were ten other men
who did not buy land, but were able to obtain leases of monastic property.
The most important of these was Edward, Earl of Derby, who, when
Burscough was suppressed, was granted a lease of the site and lands.[8]
Derby, by his attitude if not by energetic action, had been instrumental in
keeping the southern portion of Lancashire quiet during the Pilgrimage of
Grace, and he clearly deserved some reward, as he had been promised by
the King.[9] But though the Earl obtained his Burscough lease, and in 1542
a lease of Dieulacres in Staffordshire,[10] he did not make the large-scale
purchases which might have been expected from someone of his stature.
Derby was not a member of the inner circle of nobility or administration,
the Norfolks, Suffolks, Cromwells and Richs, who received free grants;[11] so
if he wanted monastic land, in Lancashire or elsewhere, he would have
to pay for it. But, as was usual with the Stanley family, the Earl was in
severe financial difficulties at this time; he had only been granted livery
of his lands in 1531,[12] after a long, and probably financially crippling
wardship to the Crown. When the Lancashire monasteries were suppressed, the Earl was eager to make what profit he could, and he bought

[1] D.K.R., ix, App. 2, 209.   [2] V.C.H., viii, 279,
[3] L. & P., xx(1), 1081 g. 12; D.K.R., x, App. 2, 287.
[4] L. & P., xviii(2), 107, g. 40.   [5] Rentale de Cokersand, 7.
[6] Watson, art. cit., Appendix A.   [7] Ducatus Lancastriae, i, 180, 236, 252.
[8] L. & P., xi, 517.   [9] Corresp., 53–5.
[10] L. & P., xvii, 1258.   [11] Savine in Fisher, Political History of England, v, App. 2.
[12] L. & P., v, 119, g. 22.

K

the goods of Burscough from the Suppression Commissioners,[1] but he
could not really afford to do so, and pestered Fitzwilliam, the Chancellor
of the Duchy, at least twice for a reduction in the purchase price.[2] In 1541
the Earl's servants were selling plate in London from suppressed religious
houses,[3] and the government obviously thought he was making illicit
profits at the Crown's expense,[4] and his difficulties must have given weight
to the suspicions. Derby, in fact, was in no position to buy any lands, and
the government would not allow him any more credit; in 1542 he owed
the King £1,000,[5] payment of which he had been putting off since 1537[6]
—it is easy to imagine Sir Brian Tuke's despair when he wrote, 'This I am
in most doubt of the payment.'[7]

Sir Thomas Butler was another Lancashire notable prevented by financial problems from acquiring the lands he might have anticipated. He was
one of the most important men in south Lancashire, a member of the
tenths commission,[8] sheriff in 1535,[9] and a correspondent of Thomas
Cromwell.[10] He turned out with his men to help Derby against the rebels
in 1536,[11] assisted in the suppression of Furness,[12] and helped to gather
evidence and put the oath of loyalty.[13] Butler, of course, could hope for
rewards, and he was granted leases immediately after the Suppression, of
Holland in 1536,[14] and of certain Furness lands in February 1538.[15] But
Butler did not buy any land, and this can only be because of his financial
position. In 1523, he was granted a life appointment as Duchy receiver for
Lancashire and Cheshire,[16] but he had to surrender the office in 1530 and
was involved in complicated financial negotiations with the King.[17] Some
years later, he had still not settled his accounts for the office, and his
guarantors were called on to make good his arrears; apparently he paid
off his debt in 1543 by transferring a large batch of cloth to the King.[18]
Also in 1543, and presumably in connection with this, he had to surrender
his lease of the Whalley lands.[19] Sir Thomas Butler, obviously, could not
afford to buy monastic lands.

Sir Thomas Southworth was of similar status, a tenths commissioner in
1535,[20] sheriff in 1541,[21] and a captain in the Scottish campaigns and the

[1] P.R.O., DL29/2198.
[2] L. & P., xi, 517, 1118.
[3] L. & P., xvi, 783.
[4] ibid., 794.
[5] ibid., xvii, 274, ii.
[6] L. & P., Addenda, 1222.
[7] L. & P., xvii, 274, ii.
[8] L. & P., viii, 149, g. 63.
[9] ibid., ix, 144; Somerville, *Duchy of Lancaster*, 463.
[10] L. & P., xi, 919; xii(1), 348.
[11] ibid., xi, 1251.
[12] L. & P., xii(1), 832, 840, 880.
[13] L. & P., xi, 1253; xii(1), 578.
[14] P.R.O., DL29/2303.
[15] L. & P., xiii(1), 384, g. 69.
[16] Somerville, *Duchy of Lancaster*, 495.
[17] Watson, art. cit., 25, 53.
[18] Somerville, op. cit., 495-6.
[19] L. & P., xviii(1), 346, g. 22. In the same year Butler had to pledge his sub-lease of
Warrington rectory as security for the £500 he was to pay the King (*Church Goods*, ii, 59).
[20] L. & P., viii, 149, g. 63.
[21] Somerville, op. cit., 463.

county musters,[1] while he had assisted the Earl of Derby against the rebels in 1536.[2] But Southworth too had to be satisfied with only a lease, the farm of part of the Whalley demesnes, and lands in Whitton and Little Harwood, granted in 1540.[3] As Southworth was the only other man of status among the lessees who did not buy lands, it is reasonable to suppose that he too, like Butler and Derby, could not afford to do so. It has been suggested[4] that the older gentry, of established families, could not afford to add to their estates, for their wealth was completely tied up in land. This was probably true of Southworth, and if his estate management was as conservative as his cast of mind[5] it would not be surprising if he had no ready cash for purchases.

The other lessees were men of lesser rank, only one of whom held any local office. William Sandys, father of the Elizabethan archbishop, was appointed to the commission of the peace for Furness in March 1538,[6] and was soon active with Sir John Lamplieu, deputy-steward of the liberty, in holding the courts in the area.[7] Sandys had been acting as the receiver for the Furness lands since the Suppression,[8] and in 1540 he was officially appointed Duchy receiver for the possessions.[9] He was therefore in a very good position to obtain grants, and in 1538 he was given the leases of three iron smithies, two farms, and a fishery in Furness Fells.[10] The remaining leases, to Henry Markland and George Shuttleworth from Whalley,[11] and to Nicholas Simpson, Adam Bardsey, and Richard Morgan from Furness,[12] were all minor matters, and were probably secured by intercession with local officials.

There is a clear distinction, among the twenty-four grantees who have been mentioned, between those able to purchase lands and those who only obtained leases. Except for those whose financial circumstances precluded any investment in more land, the lessees were all men of lower social status than the fourteen purchasers; the purchasers, except for Crimbleholme, who seems to have been out for speculative gains, were all substantial gentry who had some connection, however tenuous, with the government, and had proved their worth in local administration. These were the 'new monastics', those who really profited from the Suppression. The Crown's gain was largely ephemeral,[13] as lands were sold off to pay for the expensive Scots wars, and the promised schools and hospitals which

---

[1] L. & P., xix(1), 532; (2), App. 8. [2] L. & P., xi, 1251.
[3] L. & P., xv, 831, g. 12.
[4] J. Youings, *Devon Monastic Lands: Calendar of Particulars for Grants*, xxviii.
[5] In 1568 he expressed a determination to 'follow the faith of his fathers' and to 'die in the faith wherein he was baptised'—quoted by V. J. K. Brook, *Life of Archbishop Parker*, 213. He was clearly of an extreme conservative temperament, and it may be indicative that in 1544 at least he was unable to sign his own name—L. & P., xix(1), 532.
[6] ibid., xiii(1), 646, g. 31. [7] *Furness Coucher*, 664-7.
[8] P.R.O., DL29/2506. [9] Somerville, op. cit., 487.
[10] L. & P., xiii(1), 1520. [11] ibid., xv, 282, g. 72; xvii, 443, g. 70.
[12] ibid., xiii(1), 1520. [13] Knowles, *Religious Orders*, iii, 400.

were to replace the social activities of the monasteries were never built. If the Suppression benefited anyone, it was a small group of local gentlemen who were able to expand their possessions, income, and influence at the expense of the old institutions.

But it is difficult to see the grantees as a class of land-hungry Protestant exploiters, eager to dismantle the Catholic Church and enrich themselves on the proceeds. Of the fourteen purchasers considered, the families of twelve were largely Catholic under Elizabeth,[1] they do not seem to have been particularly aggressive landlords, and they were no more litigious than any other Lancashire gentry. In fact, the only thing they seem to have had in common was that, in the years immediately following the Suppression, they were in the best position to press the government to sell them lands; this was the only distinction between them and the other landlords which is immediately obvious, although it is probably also true that many of those who did not buy lands were unable to do so because their wealth was so tied in land that they had no ready capital for investment.

The pattern in Lancashire is remarkably similar to that found in Devon by Dr. Youings; the bulk of the purchasers were local gentlemen who by services to the Crown had managed to acquire influence at Court, and by their local offices had acquired a knowledge of monastic estates which enabled them to choose the land they wanted.[2] But the grantees in Lancashire were not the 'new men' which the conventional interpretations of the period lead one to expect; with one or two exceptions, they were of established county families, conservative in religion, and government servants because they were first the leaders of local society, rather than vice versa. The 'new monastics', like the monks they replaced, illustrate the essentially conservative character of Lancashire society.

[1] Thomas Holt of Gristlehurst—*Lord Burghley's Map of Lancashire*, 211, William Eccleston—ibid., 200; John Kechyn—ibid., 169-70; John Braddyll—ibid., 183-4; Lord Mounteagle—ibid., 167; Sir Richard Houghton—ibid., 175, 184, 192; Robert Holt of Stubley—ibid., 210; Sir Alexander Radcliffe—ibid., 221, 222; Thurstan Tildesley—ibid., 171, 215; Richard Crimbleholme—V.C.H., vii, 60; William Thornborough—*Lord Burghley's Map of Lancashire*, 165; John Holcroft—ibid., 206.
[2] E.H.R., lxix, 31; *Devon Monastic Lands: Calendar of Particulars for Grants*, xxii.

CONCLUSION

LANCASHIRE MONASTERIES AND LANCASHIRE RELIGION

THE Lancashire monasteries, in the half-century before their suppression, shared all the faults of the pre-Reformation Church. Their inmates were sometimes loose in morals and lax in observance, while the institutions themselves had often lost all spiritual zeal and become merely parts of a static and worldly ecclesiastical structure. But though monasteries and Church were as bad as corresponding organisations in the south of England, neither had lost the respect and affection of the local people, and neither succumbed easily to the attacks to which they were subjected in the sixteenth century.

The Church in Lancashire was backward and slow in its evolution, and the Reformation came well before even church building and the organisation of parishes were complete. There were fifty-six parishes by Pope Nicholas' survey in 1291,[1] and only one more had been added before 1541,[2] while there were eighty-six chapels before 1541.[3] But by 1650 there were sixty-two parishes and 128 chapelries.[4] When the south of England was growing tired of Catholicism and either falling into a secularist anti-clericalism or looking for a new religion, the old Church in Lancashire was passing through a period of rapid expansion, with forty-six new chapels being founded between 1470 and 1548.[5] The Reformation in Lancashire collided, as it did in Wales,[6] with a revitalised medieval Catholicism, in which both the physical structure of the Church and the spiritual life of the people were extended. In such a situation, Protestantism could not be expected to make any strong impact, especially as the political and social structure of the county was as undeveloped as its religion.

Conflicts between organised bands of retainers were still common,[7] feudal oaths were still taken,[8] and the Earl of Derby was still a semi-independent potentate. The trading connections of the county were with 'Catholic' rather than 'Protestant' areas, with Yorkshire, Northumberland, and Durham, rather than with London and the south, and with

[1] Tupling, 'Pre-Reformation Churches & Chapelries', Trans. L. & C. Antiq. Soc., vol. 67, p. 6.
[2] ibid.   [3] Tupling, art. cit., 12–16.
[4] Jordan, Social Institutions of Lancashire, Cheth. Soc., 3rd Series, xi, pp. 75–6.
[5] Tupling, art. cit., 9.
[6] G. Williams, The Welsh Church from Conquest to Reformation, 264–8.
[7] e.g. L. & P., viii, 984, 1108.
[8] History of Warrington Friary, 56; West, Antiquities, liii; Bouch & Jones, The Economic and Social History of the Lake Counties, 26–7.

Spain, Portugal, and Ireland, rather than with Germany or the Low Countries. Perhaps most important of all, Lancashire was probably the least well controlled of the counties of England, so that any government had the greatest difficulty in forcing its will on the people. The Council in London could control most of southern England and the Midlands, while there was a short-lived Council in the West. Wales and the west Midlands were under the thumb of the Council in Wales and the Marches, and the north, north-east, and the extreme north-west were controlled by the Council in the North. Lancashire, however, was left outside the jurisdiction of the Council in the North, presumably from a fear of offending the powerful Earls of Derby, but the nearest border of Lancashire was 150 miles from London. Church control was equally weak; before 1541 half of Lancashire was within the diocese of Lichfield, and the rest in the diocese of York, and so the Church in the county was administered from cities far away, from which the bishops could have exercised little real influence. Even after the reform of 1541, the cathedral city was Chester, and the two archdeaconries of Chester and Richmond were held 'in commendam' by the bishop. In Lancashire, as in Ireland,[1] the weakness of both secular and ecclesiastical control meant that the government had the greatest difficulty in forcing even the minimum of observance of the new religion upon an unwilling people. Lancashire, too, was a poor and underdeveloped county, and, though sixth in size, it was thirty-sixth in wealth of the counties of England.[2] In such a county, with small and isolated communities tied to subsistence agriculture, new ideas could permeate with only the greatest difficulty.

The factors which kept Lancashire religion backward and cut off from the currents of the religious history of the rest of England also affected the monasteries. There was no religious house in Lancashire until 1084, when a small priory was established at Lancaster, and the bulk of the Lancashire houses were twelfth- and thirteenth-century foundations. As has been suggested,[3] the monastic population of the county was still increasing in the period before the Suppression, which must indicate that the monasteries were taking part in the rapid and vital expansion of the Church in Lancashire in the early sixteenth century. It has been argued[4] that the religious houses were still integral parts of Lancashire society, because of the slow change of the county, and, as the Lancashire Church was not ready for the Reformation, so the Lancashire monasteries had not yet become irrelevant and unnecessary to the religious and social aspirations of the county, as those in the south had become. When the Elizabethan government tried to force Protestantism on the county, the local justices

[1] R. Dudley Edwards, *Church and State in Tudor Ireland*, viii, xxxiv–xxxv.
[2] Jordan, op. cit., 2.
[3] See above, Chapter One.
[4] ibid. and Chapter Five.

simply refused to enforce the orders of the Privy Council and the recusancy laws,[1] and when the Henrician government suppressed the religious houses, the county reacted in rebellion.

The Pilgrimage of 1536–7 was made more serious in Lancashire by the
harshness of the Duchy Commissioners, who treated the monks ejected
from the smaller houses with far less generosity than characterised the
Augmentations administration. The revenues of the Duchy were de-
clining,[2] and the Act of 1540 which transferred the Furness estates to the
Duchy[3] declared that this was necessary to maintain the revenues which
had been hard hit by the reduction in Duchy lands. The Duchy was
therefore eager to displace the monks as cheaply as possible, so payments
to the ex-religious and their servants in Lancashire were very small, and
was anxious to secure as much monastic land as possible, so only one
house was exempted from suppression to accommodate the large number
of monks who wished to remain in religion, and many who wished to do
so could not.[4] The Augmentations officials who surveyed Furness and
Cockersand, and the Earl of Sussex at Whalley, followed more generous
policies, partly because of the more generous practice of the other departments, and partly because they had learned the lesson of the Pilgrimage.[5]

Though the Lancashire monasteries exemplified the conservatism of the
county, and the monks of at least one house were outspoken in their
opposition to the reform movement, they made little active contribution
to the county's resistance to change. Many of the ex-religious were assimilated quite easily into the Henrician Church, and none of them is known
to have taken part in any further resistance to royal policies. Perhaps they
had no wish to share the fate of their brethren at Whalley and Cartmel,
for eleven of the one hundred and thirty-two Lancashire monks were
executed, imprisoned, or forced to flee for their lives. Of those who lived
on into Elizabeth's reign, at least the two surviving canons of Cartmel and
one of the Whalley monks married. Except for the eleven who suffered, the
Suppression does not seem to have had a catastrophic effect on the religious, and over one-third of them, instead of being isolated in the
monasteries, were integrated into the parochial structure of the Church.
Similarly, the great transfer of property does not appear to have had any
serious effects, and, for the bulk of the monastic tenants, the Suppression
can have meant little but a change of landlord. No new class of property
magnates was created, and as the bulk of the land which was alienated by
the Crown passed into the hands of those who were already substantial
gentry, the lands formerly held by the monasteries were integrated into
the normal landowning pattern of the county.

[1] e.g. see the report of 1591 printed Morris, *Diocesan Histories; Chester*, 144–7.
[2] Somerville, *History of the Duchy of Lancaster*, 292.
[3] 32 Henry VIII, c. 57.
[4] See above, Chapter Four.
[5] L. & P., xii(2), 206.

But it can hardly be doubted, though proof is difficult, that the vitality, generosity, splendour, and utility of some of the Lancashire houses contributed towards the attachment of the people to the old faith. The proximity of Whalley Abbey may have been one of the reasons for the later recusancy of the Ribble valley, and of the Southworth, Sherburne, and Towneley families, which dominated Lancashire Catholicism under Elizabeth. The influence of Burscough may have been a factor in the recusancy of the coastal area, and of Lydiate, Aughton, Ince-Blundell, and Crosby. But it was not so much that the monasteries were one of the causes of Lancashire recusancy, as that the importance of the monasteries and Lancashire recusancy were both the product of the slow evolution and conservatism of the county. The later history of the monasteries in Lancashire is one aspect of the county's resistance to religious reform.

APPENDIX A

THE MONKS OF LANCASHIRE
BEFORE THE SUPPRESSION

i. *Burscough Priory*—Augustinian Canons
There were five canons according to the 'Brief Certificate'—P.R.O.,
  DL43/5/7, f. 4.
Hugh Huxley, prior—F.O.R., 65; P.R.O., DL43/4/6; DL42/30, f. 185.
William Aspinall—F.O.R., 65; *Lancs & Ches. Wills & Inventories*, ii, 55.
Richard Castello—F.O.R., 66.
Hugh Woodheaver—F.O.R., 66; *Church Goods*, 113.
Ralph Evers—F.O.R., 66.

Also the following, not normally resident:
Robert Madoke, Vicar of Ormskirk—*Valor*, v, 223; V.C.H., iii, 244.
Roger Mason, Vicar of Huyton—V.C.H., iii, 154; *Lancs & Ches. Wills*,
  181.

ii. *Cartmel Priory*—Augustinian Canons
There were ten canons according to the 'Brief Certificate'—P.R.O.,
  DL43/4/11.
Richard Preston, prior—F.O.R., 65; P.R.O., DL43/4/12; DL41/11/50;
  DL42/30, f. 185.
William Pannell—F.O.R., 65; P.R.O., DL43/4/12; PL26/13/6.
Richard Bakehouse—F.O.R., 65; P.R.O., DL43/4/12; PL26/13/6.
John Ridley—F.O.R., 65; P.R.O., DL43/4/12; PL26/13/6.
Augustine Fell—F.O.R., 65; P.R.O., DL43/4/12; PL26/13/6.
Thomas Briggs—F.O.R., 65; P.R.O., DL43/4/12; PL26/13/6.
Thomas Person—F.O.R., 65; P.R.O., DL43/4/12; PL26/13/6.
James Eskrigge, sub-prior—F.O.R., 65; P.R.O., DL43/4/12; PL26/12/6.
Brian Willan, cellarer—F.O.R., 65; P.R.O., DL43/4/12; PL26/13/6.
John Cowper—F.O.R., 65; P.R.O., DL43/4/12; PL26/13/6.

iii. *Cockersand Abbey*—Premonstratensian Canons
There were twenty-two canons according to the 'Brief Certificate'—
  P.R.O., DL43/5/7, f. 1.
Robert Poulton, abbot—P.R.O., DL43/5/4; *Cock. Chart*, 1154; L. & P.,
  xiv(1), 1355, p. 602.
Richard Aldcliffe, prior—P.R.O., DL43/5/4; *Cock. Chart.*, 1154; L. & P.,
  xiv(1), 1355, p. 602.
John Preston—P.R.O., DL43/5/4; *Cock. Chart.*, 1154; L. & P., xiv(1),
  1355, p. 602.

The following P.R.O., DL43/5/4; *Cock. Chart.*, 1154; L. & P., xiv(1), 1355, p. 602:
James Kirkland
Edward Garstang
Thomas Dalton
Oliver Burton
William Whalley
Brian Furness
Robert Forton
Leonard Bentham
John Downham
Ralph Plumpton
Richard Salley
Roger Claughton, sub-prior
Richard Preston
Edward Bethom, cellarer
John Holm
Robert Catterall
Ralph Orton

James Wainwright—P.R.O., DL43/5/4; *Cock. Chart.*, 1154.
Abraham Clitheroe—P.R.O., DL43/5/4; *Valor*, v, 260; *Lancs Chantries*, ii, 233–4.

The following arrived at the house after 1536:
William Lancaster—*Cock. Chart.*, 1154; L. & P., xiv(1), 1355.
Robert Chapman—ibid.

The following were also canons:
James Dugdale—C.A.P., ii, 125, 126; *Valor*, v, 263; V.C.H., vii, 297.
Thomas Kellett—C.A.P., ii, 120, 125, 127; *Duchy Pleadings*, 107; *Cock. Chart.*, 1185.

iv. *Conishead Priory*—Augustinian Canons
There were nine canons in the 'Brief Certificate'—P.R.O., DL43/5/7, f. 3.
Thomas Lord, prior—F.O.R., 67; P.R.O., DL41/11/59, fos. 1, 2, 8, & 9; *Valor*, v, 295.
Thomas Bakehouse—F.O.R., 67.
George Cansforth—F.O.R., 67; P.R.O., DL41/11/59, f. 11; DL29/2313, m. 8.
Christopher Preston—F.O.R., 67.
Nicholas Wilson—F.O.R., 67.
Christopher Poole—F.O.R., 67; V.C.H., viii, 341.
Thomas Heysham—F.O.R., 67.
Richard Scotsands—F.O.R., 67.

Also not normally resident:
William Harrington, Warden of Kendal Hospital—F.O.R., 45; *Valor*, v, 268.

v. *Furness Abbey*—Cistercian
The surrender was signed by thirty monks
Roger Pyle, abbot—West, *Antiquities*, App. X, No. 7; *Richmond Wills*, 21.
Brian Garner, prior—West, loc. cit.; F.O.R., 97; L. & P., xii(1), 840, Nos. 2 & 3.
John Thornton—West, loc. cit.; F.O.R., 97; L. & P., xii(1), 840, No. 3, ii.
John Harrington—ibid.
Richard Scales, or Bussyn—West, loc. cit.; F.O.R., 97.
Matthew Kirkby—West, loc. cit.; F.O.R., 97; L. & P., xii(1), 842.
Thomas Settle—West, loc. cit.; F.O.R., 97; L. & P., xii(1), 841, No. 3, ii.
John Troughton—West, loc. cit.; F.O.R., 97.
Roger Preston—ibid.
Thomas Snell—ibid.; Beck, *Annales*, App. IX.
Hugh Brown—West, loc. cit.; F.O.R., 97; Beck, *Annales*, App. IX.

The following—West, loc. cit.; F.O.R., 97:
James Lancliffe
Christopher Carre
William Newark
Anthony Plummer
James Forster—L. & P., xii(1), 841, No. 3, ii.
Christopher Massrudder—West, loc. cit.; F.O.R., 97; L. & P., xii(1), 841, Nos. 2 & 4.
William Barwick—West, loc. cit.; F.O.R., 97.
William Rigge—ibid.; L. & P., xii(1), 841, No. 3.
Christopher Whalley, or Brown—West, loc. cit.; F.O.R., 97; L. & P., xii(1), 841, Nos. 2, 3, and 3, ii.
Giles Bolland—West, loc. cit.; F.O.R., 97; or Taylor, Beck, *Annales*, App. IX.
Stephen Skipton—West, loc. cit.; F.O.R., 97.
William Forest—ibid.; L. & P., xii(1), 841, No. 3.
Richard Martindale—West, loc. cit.; F.O.R., 97; L. & P., xii(1), 841, No. 3.

The following—West, loc. cit.; F.O.R., 97:
Robert Kechyn
Stephen Stanforth
Edward Blomer
Thomas Hornby
Michael Hammerton—L. & P, xii(1), 841, Nos. 2 & 3.

There were also:
Michael Thornborough—F.O.R., 97; V.C.H., vii, 265.
Edmund Stanford, Vicar of Millom—F.O.R., 94; *Valor*, v, 267.
John Broughton—L. & P., xii(1), 841, No. 3.
Henry Salley—L. & P., xii(1), 841, No. 3; ibid., 842.
James Proctor—F.O.R., 21.
Thomas Hartley, Vicar of Urswick—F.O.R., 53; V.C.H., viii, 337.
Roger Waller, Vicar of Dalton—F.O.R., 97; *Valor*, v, 272; V.C.H., viii,
    316.
Richard Banke, Vicar in I.O.M.—L. & P., vi, 787; P.R.O., SC12/9/73.

vi. *Holland Priory*—Benedictine
There were five monks in the 'Brief Certificate'—P.R.O., DL43/5/7,
    f. 5.
Peter Prescot, prior—F.O.R., 65; P.R.O., 41/11/47; DL42/30, f. 185.
John Codling—F.O.R., 65; P.R.O., 41/11/47.
Hugh Fairclough—F.O.R., 65.
John Ainsdale—F.O.R., 65; P.R.O., 41/11/47.
James Smith—F.O.R., 65; P.R.O., 41/11/47.

vii. *Hornby Priory*—Premonstratensian cell of Croxton

There were three canons in 1536:
William Halliday, prior—D.K.R., viii, App. 2, 23; L.R.S., Vol. 53, 141;
    F.O.R., 173; L. & P., xiv(1), 1355, p. 598.
Robert Derby—D.K.R., viii, App. 2, 23; *Lancs Chantries*, 232–3.
John Fletcher—D.K.R., viii, App. 2, 23.
There were also three canons in 1538:
John Consyll, prior—D.K.R., viii, App. 2, 18; L. & P., vii, 376; F.O.R.,
    173; L. & P., xiv(1), 1355, p. 598.
John Fletcher—D.K.R., viii, App. 2, 18; F.O.R., 173; L. & P., xiv(1),
    1395, p. 598.
Thomas Edynstow—ibid.

viii. *Kersall Priory*—Cluniac cell of Lenton Priory
There were usually two monks—Knowles and Hadcock, 97.

ix. *Lytham Priory*—Benedictine cell of Durham
There were usually three monks—Knowles and Hadcock, 70; *Duchy
    Pleadings*, i, 206–9.
Richard Blackstone was the last prior—Dugdale, *Monasticon*, iv, 283.

x. *Penwortham Priory*—Benedictine cell of Evesham Abbey.
There were usually three monks—V.C.H., ii, 105.
Their last prior was Richard Hawkesbury—L. & P., x, 364.

xi. *Whalley Abbey*—Cistercian

John Paslew, abbot—Whitaker, i, 114; P.R.O., PL26/13/6; L. & P., xii(1), 632.

William Haydock—P.R.O., PL26/13/6; receiver for Rochdale, *Valor*, v, 229.

Christopher Smith, prior—F.O.R., 91; Whitaker, i, 114; *Whalley Act Book*, 1–125.

Thomas Horowode—P.R.O., PL26/13/6; F.O.R., 91.

James More, kitchener—F.O.R., 91; Whitaker, i, 188.

William Chatburne, bursar—F.O.R., 91; Whitaker, i, 114.

Richard Wood—F.O.R., 91; *Valor*, v, 230.

Richard Marstyn—F.O.R., 91.

Robert Parish, Vicar of Whalley—F.O.R., 91; *Valor*, v, 229; V.C.H., vi, 358.

John Foster—F.O.R., 91.

William World, or Whalley—F.O.R., 91; L. & P., xii(1), 621.

John Holden—F.O.R., 91. Whitaker, i, 115.

Richard Morten—F.O.R., 91.

Miles Whitaker—ibid.

Henry Clitheroe—ibid.

Ralph Catterall—ibid.

Christopher Cromboke—F.O.R., 96.

Thomas Hockson—ibid.

James Mitchell—ibid.

John Chester—F.O.R., 110. Last bursar, Whitaker, i, 114.

Francis Green—F.O.R., 110.

John Lawe—ibid.

Thomas Blackburn—ibid.

John Estgate—P.R.O., PL26/13/6; L. & P., xii(1), 706.

Edward Manchester, or Pedley—L. & P., x, 23; Wood, *Athenae*, ii, 103; V.C.H., vi, 358.

Ralph Lynney, Vicar of Blackburn—P.R.O., E315/237, f. 3; *Valor*, v, 229; V.C.H., vi, 241.

Laurence Forest—Whitaker, i, 114; *Whalley Act Book*, 129 ff.; L. & P., xii(1), 621; *Duchy Pleadings*, ii, 38.

PURCHASERS OF MONASTIC LANDS

Burscough
Site and lands granted free to Sir William Paget, 1547. P.R.O., DL42/23, fos. 10-12.

Cartmel
Thomas Holcroft—site and part of the lands, 1540. L. & P., xvi, 305, g. 56.
Henry Audley, of St. Albans—Humphreyhead in Cartmel, 1545. L. & P., xx(1), 465, g. 99; D.K.R., ix, App. 2, 160.

Cockersand
John Braddyll—rents and services, 1545. L. & P., xx(1), 465, g. 64.
William Eccleston—Singleton in Kirkham, 1543. L. & P., xviii(2), 107, g. 40; D.K.R., ix, App. 2, 205.
Thomas Holt—manors of Counscough and Forton, etc., 1543. L. & P., xviii(2), 107, g. 1; D.K.R., ix, App. 2, 230.
John Kechyn—site and lands in Cockerham and Garstang, 1543. L. & P., xviii(2), 241, g. 2; D.K.R., x, App. 2, 224.
Anthony Brown—various lands, 1551. C.P.R., Edward VI, iv, 168.
James Brown, of London—manor of Westhoughton, 1545. L. & P., xx(1), 846, g. 76; D.K.R., ix, App. 2, 179.
Richard Pymonde—lands in Caton, Claughton, and Gressingham, 1544. L. & P., xix(1), 1035, g. 75; D.K.R., x, App. 2, 257.
Laurence Rowsthorne, of Berkshire—manor of Hutton, 1546. L. & P., xxi(1), 504, g. 16; D.K.R., x, App. 2, 263.
Richard Steven and George Buck—various lands, 1546. L. & P., xxi(2), 476, g. 55; D.K.R., x, App. 2, 277.

Conishead
Site and part of lands granted free to Sir William Paget, 1547. P.R.O., DL42/23, fos. 10-12.
William Thornborough—lands in Westmorland, 1545. L. & P., xx(1), 1081, g. 12; D.K.R., x, App. 2, 283.
John Benson, of Grasmere—lands in Grasmere, 1545. L. & P., xx(1), 1081, g. 6; D.K.R., ix, App. 2, 170.

Holland
John Holcroft—site and lands, 1545. L. & P., xx(1), 846, g. 70; D.K.R., ix, App. 2, 229; Dugdale, *Monasticon*, iv, 412.

Hornby

Lord Mounteagle and Henry Croft—site and lands, 1544. L. & P.,
xix(2), 690, g. 37; D.K.R., App. 2, 241.

Lord Mounteagle and Henry Croft—lands in Melling, 1546. L. & P.,
xxi(1), 1383, g. 107; D.K.R., x, App. 2, 276.

Kersall

Baldwin Willoughby, sewer of the chamber—site and lands, 1540. L. & P.,
xv, 942, g. 102; Dugdale, op. cit., v, 110.

Lytham

Thomas Holcroft—site and lands, 1554. C.P.R., Philip and Mary, i,
500–1; Dugdale, op. cit., iv, 283.

Penwortham

John Fleetwood—manor, site, and rectories, 1543. L. & P., xviii(1), 100,
g. 18; Dugdale, op. cit., iii, 421.

Whalley

John Braddyll—lands in Clayton, etc., 1545. L. & P., xx(1), 465, g. 64.

John Braddyll—various lands, 1545. L. & P., xx(1), 846, g. 75.

John Braddyll and Richard Assheton—site and part of lands, 1553.
C.P.R., Edward VI, v, 80–1; *Whalley Coucher*, 1175.

Richard Crimbleholme—lands in Whalley and Blackburn, 1543. L. & P.,
xviii(1), 623, g. 79.

Thomas Holcroft—various lands, 1540. L. & P., xv, 611, g. 31.

Thomas Holcroft—reserved rents on earlier grant, 1546. L. & P., xxi(2),
200, g. 1.

Robert Holt—lands in Clitheroe, Rochdale, and Whalley, 1542. L. & P.,
xvii, 220, g. 75.

Thomas Holt—lands in Rochdale and Chadderton, 1542. L. & P., xvii,
220, g. 74.

Thomas Holt—lands in Cronton, Staining, etc., 1543. L. & P., xviii(2),
107, g. 1.

Sir Richard Houghton—Stanworth, Wheleton, etc., 1540. L. & P., xv,
611, g. 11.

Sir Alexander Radcliffe—lands in Eccles, 1540. L. & P., xv, 942, g. 4.

Thurstan Tildesley—lands in Coppull, Westwood, etc., 1540. L. & P.,
xv, 942, g. 5.

John Bellow of Grimsby and John Broxholme of London—lands in
Wigan, 1546. L. & P., xxi(2), 476, g. 96; D.K.R., ix, App. 2, 170.

APPENDIX C

LESSEES OF MONASTIC LANDS

Burscough
Earl of Derby—site and demesne, 1536. P.R.O., DL29/2198; L. & P.,
xi, 517.

Cartmel
Thomas Holcroft—site and demesne, 1536. P.R.O., DL29/2228.

Cockersand
Thomas Wolsey, of Claughton—lands in Claughton and Ellel, 1539.
L. & P., xv, 1032.
James Brown, of London—manor of Westhoughton, 1542. L. & P., xvii,
1258.

Conishead
Lord Mounteagle—site and demesne, 1536. P.R.O., DL29/2273.

Furness
William Sandys and John Sawrey—iron smithies in Furness Fells, 1537–8.
L. & P., xiii(1), 1520.
William Sandys—farms and a fishery in Furness Fells, 1537–8. ibid.
Adam Bardsey—sheepcote in Furness Fells, 1537–8. ibid.
Richard Morgan and John Askew—water mills in Dalton, 1537–8. ibid.
Nicholas Simpson—lands in Dalton, 1537–8. ibid.
Thomas Cromwell—site and lands in Dalton, 1539. L. & P., xv, 1032.
Sir Thomas Curwen—site and demesne, 1540. L. & P., xvi, 305, g. 29.
John Aylyf, the King's surgeon—a fishery near Lancaster, 1537–8. L. & P.,
xiii(1), 1520.
John Booth, of the Household—lands in Colton, 1537–8. ibid.

Holland
Sir Thomas Butler—site and demesne, 1536. P.R.O., DL29–2303.

Whalley
Sir Thomas Butler—lands in Whalley, 1538. L. & P., xiii(1), 384, g. 69.
Thomas Holcroft—manor of Billington, 1540. L. & P., xv, 436, g. 68.
Sir Richard Houghton—manor of Wheleton, etc., 1539. L. & P., xiv(1),
1192, g. 15.
John Kechyn—lands in Whalley, Clitheroe, Penhulton, etc., 1543.
L. & P., xviii(1), 346, g. 21.

John Kechyn—part of the manor of Whalley, 1543. ibid,, g. 22.

Henry Markland—lands in Markland, 1540. L. & P., xv, 282, g. 72.

George Shuttleworth—lands in Whalley and Clayton, 1542. L. & P., xvii, 443, g. 70.

Sir Thomas Southworth—part of the demesne, 1540. L. & P., xv, 831, g. 12.

BIBLIOGRAPHY

Only works and documents cited in the footnotes are listed, and not all those consulted.

PRIMARY SOURCES

i. *Manuscript*
Borthwick Institute, York
R/I/26—Register of Archbishop Bainbridge, 1508–14.
R/I/28—Register of Archbishop Lee, 1531–44.
R/I/29—Register of Archbishops Holgate and Heath, 1547–57.

British Museum
Cotton MSS., Cleopatra E iv—Various Suppression documents.
Cotton MSS., Vespasian D xvii—Chronicle of Thomas Talbot of Salesbury.

Cheshire Record Office
EDA12/1—Proceedings of the 1535 Ecclesiastical Commissioners at Wigan.
EDC1/4—Consistory Court Book, 1529–31.
EDC1/8—Consistory Court Book, 1531–2.
EDC1/5—Consistory Court Book, 1533–4.
EDC1/6—Consistory Court Book, 1534.
EDC1/7—Consistory Court Book, 1535–8.
EDC2/1—Consistory Deposition Book, 1529–32.
EDV1/1—Visitation Correction Book, 1554, 1556.
EDV2/1—Visitation Call Book, 1538, 1541.
EDV2/4—Visitation Call Book, 1548.

Corpus Christi College, Cambridge
MS. 170—Letter Book of N. Collys, Notary. f. 123—Citation of Miles Burre and William Payne before the Archbishop of York, 1501. f. 144—Commission for the dispute between Prior Hale and the Archdeacon of Richmond.

Lancashire Record Office
DDTo/B21—Whalley Abbey Accounts, 1520.

Lichfield Record Office
B/A/I—Register of Bishop Arundel, 1496–1502.
B/A/I—Register of Bishop Boulers, 1453–9.
B/A/I—Register of Bishop Hales, 1459–90.

B/A/I—Register of Bishop Lee, 1534–43.
B/V/I/I—Visitations of Religious Houses, 1517–24.

Public Record Office
Duchy of Lancaster Records
DL3/3, K.1, N.D.—Pleadings, Thomas Kendall v. Alexander, Abbot of Furness, 1530.
DL3/4, K.5, N.D.—Pleadings, Thomas Kirkby, priest, v. Thomas Halsall, etc.
DL3/6, P.3.—Pleadings, Poulton and Bispam v. Ralph, Prior of Lytham, 1532.
DL3/6, R.1.—Pleadings, Rex v. Alexander, Abbot of Furness, 1530.
DL3/34, P.1.—Pleadings, Gabriel and Thomas Proctor v. Earl of Cumberland, 1542.
DL5/6—Books of Decrees and Orders, 24–30 Henry VIII.
DL12/7/39—Warrant enforcing the White Hall settlement, 1536.
DL28/7/5—Various Accounts, Receiver-General's Account, 1536.
DL29/158—Minister's Account, miscellaneous documents.
DL29/2198—Minister's Account, Burscough, 1536.
DL29/2228—Minister's Account, Cartmel, 1536.
DL29/2273—Minister's Account, Conishead, 1536.
DL29/2303—Minister's Account, Holland, 1536.
DL29/2313—Receiver's Account, Lancashire priories, 1536.
DL29/2317—Receiver's Account, Lancashire priories, 1539.
DL29/2505—Minister's Account, Furness, 1537–8.
DL29/2507—Minister's Account, Furness, 1540.
DL29/2523—Receiver's Account, Furness, 1537–8.
DL29/2525—Receiver's Account, Furness, 1540.
DL41/11/36—Inventory of Burscough, 1510.
DL41/11/47—Inventory of Holland, 1536.
DL41/11/49—Obligations for five Lancashire monasteries, 1536.
DL41/11/50—'Commandment' to the Prior of Cartmel, 1536.
DL41/11/59—f. 1—'Commandment' to the Prior of Conishead, 1536.
  f. 2—Letter, Thomas Sherburne to Thomas Burgoyne, 1536.
  f. 3—Letter, Anthony Fitzherbert to Thomas Burgoyne, 1536.
  f. 4—Letter, Prior of Conishead to Thomas Burgoyne, 1536.
  f. 5—Letter, Thomas Wharton to the Commissioners, 1536.
  f. 6—Letter, William Gerard to the Commissioners, 1536.
  f. 7—Letter, Richard Duckett to Thomas Burgoyne, 1536.
  f. 8—Conishead's first offer, 1536.
  f. 9—Conishead's second offer, 1536.
  f. 10—List of lead at Conishead, 1536.
  f. 11—Petition of George Cansforth, 1536.
  f. 12—Agreement of Richard Duckett and Sir William Harrington.

DL41/12/10—Draft commission to Chancellor of Duchy, 1536.
DL41/12/11—Questions from Duchy to Augmentations, 1536.
DL41/12/12—Answers of Augmentations Attorney.
DL41/158/22—Petition of Richard Johnson.
DL42/22—Register of grants, temp. Henry VIII.
DL42/23—Register of Grants, temp. Edward VI and Philip and Mary.
DL42/30—Book of enrolments of leases and grants.
DL43/4/11—'Brief Certificate' of Cartmel, 1536.
DL43/4/12—'Declaration of Survey' of Cartmel, 1536.
DL43/5/2—'Valor' of Lancashire monastic rents, 1536.
DL43/5/4—'Declaration of Survey' of Cockersand, 1536.
DL43/5/7—f. 1—'Brief Certificate' of Cockersand, 1536.
    f. 2—'Brief Certificate' of Cartmel, 1536.
    f. 3—'Brief Certificate' of Conishead, 1536.
    f. 4—'Brief Certificate' of Burscough, 1536.
    f. 5—'Brief Certificate' of Holland, 1536.
DL43/5/11—Rental of Conishead.
DL43/5/12—Rental of Hornby.
DL43/5/14—List of Lancashire commissioners.

Exchequer Records
E101/76/17—Report of 1553 pensions survey.
E315/93, 102—Books of decrees and orders, Court of Augmentations.
E315/232, 237, 427—Enrolments of leases and pensions, Court of Augmentations.
E321/18/29—Complaint against Sir Thomas Langton.
E321/39/11—Enquiry into the lease of Westhoughton.
E334/1, 2—Composition Books, First-Fruits and Tenths Office.

Palatinate of Lancaster Records
PL25/29—Assizes at Lancaster, 1537.
PL26/13/6—Indictment of the monks of Whalley and Cartmel, 1537.

Special Collections
SC6/708—Receiver's Account, Durham Priory, including Lytham, 1541.
SC6/1797—Receiver's Accounts, Whalley Abbey, 1537.
SC6/1827—Receiver's Account, Croxton Abbey, including Hornby, 1538.
SC6/7304—Receiver's Account, various monasteries, including Cockersand, 1539.
SC6/7470—ibid, 1539.
SC6/7471—ibid, 1540.
SC11/376—Survey of the possessions of Furness, 1537.
SC12/9/73—Rental of Roger, Abbot of Furness.
SC12/13/74—Survey of Kersall demesnes.

ii. *Printed*

Act Book of the Ecclesiastical Court of Whalley Abbey, ed. A. M. Cooke, Chetham Society, New Series, Vol. 44, 1901.

Acts of the Privy Council of England, ed. J. R. Dasent, 32 vols., 1890–1907.

'Aske's Examination', ed. M. Bateson, E.H.R., v, 1890, 550–73.

'Aske's Narrative', ed. M. Bateson, E.H.R., v, 1890, 330–45.

Bowker, M., ed., *An Ecclesiastical Court Book for the Diocese of Lincoln, 1514–1520*, Lincoln Record Society. Vol. 61, 1967.

Calendar of Patent Rolls, Edward VI, 6 vols., 1924–9.

Calendar of Patent Rolls, Philip and Mary, 4 vols., 1936–9.

Calendar of State Papers, Domestic, Addenda, 1547–65, ed. M. A. E. Green, 1872.

Chartulary of Cockersand Abbey, ed. W. Farrer, Chetham Society, New Series, Vols. 38–40, 43, 1898–1900.

Clifford Letters of the Sixteenth Century, ed. A. G. Dickens, Surtees Society, Vol. 172, 1957.

Collectanea Anglo-Premonstratensia, ed. F. A. Gasquet, Camden Society, Third Series, Vols. 6, 10, 12, 1904–6.

Correspondence of Edward, Third Earl of Derby, ed. T. N. Toller, Chetham Society, New Series, Vol. 19, 1890.

Coucher Book of Furness Abbey, ed. J. Brownbill, Chetham Society, New Series, Vols. 74, 76, 78, 1915–19.

Coucher Book of Whalley Abbey, ed. W. A. Hulton, Chetham Society, Old Series, Vols. 10, 11, 16, 20, 1847–9.

Documents relating to the Priory of Penwortham, ed. W. A. Hulton, Chetham Society, Old Series, Vol. 30, 1853.

Ducatus Lancastriae, Calendar of Pleadings and Inquisitions, ed. Harper, Caley, and Minchin, 3 vols., 1823–34.

Dugdale, W., *Monasticon Anglicanum*, ed. Caley, Ellis, and Bandinel, 6 vols. in 8, 1817–30.

Elton, G. R., ed., *The Tudor Constitution*, 1960.

Heraldic Visitation of the Northern Counties, 1530, ed. W. H. D. Longstaffe, Surtees Society, Vol. 41, 1853.

History of the Chantries within the County Palatine of Lancaster, Reports of the Chantry Commissioners, ed. F. R. Raines, Chetham Society, Old Series, Vols. 59, 60, 1862.

Inventories of Church Goods in the Churches and Chapels of Lancashire, 1552, ed. J. E. Bailey, Chetham Society, Old Series, Vols. 107, 113, 1879–1888.

Lancashire and Cheshire Cases in the Court of Star Chamber, ed. R. Stewart-Brown, Lancashire and Cheshire Record Society, Vol. 71, 1916.

Lancashire and Cheshire Wills, and Inventories, ed. G. J. Piccope, Chetham Society, Old Series, Vols. 33, 51, 1857–60.

Leland, J., *De Rebus Britannicis Collectanea*, ed. T. Hearne, 6 vols., 1715.

Letters and Papers, Foreign and Domestic, of the Reign of Henry VIII, ed. Brewer, Gairdner, and Brodie, 23 vols. in 38, 1862–1932.

List of the Clergy in Eleven Deaneries of the Diocese of Chester, 1541–2, Lancashire and Cheshire Record Society, Vol. 33, 1896.

Lord Burghley's Map of Lancashire, 1590, ed. J. Gillow, Catholic Record Society, Vol. 4, 1907.

Pleadings and Depositions in the Duchy Court of Lancaster, ed. H. Fishwick, Lancashire and Cheshire Record Society, Vols. 32–5, 1896–7.

Pott's Discovery of Witches in the County of Lancaster, ed. J. Crossley, Chetham Society, Old Series, Vol. 6, 1845.

Register of the Archbishop of Canterbury's Faculty Office, ed. D. S. Chambers, 1966.

Register of the Parish of Cartmel, Lancashire Parish Register Society, Vol. 28.

Register of the Parish of Great Harwood, Lancs Parish Register Soc., Vol. 75.

Register of the Parish of Whalley, Lancs Parish Register Soc., Vol. 7.

Register or Chronicle of Butley Priory, ed. A. G. Dickens, 1951.

Rentale de Cokersand, 1501, ed. F. R. Raines, Chetham Society, Old Series, Vol. 57, 1862.

Report of the Deputy Keeper of the Public Records, Vol. VIII, 1847.

Report of the Deputy Keeper of the Public Records, Vol. IX, 1848.

Report of the Deputy Keeper of the Public Records, Vol. X, 1849.

Rhymer, T., *Foedera,* Vol. xiv, 1712.

Richmond Wills, ed. J. Raine, Surtees Society, Vol. 26, 1853.

State of the Ex-Religious and Former Chantry Priests in the Diocese of Lincoln, ed. G. A. J. Hodgett, Lincoln Record Society, Vol. 53, 1959.

Statuta Capitulorum Generalium Ordinis Cisterciensis, ed. J.-M. Canivez, 8 vols., 1933–41.

Statutes of the Realm, 11 vols., 1810–28.

Talbot, C. H., ed., *Letters of the English Abbots to the Chapter at Citeaux, 1442–1521,* Camden Society, Fourth Series, Vol. IV, 1967.

Tudor Royal Proclamations, ed. Hughes and Larkin, Vol. I, 1964.

Valor Ecclesiasticus, ed. Caley and Hunter, 6 vols., 1810–34.

Visitation of Lancashire, 1533, ed. W. Langton, Chetham Society, Old Series, Vols. 98, 110, 1876–82.

Wilkins, D., *Concilia Magna Britanniae et Hiberniae,* 4 vols., 1737.

SECONDARY WORKS

Ashmore, O., 'The Whalley Abbey Bursar's Account for 1520', Transactions of the Historic Society of Lancashire and Cheshire, Vol. 114, 1962.

Baskerville, G., *The English Monks and the Suppression of the Monasteries,* 1937.

Beaumont, W., *History of Warrington Friary,* Chetham Society, Old Series, Vol. 83, 1872.

Beck, T. A., *Annales Furnesienses*, 1844.

Bouch, C. M. L. & Jones, G. P., *Economic and Social History of the Lake Counties, 1500–1830*, 1961.

Brigg, M., 'The Forest of Pendle in the Seventeenth Century', Transactions of the Historic Society of Lancashire and Cheshire, Vol. 113, 1961.

Brook, V. K. J., *Life of Archbishop Parker*, 1962.

Burnet, G., *History of the Reformation of the Church of England*, ed. N. Pocock, 6 vols., 1865.

Clebsch, W. A., *England's Earliest Protestants, 1520–1535*, 1964.

Colvin, H. M., *The White Canons in England*, 1951.

Dickens, A. G., 'Edwardian Arrears in Augmentations Payments', E.H.R., Vol. 55, 1940.

'Royal Pardons for the Pilgrimage of Grace', Y.A.J., Vol. 33, 1936.

Dodds, M. H. & R., *The Pilgrimage of Grace and the Exeter Conspiracy*, 1915.

Edwards, R. Dudley, *Church and State in Tudor Ireland*, 1935.

Elton, G. R., *The Tudor Revolution in Government*, 1953.

Fisher, H. A. L., *Political History of England*, Vol. 5, 1485–1547, 1906.

Hodgett, G. A. J., 'The Unpensioned Ex-religious in Tudor England', J. Eccl. Hist., Vol. 13, 1962.

Hughes, P., *The Reformation in England*, Vol. 1, 1950.

Jordan, W. K., *The Social Institutions of Lancashire*, Chetham Society, Third Series, Vol. 11, 1962.

Ker, N. R., *The Medieval Libraries of Great Britain*, Royal Historical Society, second edition, 1964.

Knowles, M. D., *The Religious Orders in England*, Vol. 3, 1959.

Knowles, M. D. & Hadcock, R. N., *Medieval Religious Houses*, 1954.

Mason, R. J., *The Income, Administration and Disposal of Monastic Lands in Lancashire, from the Suppression to 1558*, unpublished M.A. thesis, University of London, 1962.

McRoberts, D., ed., *Essays in the Scottish Reformation*, 1962.

Merriman, R. B., *The Life and Letters of Thomas Cromwell*, 1902.

Morris, R. H., *Diocesan Histories; Chester*, 1895.

Oxley, J. E., *The Reformation in Essex*, 1965.

Raines, F. R., *The Vicars of Rochdale*, Chetham Society, New Series, Vols. 1, 2, 1883.

Richardson, W. C., *History of the Court of Augmentations*, 1961.

Savine, A., *English Monasteries on the Eve of Dissolution*, 1909.

Somerville, R., *History of the Duchy of Lancaster, 1265–1603*, Vol. I, 1953.

Stone, L., *The Crisis of the Aristocracy, 1558–1640*, 1965.

Strype, J., *Ecclesiastical Memorials*, 3 vols. in 6, 1822.

Tempest, A. C., 'Nicholas Tempest, a Sufferer in the Pilgrimage of Grace', Y.A.J., Vol. 11, 1890.

Tupling, G. H., 'Pre-Reformation Parishes and Chapelries', Transactions
    of the Lancashire and Cheshire Antiquarian Society, Vol. 67, 1957.
Victoria History of the County of Lancashire, 8 vols., 1906–14.
Wallis, J. E. W., *History of the Church in Blackburnshire*, 1932.
    'Narrative of the Indictment of the Traitors of Whalley and Cartmel',
    Chetham Society, New Series, Vol. 90, 1931.
Watson, J. B., 'The Lancashire Gentry and the Public Service, 1529–58',
    Transactions of the Lancashire and Cheshire Antiquarian Society,
    Vol. 73, 1963.
West, T., *Antiquities of Furness*, 1732.
Whitaker, T. D., *History of the Original Parish of Whalley*, ed. Nicholas and
    Lyons, 1872.
Williams, G., *The Welsh Church from Conquest to Reformation*, 1962.
Wood, A., *Athenae Oxonienses*, ed. Bliss, 1813–20.
Woodward, G. W. O., *The Dissolution of the Monasteries*, 1966.
    'The Exemption from Suppression of Certain Yorkshire Priories',
    E.H.R., Vol. 76, 1961.
Youd, G., 'The Common Fields of Lancashire', Transactions of the His-
    toric Society of Lancashire and Cheshire, Vol. 113, 1961.
Youings, J., Introduction to *Devon Monastic Lands; Calendar of Particulars
    for Grants, 1536–1558*, Devon and Cornwall Record Society, New
    Series, Vol. I, 1955.
    'The Terms of the Disposal of the Devon Monastic Lands, 1536–1558',
    E.H.R., Vol. 69, 1954.

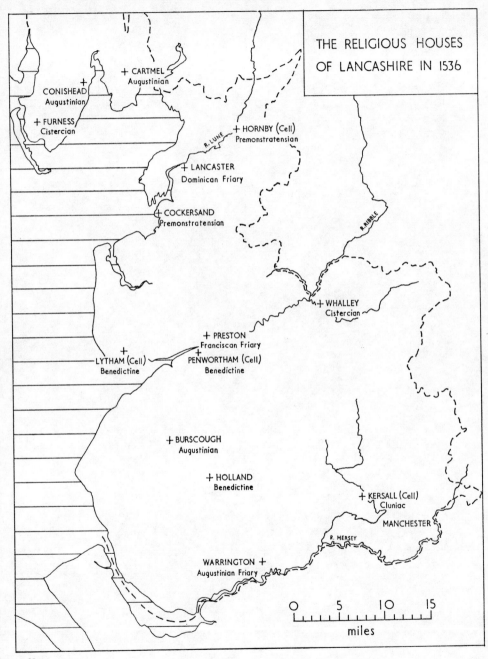

THE RELIGIOUS HOUSES
OF LANCASHIRE IN 1536

+ CARTMEL
Augustinian

CONISHEAD
Augustinian

+ FURNESS
Cistercian

R. LUNE

+ HORNBY (Cell)
Premonstratensian

+ LANCASTER
Dominican Friary

R. RIBBLE

+ COCKERSAND
Premonstratensian

+ WHALLEY
Cistercian

+ PRESTON
Franciscan Friary

LYTHAM (Cell)
Benedictine

+ PENWORTHAM (Cell)
Benedictine

+ BURSCOUGH
Augustinian

+ HOLLAND
Benedictine

+ KERSALL (Cell)
Cluniac

MANCHESTER

R. MERSEY

WARRINGTON +
Augustinian Friary

0   5   10   15

miles

M

INDEX

The following abbreviations are used: Cl.—Cluniac; O. Cist.—Cistercian; O.F.M.—Franciscan; O.P.—Dominican; O. Prem.—Premonstratensian; O.S.A. —Augustinian; O.S.B.—Benedictine.

agriculture, in Lancs, 50–1

Ainsdale, John, O.S.B. Holland, 115– 116, 143

Ainsworth, Christopher, 9

Aldcliffe, Richard, O. Prem. Prior of Cockersand, 34, 143

Aldingham, parish, 18

Alexander VI, Pope, 8

alms, *see* charity

almsmen, 34, 39, 41n., 48, 53, 54

Armerer, Thomas, 32

Arundel, John, Bishop of Lichfield, 6

Ashburner, William, priest, 52

Ashton, parish, 50

Aske, Robert, 53, 54, 55, 56, 57, 64, 66, 67, 70, 71, 73, 74, 75, 76, 79, 81, 89, 93

Askew, John, 150

Aspinall, William, O.S.A. Burscough, 114, 143

Asshawe, Laurence, 134

Asshawe, Roger, 37

Asshe, Hugh, 132

Asshe, Richard, 132

Assheton, John, 31, 105

Assheton, Richard, 130

Assheton, Sir Richard, 32

Astley, John, 132

Atkinson, ?, 69, 70, 71, 76, 82, 90

Audley, Henry, 109, 127, 148

Audley, Thomas, Lord Chancellor, 30, 82, 100, 109, 134

Augmentations, Court of, 17, 30, 32 & n., 39, 40, 42, 48, 51, 100, 104, 105, 107, 109, 110, 111, 113, 120, 121, 126, 129, 130, 134 & n., 135, 140

Attorney of, *see* Onley, John

Chancellor of, *see* Rich, Sir Richard

Aylyf, John, 128, 150

Bakehouse, Richard, O.S.A. Cartmel, 143

Bakehouse, Thomas, O.S.A. Conishead, 144

Banaster, Henry, 89

Banke, Alexander, O. Cist. Abbot of Furness, 14–16, 17, 18, 19, 20, 56, 58

Banke, Richard, O. Cist. Furness, 18, 120, 146

Bankes, Robert, 76

Bannester, Nicholas, 81

Bardsey Adam, 137, 150

Bardsey, Christopher, 15–16, 75

Bardsey, John, 7–8

Barlings, Abbot of, *see* Macrell, Mathew

Barlow, Edward, 8

Barnes, Robert, O.S.A. Friar, 52

Barrett, William, 83, 89, 90

Barton, Andrew, 133

Barwick, William, O. Cist. Furness, 59, 145

Baskerville, G., 113

Bateson, Giles, 131

Battlefield College, Salop, 120

Bedfordshire, 123

Belling, John, 9

Bellingham, Sir Robert, 69

Bellow, John, 127, 149

Benson, John, 127, 148

Bentham, Leonard, O. Prem. Cocker-sand, 34, 144

Bentham, William, O. Prem. Cocker-sand, 11, 12

Berwick Herald, 66

Bethom, Edward, O. Prem. Cocker-sand, 34, 144

Bigod, Sir Francis, 73